The Southern Baptist Convention & Civil Rights, 1954–1995

Monographs in Baptist History

VOLUME 22

SERIES EDITOR
Michael A. G. Haykin, The Southern Baptist Theological Seminary

EDITORIAL BOARD
Matthew Barrett, Midwestern Baptist Theological Seminary
Peter Beck, Charleston Southern University
Anthony L. Chute, California Baptist University
Jason G. Duesing, Midwest Baptist Theological Seminary
Nathan A. Finn, North Greenville University
Crawford Gribben, Queen's University, Belfast
Gordon L. Heath, McMaster Divinity College
Barry Howson, Heritage Theological Seminary
Jason K. Lee, Cedarville University
Thomas J. Nettles, The Southern Baptist Theological Seminary, retired
James A. Patterson, Union University
James M. Renihan, Institute of Reformed Baptist Studies
Jeffrey P. Straub, Independent Scholar
Brian R. Talbot, Broughty Ferry Baptist Church, Scotland
Malcolm B. Yarnell III, Southwestern Baptist Theological Seminary

Ours is a day in which not only the gaze of western culture but also increasingly that of Evangelicals is riveted to the present. The past seems to be nowhere in view and hence it is disparagingly dismissed as being of little value for our rapidly changing world. Such historical amnesia is fatal for any culture, but particularly so for Christian communities whose identity is profoundly bound up with their history. The goal of this new series of monographs, Studies in Baptist History, seeks to provide one of these Christian communities, that of evangelical Baptists, with reasons and resources for remembering the past. The editors are deeply convinced that Baptist history contains rich resources of theological reflection, praxis and spirituality that can help Baptists, as well as other Christians, live more Christianly in the present. The monographs in this series will therefore aim at illuminating various aspects of the Baptist tradition and in the process provide Baptists with a usable past.

The Southern Baptist Convention & Civil Rights, 1954–1995

Conservative Theology, Segregation, and Change

David Roach

☙PICKWICK *Publications* • Eugene, Oregon

THE SOUTHERN BAPTIST CONVENTION & CIVIL RIGHTS, 1954–1995
Conservative Theology, Segregation, and Change

Monographs in Baptist History Volume 22

Copyright © 2021 David Roach. All rights reserved. Except for brief quotations in critical publications or reviews, no part of this book may be reproduced in any manner without prior written permission from the publisher. Write: Permissions, Wipf and Stock Publishers, 199 W. 8th Ave., Suite 3, Eugene, OR 97401.

Pickwick Publications
An Imprint of Wipf and Stock Publishers
199 W. 8th Ave., Suite 3
Eugene, OR 97401

www.wipfandstock.com

PAPERBACK ISBN: 978-1-6667-1748-8
HARDCOVER ISBN: 978-1-6667-1749-5
EBOOK ISBN: 978-1-6667-1750-1

Cataloguing-in-Publication data:

Names: Roach, David, author.

Title: The Southern Baptist Convention & civil rights, 1954–1995 : conservative theology, segregation, and change / by David Roach.

Description: Eugene, OR: Pickwick Publications, 2021 | Series: Monographs in Baptist History 22 | Includes bibliographical references.

Identifiers: ISBN 978-1-6667-1748-8 (paperback) | ISBN 978-1-6667-1749-5 (hardcover) | ISBN 978-1-6667-1750-1 (ebook)

Subjects: LCSH: Southern Baptist Convention—History—20th century. | Racism—Religious aspects—Baptists. | Civil rights—Religious aspects—Baptists—History of doctrines—20th century.

Classification: BX6462.3 R63 2021 (print) | BX6462.3 (ebook)

Unless otherwise indicated, all Scripture quotations are from the ESV® Bible (The Holy Bible, English Standard Version®), copyright © 2001 by Crossway, a publishing ministry of Good News Publishers. Used by permission. All rights reserved.

12/14/21

To Erin,
Caroline, Mallory, and Hutton

Contents

Introduction | ix

CHAPTER 1
Segregation in the Southern Baptist Convention | 1

CHAPTER 2
Conservative Theology, Segregation, and Change | 20

CHAPTER 3
Foy Valentine and the Christian Life Commission Vision | 43

CHAPTER 4
The Experience of Southern Baptist Seminaries and Colleges | 76

CHAPTER 5
African Americans and Southern Baptists | 107

CHAPTER 6
Moderates and Race During the Southern Baptist Convention Controversy | 126

CHAPTER 7
Richard Land and Modern Conservatives on Race | 143

CHAPTER 8
Conclusion: The Way Forward | 166

Bibliography | 171

Introduction

SCHOLARS HAVE ARGUED THAT theological liberals led the Southern Baptist Convention to reject segregation and racism in the twentieth century. David Stricklin, for example, argued that during the civil rights era, radical dissenters took action against racial injustice while the Southern Baptist Convention only made statements and passed resolutions.[1] Many mainstream Southern Baptists saw no contradiction in a man serving simultaneously as a pastor and a member of the Ku Klux Klan, Stricklin said, but the dissenters reassessed the South's traditional views on race.[2] Mark Newman argued similarly that a group of progressive leaders urged Southern Baptists forward in race relations, but rank-and-file Southern Baptists lagged behind these leaders.[3] Progressives criticized racial segregation long before their mainstream contemporaries, Newman said.[4]

These arguments have merit. Liberals criticized segregation before mainstream Southern Baptists. They created racially integrated ministry opportunities. They pressed the Southern Baptist Convention to reject segregation. They spoke later against institutional racism. And they put ethnic minorities in leadership positions during the late twentieth century.

Scholars have discounted the role of conservative theology in the Southern Baptist Convention's shift away from racial segregation and prejudice. Between 1954 and 1995 Southern Baptists rejected segregation and prejudice. Throughout the period, conservative theology proved

---

1. Stricklin, *A Genealogy of Dissent*, 48–81.
2. Stricklin, *A Genealogy of Dissent*, 18–19, 66–74.
3. Newman, *Getting Right with God*, ix.
4. Newman, *Getting Right with God*, 21. See similarly K'Meyer, *Interracialism and Christian Community in the Postwar South*; Hankins, *Uneasy in Babylon*, 250; Spain, *At Ease in Zion*, 44–126.

Introduction

remarkably compatible with efforts toward racial justice. At times conservative theology was a catalyst for rejecting racial prejudice. When progressives controlled convention agencies between 1950 and 1980, they by necessity advanced racial justice by speaking in ways that did not contradict the conservative theology of the Southern Baptist rank and file. They chipped away at racial prejudice by appealing to the biblical doctrines of salvation and creation. They argued that Southern Baptists must reject segregation and prejudice in order to live consistently with the theology they professed to believe. They were, in fact, least successful at advancing racial justice when they appealed to the social gospel or appeared to draw from liberal theology. When conservatives took control of convention agencies in the 1980s and 1990s, they sought to continue the race reform efforts of their progressive predecessors, not to reverse or derail them. Conservative theology never contradicted efforts to end segregation and prejudice in the Southern Baptist Convention.[5]

By "conservative theology," this work refers to what British historian David Bebbington called evangelicalism. Bebbington identified evangelicalism as a school of thought characterized by conversionism (an emphasis on the "new birth" as life-changing religious experience), biblicism (a reliance on the Bible as ultimate religious authority), activism (a concern for sharing the faith), and crucicentrism (a focus on Christ's redeeming work on the cross).[6] For Baptist historian Tom Nettles, "evangelical" denotes a series of doctrinal affirmations including justification by faith, the necessity of the work of Christ, and the necessity of the work of the Spirit. These definitions of evangelical cover the essential points that correspond to this work's use of the term evangelical.[7] It usually includes belief in the inerrancy of the Bible, the historical accuracy of its miracle accounts, and the real existence of Adam and Eve by God's direct creation. This work uses the term "conservative theology" interchangeably with "evangelical theology."

Each chapter explores the interplay between conservative theology and advancement of racial justice in a different sphere of Southern

---

5. On race generally and race in America, see Omi and Winant, *Racial Formation in the United States*; Gould, *The Mismeasure of Man*; Jordan, *The White Man's Burden*; Myrdal, *An American Dilemma*; Du Bois, "The Conservation of Races," in *W. E. B. Du Bois: Writings*. On America and the civil rights era, see Branch, *Parting the Waters*; Branch, *Pillar of Fire*; Branch, *At Canaan's Edge*.

6. Bebbington, *Evangelicalism in Modern Britain*, 2–19. See also Noll, *The Scandal of the Evangelical Mind*, 7–10.

7. Nettles, *Beginnings in Britain*, 40–44.

Introduction

Baptist life. Chapter 1 sets the stage for the ideological change, arguing that between World War II and the Supreme Court's school desegregation decision, Southern Baptists from all theological camps advocated racial equality. Most did not believe, however, that a belief in equality conflicted with segregation. Chapter 2 shows how the changing social climate between 1955 and 1970 drove Southern Baptists to reflect on segregation and finally to reject it. Their commitment to conservative theology played an important role in the change. Chapter 3 argues that even within the theologically liberal Christian Life Commission, progressive thinkers appealed to evangelical theology to move their denomination on the race issue. Chapter 4 shows how Southern Baptist seminaries and colleges gradually integrated and appropriated conservative theology to gain support from the denomination. Chapter 5 considers how African Americans viewed the Southern Baptist Convention during the second half of the twentieth century. The chapter argues that blacks felt evangelical theology logically demanded racial inclusiveness and wondered why the Southern Baptist Convention failed to live up to the theology it professed to believe. Chapters 6 and 7 argue that by the 1980s, evangelical views had established denominational opinion in favor of racial equality and integration. Because of the widespread agreement on race, persons on both sides of a denominational controversy agreed in their approach to race despite disagreeing on a host of other issues. A brief conclusion argues that continuing to change the Southern Baptist Convention in the area of racial justice will require appealing to the Bible above all other sources.

Chapter 1

Segregation in the Southern Baptist Convention

SWEDISH SOCIOLOGIST GUNNAR MYRDAL's assessment of race relations in America during the 1940s applied well to the Southern Baptist Convention. Myrdal argued in *An American Dilemma* that a conflict existed between Americans' general moral beliefs and the specific beliefs they held regarding African Americans. He wrote:

> The "American Dilemma" referred to in the title of this book, is the ever-raging conflict between, on the one hand, the valuations preserved on the general plane which we shall call the "American Creed," where the American thinks, talks, and acts under the influence of high national and Christian precepts, and, on the other hand, the valuations on specific planes of individual and group living, where personal and local interests; economic, social, and sexual jealousies; considerations of community prestige and conformity; group prejudice against particular persons or types of people; and all sorts of miscellaneous wants, impulses, and habits dominate his outlook.[1]

The American dilemma was also the Southern Baptist dilemma. In short, Southern Baptists believed generally in equality for all people and professed that belief publicly. But at the same time, they were segregationists who did not recognize the conflict between their general beliefs and their specific beliefs regarding African Americans. On the race issue there was

---

1. Myrdal, *An American Dilemma*, 1:xliii.

a widespread failure in the Southern Baptist Convention to press for social justice or challenge the prevailing segregationist assumptions. Its more progressive moderate minority and its conservative majority participated in the failure. Even after the Supreme Court's 1954 decision outlawing segregation in public schools, Southern Baptists of every theological stripe failed to characterize segregation as a moral evil.[2] A general belief in equality never meant anything except separate but equal for Southern Baptists in the decade following World War II.

Advocates of Equality

Southern Baptists had always professed a general commitment to the idea of equality. They called for evangelization of all races, Christian treatment of all races, and ministerial education for all races. Beginning in 1849—just four years after the Southern Baptist Convention's inception—the convention addressed race relations at its annual meeting by advocating the evangelization of slaves.[3] Annual meetings returned to the topic of race in 1867 with a recommendation to evangelize the African continent, in 1870 with discussion of missions to people of African descent both at home and abroad, in 1878 with discussion of "evangelization of the colored people at the South," in 1915 with a "Report on the General Condition of the Negro," in 1918 with an address by a representative of the Negro Baptist Sate Convention of Arkansas, and in 1940 with a resolution expressing gratitude for the end of mob violence and hope for interracial understanding.[4] As in the Southern Presbyterian denomination, which appointed a permanent committee for Negro work in 1946, the Southern Baptist Convention's general support for equality increased following World War II.[5] Between 1944 and 1954 the Southern Baptist Convention took no fewer than ten official actions pertaining to race.[6] The first of those actions was adopting a 1944 report by the Social Service Commission acknowledging "the increasing acuteness of the race problem within the nation, and especially in the South, and the danger which crouches at our doors, that we shall be guilty of unchristian attitudes

---

2. Brown v. Board of Education, 347 U.S. 483 (1954).

3. "Importance of Domestic Missions," *Fifth Annual Report*, p. 39, Box 1, Folder 1, Race Relations Collection.

4. See Box 1, Folders 1–11, Race Relations Collection.

5. Thompson, *Presbyterians in the South*, 420–22. Alvis, *Religion and Race*, 17.

6. See Box 1, Folders 1–19, Race Relations Collection.

and actions."[7] By 1947 the convention had appointed both a committee on race relations and a committee on Negro ministerial education. Both ad hoc committees touted the need for equality.

The 1947 report of the Committee on Race Relations was a case in point. The committee made several recommendations concerning partnering with African-American denominations, fostering interracial brotherhood, informing the convention of current legislation related to race relations, and continuing the work of a multi-denominational interracial committee on ministerial education for African Americans known as the Inter-Convention Committee on Negro Ministerial Education.[8] The committee also chided any who dared to criticize the Southern Baptist Convention's commitment to equality:

> Frequently, it has been said that Southern Baptists are doing "little or nothing" in this field. That is because much has been unreported and much has lain unnoticed in the reports of various agencies and groups. When put together, the total effort of Southern Baptists in interracial service and co-operation indicates a rather widespread consciousness of our task and obligation.[9]

The committee argued that the Home Mission Board, American Baptist Theological Seminary, Sunday School Board, Baptist Student Unions, seminaries, Woman's Missionary Union, the Inter-Convention Committee on Negro Ministerial Education, and state conventions all carried out significant work with African Americans.[10] The only shortcoming that the committee noted among Southern Baptists was occasional indifference to racial advance: "Sampling here and there in the various states, however, reveals situations ranging from indifference to active interest and participation in inter-racial matters, and well planned programs of helpfulness."[11] All told, the committee estimated that the Southern Baptist Convention spent a total of $205,592 on "Negro work" in 1947.[12] Some

---

7. "Recommendations," *Southern Baptist Convention Proceedings*, p. 135, Box 1, Folder 12, Race Relations Collection.

8. "Friday—Morning Session," *Southern Baptist Convention Proceedings*, pp. 47–48, Box 1, Folder 14, Race Relations Collection.

9. "Committee on Race Relations," *1947 Southern Baptist Convention Annual*, 340, in "SBC Annuals."

10. "Committee on Race Relations," *1947 Southern Baptist Convention Annual*, 340.

11. "Committee on Race Relations," *1947 Southern Baptist Convention Annual*, 340.

12. "Committee on Race Relations," *1947 Southern Baptist Convention Annual*, 340.

state conventions appointed similar committees. A committee appointed by the Alabama Baptist Convention in 1940 did similar work at the state level, investigating the "Negro religious situation."[13]

The Southern Baptist representatives on the Inter-Convention Committee on Negro Ministerial Education likewise professed belief in the equality of all people. Working from 1947 to 1951 to determine how to increase the quality of ministerial education among African-American ministers, the committee was a joint undertaking of the Southern Baptist Convention, the Northern Baptist Convention, and the National Baptist Convention, Inc. For its work, the committee visited black Baptist seminaries and college departments of religion that contributed significantly to education of African-American Baptist ministers. The committee completed all its visits by May 30, 1950, and delivered its final report in 1951.[14] Especially disconcerting for Southern Baptist committee members was the inequality between educational opportunities for black and white ministers. An interim report of the Committee on Negro Ministerial Education to the Southern Baptist Convention acknowledged "that what has been done to date in this field has not been sufficient to produce an adequately trained Negro Baptist leadership."[15] The same report recommended a cooperative effort with other denominations to determine the appropriate courses of action to remedy the deficiency among black ministers. Another report likewise acknowledged a need for helping African-American ministers in major cities: "the average (black) Baptist minister was regarded as more poorly trained than the average minister of any other major denomination in these cities."[16] Victor T. Glass, a Southern Baptist working at the American Baptist Theological Seminary to train African-American ministers, wrote in 1950 to committee member Edward A. McDowell, a New Testament professor at the Southern Baptist

---

13. Flynt, *Alabama Baptists*, 449–50.

14. "Report to the Members of the Commission on Survey of Negro Baptist Ministerial Education," Box 74, "Negro Ministerial Education–1947–1950" Folder, Executive Committee Records, Administrative and Program Planning Files.

15. "Report of Committee on Negro Ministerial Education," Box 74, "Negro Ministerial Education–1947–1950" Folder, Executive Committee Records, Administrative and Program Planning Files.

16. "Survey of Negro Baptist Ministerial Education Progress Report, November 1, 1950," Box 74, "Negro Ministerial Education–1947–1950" Folder, Executive Committee Records, Administrative and Program Planning Files.

Theological Seminary, that some change was essential in order to raise the training of African Americans to an adequate level:

> There has to be something done at our school here. We cannot even attempt to do an adequate job with the great disparity among our students with respect to academic background. We should either seek to train college men here exclusively or not at all. I really wish that our three white seminaries would open their doors to college men and let us go on helping the vast number of men who need help, but who cannot do advanced theological work.[17]

Similarly, a 1950 report of the committee urged Southern Baptists to help provide "theological training for college-educated candidates for the ministry comparable to that given in our white seminaries."[18]

In addition to advocating equal educational opportunities for ministers of both races, the committee made some effort to foster increasingly fraternal relationships between white and black Baptists. African-American Baptist leader Benjamin Mays corresponded with McDowell, and their relationship eventuated in McDowell's invitation for Mays, who served as president of Morehouse College in Atlanta, to address the 1950 annual meeting of the Southern Baptist Convention in Chicago.[19] McDowell wrote to Southern Baptist leader Herschel Hobbs that Mays was "one of the outstanding Negro Christian leaders in America."[20] Another Morehouse faculty member, George D. Kelsey, at a 1948 meeting of the Inter-Convention Committee on Negro Ministerial Education, delivered a paper which so impressed Southern Baptists that Una Roberts Lawrence of the Home Mission Board sent a copy to Porter Routh of the Southern Baptist Convention's Sunday School Board.[21] Kelsey also addressed the

---

17. Victor T. Glass to Edward A. McDowell, 3 March 1950, Box 74, "Negro Ministerial Education–1947–1950" Folder, Executive Committee Records, Administrative and Program Planning Files.

18. "Report of Committee on Negro Ministerial Education," Box 74, "Negro Ministerial Education–1947–1950" Folder, Executive Committee Records, Administrative and Program Planning Files.

19. Edward A. McDowell to Benjamin Mays, 4 January 1950, Box 74, "Negro Ministerial Education–1947–1950" Folder, Executive Committee Records, Administrative and Program Planning Files.

20. Edward A. McDowell to Herschel Hobbs, 12 February 1950, Box 74, "Negro Ministerial Education–1947–1950" Folder, Executive Committee Records, Administrative and Program Planning Files.

21. Dorothy B. Armentrout to Porter Routh, 3 May 1948, Box 74, "Negro Ministerial Education–1947–1950" Folder, Executive Committee Records, Administrative and

1947 annual meeting of the Southern Baptist Convention on the topic of interracial relations, and the convention asked the Sunday School Board to publish Kelsey's address.[22] The inter-convention committee employed African-American sociologist Ira Reid of Haverford College to direct its survey of institutions training African-American ministers. Southern Baptist members of the committee praised Reid: "We were impressed with the excellent job that is being done by Dr. Ira Reid of Haverford College, the director of the survey. As you may know, he is one of the ranking sociologists of the country."[23] Some state conventions followed a similar trajectory. The Alabama Woman's Missionary Union, for example, hired a black woman to work with black women and children in 1938.[24]

At times, committee reports adopted by the Southern Baptist Convention did not reflect the sentiment of the convention at large. This reality presented an opportunity to racial progressives, for they could get segregationist messengers to adopt reports using the language of equality. This reality also worked to the disadvantage of racial progressives, however, because the language of equality did not translate into opposition of segregation.

Supporters of Segregation

Despite their general belief in equality and attempts at fraternal relationships with African American Baptists, Southern Baptists supported segregation. The Southern Baptist commitment to segregation contrasted with northern Baptists, Methodists, Episcopalians, Presbyterians, and Congregationalists, who between World War II and 1954 all repented of racial segregation and vowed to promote integration in churches and society.[25] For all their talk of equality, Southern Baptists on the Inter-Convention Committee on Negro Ministerial Education never challenged racial separation in theological education. There were even hints, in the form of decreased financial support for the American Baptist Theological Seminary, that Southern Baptists might

---

Program Planning Files.

22. *1947 Southern Baptist Convention Annual*, 48, in "SBC Annuals." The Sunday School Board published Kelsey's address as Kelsey, "Christian Love and Race Relations."

23. Edward A. McDowell to Duke K. McCall, 29 January 1951, Box 74, "Negro Ministerial Education–1947–1950" Folder, Executive Committee Records, Administrative and Program Planning Files.

24. Flynt, *Alabama Baptists*, 449; Jackson, *Women of Vision*, 86.

25. Reimers, *White Protestantism and the Negro*, 112–13.

not have been as serious as they said about providing equal opportunities within segregation. In 1951 McDowell reported to Duke McCall, executive secretary of the Southern Baptist Convention's Executive Committee, that the American Baptist Theological Seminary could not contribute to the continuation of the Negro ministerial education study because its funding from the Southern Baptist Convention had been "drastically reduced since this survey was authorized."[26] The funding issue aside, committee members made clear both that they did not recommend a change in segregated ministerial education and that rank-and-file Southern Baptists would not accept such a change if proposed. A supplementary report prepared by the committee in 1950 concluded that improving segregated schools was the answer to the dilemma of an uneducated Negro ministry:

> It would seem from the small percentage of Negroes in the total enrollment of white divinity schools that the solution to the problem of a better educated Negro ministry must lie in developing fewer but better Negro divinity schools.... A further possible reason for such a development is implied in the queries of one Negro attending one of the best northern white seminaries. He queries: "Is the Negro educated in the 'white' seminary really qualified to go back to his colored congregation and to really minister to them?" "How many of the subjects in our white seminaries are there which are being taught from the specific angle of the black man?" It would seem to the present writer that the answer must be, not many.[27]

In preparation for the release of its final report to the Southern Baptist Convention, L. S. Sedberry, Southern Baptist Convention secretary of the Commission on the American Baptist Theological Seminary, urged the committee not to press Southern Baptists in the area of race relations. Sedberry said at a 1951 meeting: "I think we ought to be careful with being too frank with data and material of the survey. It could be dynamite. We all want to do some constructive, helpful work. A doctor doesn't

---

26. Edward A. McDowell to Duke K. McCall, 29 January 1951, Box 74, "Negro Ministerial Education–1947–1950" Folder, Executive Committee Records, Administrative and Program Planning Files.

27. Frank D. Watson, "Negro Baptist Ministerial Education: A Report Based on Insights Gained through Visits to Ten Northern Theological Schools for the Joint Survey Commission on Negro Baptist Ministerial Education," p. 7, Box 74, "Negro Ministerial Education–1947–1950" Folder, Executive Committee Records, Administrative and Program Planning Files.

always tell a patient how sick he is or what all is wrong with him."[28] The committee followed Sedberry's advice, telling the 1951 annual meeting of the Southern Baptist Convention that it was "not prepared at this juncture to indicate in detail the finding of the survey."[29] In 1950 Stewart Newman, a philosophy professor at Southwestern Baptist Theological Seminary, warned McDowell that the committee should not push Southern Baptists to integrate, but rather "be wise and intelligent in seizing the opportunities that are ours in this most strategic situation."[30]

Baptists in state and local leadership also supported segregation. In Alabama, for example, the state Baptist newspaper, the *Alabama Baptist*, printed occasional calls for equality but tempered those calls with consistent advocacy of segregation. In 1945, the "Report of the Social Service Commission as Adopted by the State Convention in Annual Session at Montgomery" called for equality among the races. The report said, "Let whites accord the negro all the rights of citizenship as fast as he can qualify for them."[31] A 1946 article by A. C. Miller, at the time interracial secretary for the Baptist General Convention of Texas, similarly urged an end to prideful proclamations of racial superiority: "Racial supremacy, by whatever race it may be attained, only increases the responsibility to serve those people less advanced in their development in the spirit of him who 'came not to be ministered unto, but to minister.'"[32] Another 1946 article denounced lynchings as suppressing the rights of minority groups while a 1947 editorial called for even-handed justice for all races.[33]

But mixed with these calls for equality was an underlying commitment to segregation. The same editorial that called for even-handed justice told Baptists that "every race should develop along the line of its inherent

---

28. "Minutes of the Meeting of the Joint Convention Committee on Negro Ministerial Education, January 24, 1951," p. 2, Box 74, "Negro Ministerial Education–1947–1950" Folder, Executive Committee Records, Administrative and Program Planning Files.

29. *1951 Southern Baptist Convention Annual*, 390, in "SBC Annuals."

30. Stewart A. Newman to Edward A. McDowell, 23 September 1950, Box 74, "Negro Ministerial Education–1947–1950" Folder, Executive Committee Records, Administrative and Program Planning Files.

31. L. E. Barton, "Report of the Social Service Commission As Adopted by the State Convention in Annual Session at Montgomery," *Alabama Baptist*, 29 November 1945, 5.

32. A. C. Miller, "God, Others, and Us," *Alabama Baptist*, 17 January 1946, 7.

33. William Kernan, "Lesson of the Georgia Lynchings," *Alabama Baptist*, 3 October 1946, 7. L. L. Gwaltney, "The White and Colored Races," *Alabama Baptist*, 23 January 1947, 3.

genius and not seek amalgamation with other races, for a hybrid people would have all of the weaknesses and none of the strengths of the races from which they sprang."[34] Likewise, the 1947 report of the Alabama Baptist Convention's Social Service Commission defended segregationism by denouncing as dangerous "radical demands, by Federal government agencies and others, for the rapid and complete removal of age-long discriminations by legislation."[35] Even a hardline defense of segregation found its way onto the *Alabama Baptist*'s editorial page. Horace C. Wilkinson, an Alabama judge and Baptist layman, argued in 1948 that racial purity is a gift from God and that "the Christian religion does not call for or demand social and political equality of the Negro in the United States." Citing Genesis, Jeremiah, and Deuteronomy for biblical support, Wilkinson said integration would lead to race mixing, which would lead to deterioration of both the Christian church and society in general:

> There are many reasons why segregation is desirable but the main reason is that we know beyond a reasonable doubt and to a moral certainty that social association and political intimacies between people of different races inevitably brings about and leads to intermarriage. We also know that intermarriage destroys racial purity. The destruction of racial purity is the destruction of one of God's priceless gifts to man.[36]

Southern Baptist leader M. E. Dodd, pastor of the First Baptist Church in Shreveport, Louisiana, praised Jim Crow laws as protecting Negroes and spoke against any efforts to integrate education.[37] In the same year, an editorial by Alabama editor L. L. Gwaltney faulted the Ku Klux Klan only for its methods, but not for its objectives. "One cannot believe that those men were actually vicious in their hearts but they are badly wrong in their methods," Gwaltney wrote regarding the Klan's harassment of white women who were training Negro women to become Girl Scout leaders.[38] When Hugh Brimm, executive secretary-treasurer of the Southern Baptist Convention's

---

34. L. L. Gwaltney, "The White and Colored Races," *Alabama Baptist*, 23 January 1947.

35. J. C. Stivender, "Report of the Social Service Commission to Alabama Baptist Convention, 1947," *Alabama Baptist*, 15 January 1948, 5.

36. Horace C. Wilkinson, "The Matter of Segregation," *Alabama Baptist*, 5 February 1948, 8.

37. Religion News Service, "Southern Baptist Leader Opposes Civil Rights Program," *Alabama Baptist*, 10 June 1948, 1.

38. L. L. Gwaltney, "The Klan Reasserts Itself," *Alabama Baptist*, 24 June 1948, 1.

Social Service Commission, suggested that the Dixiecrat political party was based on white supremacy and held a philosophy akin to that of Hitler and Mussolini, the *Alabama Baptist*'s Hal D. Bennett responded with a harsh editor's note: "My opinion is that our good Dr. Brimm either is misquoted or doesn't know what he is talking about."[39] In 1949, Baptists in Birmingham debated whether Baptist hospitals should accept federal funds, and one argument against accepting the funds was that acceptance might prohibit racial discrimination.[40] Like both the Committee on Race Relations and the Inter-Convention Committee on Negro Ministerial Education, Alabama Baptists reflected the Southern Baptist consensus on race relations during this period. Consciousness regarding race issues was rising and most Southern Baptists desired equal opportunities for both races, but they saw no reason to question the prevailing system of segregation.

Similar Attitudes on Both Sides

Between 1945 and 1954 Southern Baptists across the theological spectrum held similar positions. Conservatives and moderates virtually all desired some form of equality within the segregated system. There were a few exceptions. Clarence Jordan, liberal New Testament scholar and racial progressive, established the interracial Koinonia Farm in the 1940s. Walter Nathan Johnson, also a racial and theological progressive, conducted interracial seminars during the same period. Both Jordan and Johnson, however, conducted their activities outside the mainstream of Southern Baptist life.[41] Within the denominational structure, a large degree of homogeneity prevailed between World War II and the United States Supreme Court's decision to end segregation in public schools.

Illustrative of this trend were the writings of a moderate, North Carolina pastor Das Kelly Barnett, and a conservative, Alabama pastor L. E. Barton. Barnett, pastor of the Baptist Church of Chapel Hill in Chapel Hill, North Carolina, published between 1946 and 1949 a journal called *Christian Frontiers*. The journal occupied the theological left of the Southern Baptist Convention, criticizing Baptists for their lack of theological

---

39. Religion News Service, "Baptist Leader Encouraged on Attitude toward Negro," *Alabama Baptist*, 30 September 1948, 7.

40. Flynt, *Alabama Baptists*, 452.

41. See K'Meyer, *Interracialism and Christian Community in the Postwar South*; Stricklin, *A Genealogy of Dissent*, 8–22.

tolerance, lauding the usefulness of the historical-critical method of studying Scripture, and recommending books by such authors as Emil Brunner, Reinhold Niebuhr, Albert Camus, and Henry Sloane Coffin.[42] W. O. Carver, a Southern Baptist Theological Seminary professor who was no conservative, criticized a 1946 article in *Christian Frontiers* as being "vicious in its interpretation of the Scripture" and "pagan in its conception of Jesus."[43] Among the issues *Christian Frontiers* addressed was race prejudice, and the journal printed numerous articles attacking perceived injustices. A May 1946 editorial encouraged Southern Baptists to speak out on difficult issues like racism rather than limiting their resolutions to topics that were uncontroversial.[44] In the same issue, Lee C. Sheppard, pastor of Pullen Memorial Baptist Church in Raleigh, North Carolina, urged equal opportunities for people of all races:

> What we want for white people, we want also for our colored brethren. For our sakes, as well as for theirs, in all our strivings toward the richer, fuller life, we would include our Negro friends who work with us and for us. . . . For them we want equal opportunities—in the exercise of the franchise, local and national; equal opportunity to work that they may make real contributions to the wealth and health of all of us; equal opportunity for educational and vocational training; equal pay for equal quality and quantity of work.[45]

Articles in other issues criticized stereotypes of African Americans and argued Jesus would never countenance racial superiority of any kind. The publication even pushed for an antilynching law and spoke against those who used African Americans as scapegoats for the South's problems.[46] Yet

---

42. See, for example, George B. Cutten, "Intolerant Baptists," *Christian Frontiers*, March 1946, 90–96; Franklin W. Young, "The Historical Method and Biblical Studies," *Christian Frontiers*, April 1946, 111–20; "Books," *Christian Frontiers*, January 1947, 32–35; "Book Reviews," *Christian Frontiers*, February 1948, 236–37.

43. W. O. Carver to Das Kelley Barnett, 14 February 1946, Box 9, Folder 1, W. O. Carver Papers.

44. "More Resolutions, Please, Southern Baptists," *Christian Frontiers*, May 1946, 139–40.

45. Lee C. Sheppard, "Industrialization of the South," *Christian Frontiers*, May 1946, 166.

46. Das Kelley Barnett, "The Negro and the Ballot," *Christian Frontiers*, June 1946, 181–82. W. O. Carver, "What Think Ye of the Christ?," *Christian Frontiers*, June 1946, 183–90. John Arch McMillan, "Forty-One Lynchings," *Christian Frontiers*, November 1946, 275–76. Raven McDavid, "Patterns of Fascism—Southern Style," *Christian*

in its first year and a half of publication, *Christian Frontiers* made only one explicit attack against segregation, when missionary G. W. Strother argued that segregation in America hurt the cause of missions abroad.[47] For Barnett, the liberal spirit did not translate into open resistance of the segregationist status quo.

The story was very much the same for Barton, pastor of the First Baptist Church in Jasper, Alabama. Barton made clear in both his private correspondence and public writings that he stood against anyone who cast doubt on the authority or the inspiration of the Bible, or raised questions about historic Christian orthodoxy. In 1941, Barton criticized as "modernist" an article by Barnett in Southern Seminary's journal, the *Review and Expositor*, in which Barnett said of the Bible, "God did not entrust His revelation to a book." Barton was particularly distressed that "the Barnett article was published in the seminary magazine, and, as there was no dissent, with the seeming approval of the seminary."[48] Despite his theological differences with Barnett, Barton's published statements on the issue of race sounded similar to those of his more liberal contemporary. The 1945 report of the Alabama Social Service Commission, which Barton wrote as the commission's chair, argued strongly for equality of all races. "Let our nation rise to such a level of judicial justice that the rights of a negro, and of a poor white man, will be just as inviolate and sacrosanct in our courts as the rights of the rich who have money and influence to defend themselves," Barton wrote.[49] His report additionally called for equal wages for all men who perform a hard day's labor, regardless of race. Still, along with these calls for equality, Barton never said a word challenging Alabama's segregated system.

The cases of Barnett and Barton illustrated an approach that had numerous manifestations. J. B. Weatherspoon, chairman of the Social Service Commission and a professor at Southern Seminary, like Barnett and Barton, advocated racial equality. By many accounts Weatherspoon was Southern Baptists' most vocal spokesman for racial equality. While serving on the Social Service Commission, Weatherspoon worked tirelessly to expand the commission's budget and was instrumental in hiring Brimm as the first

---

Frontiers, December 1946, 328–40.

47. G. W. Strother, "Three Vital Issues," *Christian Frontiers*, February 1947, 47–53.

48. L. E. Barton to W. O. Carver, 8 December 1941, Box 9, Folder 1, W. O. Carver Papers.

49. L. E. Barton, "Report of the Social Service Commission as Adopted by the State Convention in Annual Session at Montgomery," *Alabama Baptist*, 29 November 1945, 5.

full-time employee devoted to social causes. The year 1954 marked one of Weatherspoon's greatest achievements in the area of race relations. That year, after the United States Supreme Court outlawed segregation in public schools, the Southern Baptist Convention's Christian Life Commission presented a recommendation to the convention that it affirm the court's ruling. Messengers to the denomination's annual meeting in St. Louis debated the recommendation vigorously, and there appeared to be a groundswell of opposition. But then Weatherspoon stepped to the podium and pleaded for messengers to affirm the Supreme Court:

> Now, what this Committee is doing tonight is not to argue the question, but to face the situation. And only to say, that we Southern Baptists are not going to go in another direction, when we have over our heads a banner that reads "Forward in Jesus Christ." We are not going to shut our eyes to the fact that now in a critical period, our nation needs men of faith, men who believe in Jesus Christ, not to put our feet in the mud, but we need to lift our heads, and to raise our minds to understand as far as we can, what is the Christian thing to do in a most difficult time. And if we withdraw this from our consideration tonight, we are saying to the United States of America, "Count Baptists out in the matter of equal justice," and I do not believe we want to do that.[50]

Upon hearing Weatherspoon's address, messengers voted to approve the Christian Life Commission's recommendation with fewer than fifty negative votes in a convention of approximately nine thousand messengers. The convention's action was similar to that of Southern Presbyterians, who passed a declaration against discrimination following the Supreme Court's decision in 1954.[51]

But even Weatherspoon avoided challenging the segregationist status quo. Files of Weatherspoon's sermons from the 1940s, 1950s, and 1960s do not include a single sermon specifically on the topic of race.[52] When Weatherspoon spoke about segregation the year following the Supreme Court decision, he stressed that Christians are obligated to obey the law regarding segregation in public education but need not worry that the

---

50. J. B. Weatherspoon, "Address to Southern Baptist Convention, 1954," Box 1, Folder 19, Race Relations Collection.

51. Reimers, *White Protestantism and the Negro*, 115.

52. See Series 4, Box 3, Folders 26–28, J. B. Weatherspoon Papers. Weatherspoon did preach on the need generally to address social issues. See, for example, J. B. Weatherspoon, "Jesus is Lord," in Valentine, *Christian Faith in Action*, 1–10.

court's ruling cancels the right of private schools to remain segregated.[53] There is no legal code for private and personal dealings, he argued, and believers need only ask themselves whether their conduct meets the "full requirement of the Christian spirit."[54] Wayne Ward, a friend and colleague of Weatherspoon's at Southern Seminary, believed that Weatherspoon failed to speak against segregation because "like everyone else," he feared how rank-and-file Southern Baptists might react.[55] Historian Martin Marty argued that mainstream Protestants were also unable to break down boundaries of race.[56] Yet Southern Baptists defended segregation with particular firmness. On the left, on the right, and in the middle of the theological spectrum, Southern Baptists between 1945 and 1954 expressed conviction regarding equality for the races, but generally they did not challenge segregation. A Southern Baptist's theological viewpoint did not apparently make much difference when it came to race relations.

Reactions to *Brown v. Board of Education*

Neither did Southern Baptist opinions vary by geography. When the Supreme Court handed down its *Brown v. Board of Education* decision on May 17, 1954, reactions from every state in the South confirmed that Southern Baptists tended to call for equality but not oppose segregation. The state Baptist papers were a telling forum for public opinion because they printed both editorials by Baptist leaders and letters from readers. Generally, state Baptist papers divided into three categories in their responses to the Supreme Court's decision. One group of papers expressed some sympathy with the integrationist cause. A second group refused to take a position either for or against the court's decision but urged restraint, calm, and respect for law on the part of all Baptists. The third group spoke explicitly against the desegregation ruling. In no state paper did the editorial staff take a position against segregation. Further, in papers that included letters

---

53. J. B. Weatherspoon, "Justice in Race Relations," Series 3, Box 2, Folder 29, J. B. Weatherspoon Papers.

54. J. B. Weatherspoon, "Justice in Race Relations," Series 3, Box 2, Folder 29, J. B. Weatherspoon Papers.

55. Wayne Ward, interview by author, audio recording, Louisville, Kentucky, 12 February 2008.

56. Marty, *Pilgrims in Their Own Land*, 388.

from readers, anti-segregation articles typically provoked letters to the editor arguing the opposite position.

The three most progressive papers following the *Brown* decision were North Carolina's *Biblical Recorder*, Texas' *Baptist Standard*, and Virginia's *Religious Herald*. Yet even in these papers the reaction was mixed. Only the *Biblical Recorder* advertised racially integrated activities in the months following *Brown*.[57] Its editorial stance did not oppose segregation, but argued that the decision was almost inevitable and must be met with calm.[58] A letter to the editor opposed integration and pointed out that Baptists historically had not viewed segregation as unchristian.[59] In Virginia the situation was much the same. While the editor took no official position on the ruling and urged obedience to the law, two articles by Southern Seminary professor Guy Ranson commended the Supreme Court and urged desegregation.[60] A letter from a reader, however, argued against Ranson's articles and said blacks should be thankful for what the South had done for them already rather than striving for social equality.[61] Texas' *Baptist Standard* published an editorial arguing that the *Brown* decision must be obeyed simply because it was the law of the land.[62] The *Baptist Standard* was the only paper in the South to publish an article admonishing Southern Baptists to change their attitudes regarding segregation. Foy Valentine, then-director of the Christian Life Commission of Texas, argued regarding the attitudes of those opposed to the Supreme Court's decision that "whatever else may be said about these attitudes, they cannot be justified by the New Testament or by the spirit and teachings of Christ."[63] The *Baptist Standard* featured no letters from readers.

---

57. "Interracial Institutes to Be Held in July," *Biblical Recorder*, 5 June 1954, 15; "Walt N. Johnson Interracial Retreat," *Biblical Recorder*, 5 July 1954, 5.

58. "Don't Blame the Supreme Court," *Biblical Recorder*, 29 May 1954, 5, 8; "Proud of the South," *Biblical Recorder*, 5 June 1954, 5.

59. "R. C. Bolen, "Convention Action on Segregation," *Biblical Recorder*, 24 July 1954, 15.

60. "The End of Segregation," *Religious Herald*, 27 May 1954, 10–11; Guy H. Ranson, "Baptists and the Supreme Court Decision," *Religious Herald*, 15 July 1954, 16; Guy H. Ranson, "Was 'Separate But Equal' Legal?," *Religious Herald*, 12 August 1954, 5, 16.

61. J. Clinton Hogg, "Christianity and Segregation," *Religious Herald*, 26 August 1954, 11.

62. "Segregation's Problems," *Baptist Standard*, 10 June 1954, 2.

63. Foy Valentine, "A Christian Solution," *Baptist Standard*, 15 July 1954, 6.

The largest number of state papers, fell into the second category—those that took no position on the ruling itself but urged Baptists to remain calm and behave in a Christian manner. Two of these papers, Florida's *Baptist Witness* and Tennessee's *Baptist and Reflector*, printed an article opposing segregation. In both cases it was the same anti-segregation article reprinted from a Missouri pastor, and other content made clear that the article did not reflect the opinions of the editors or the readers.[64] Neither paper printed any other article in 1954 advocating an anti-segregation position. The *Baptist and Reflector*'s own editorials urged blacks and whites to approach the Supreme Court decision with wisdom, patience, and a Christian spirit.[65] The *Baptist Witness*'s editorials urged readers to respect the law and observed regarding the Southern Baptist Convention's approval of the *Brown* decision that "not a few of the brethren felt we would have been better off to have said nothing whatever about the antisegregation decision, but obviously the great majority of the messengers felt that it would have been less than Christian to simply ignore the issue."[66]

The state Baptist papers in Alabama, Arkansas, Kentucky, Mississippi, and South Carolina took similar approaches to the 1954 desegregation decision. The *Alabama Baptist* urged restraint and caution by southerners of all races immediately following the decision, and later in the year spoke against efforts to give government money to private schools that were seeking to avoid desegregation.[67] The *Arkansas Baptist* took no position on the ruling and noted its purposeful lack of a position twice during 1954 in editor's notes attached to articles dealing with race.[68] Kentucky's Baptist paper printed only a handful of articles touching on the topic of race during 1954. Among those articles were two editorials. One stressed the need for calm and seeking

---

64. R. Lofton Hudson, "Is Segregation Christian?," *Baptist Witness*, 5 August 1954, 2; R. Lofton Hudson, "Is Segregation Christian?," *Baptist and Reflector*, 5 August 1954, 4.

65. Richard N. Owen, "The Supreme Court Decision Will Be Implemented through the Christian Spirit," *Baptist and Reflector*, 3 June 1954, 2.

66. "A Convention With Apprehensions," *Baptist Witness*, 16 June 1954, 4. See also "The Ruling Against Segregation," *Baptist Witness*, 27 May 1954, 4.

67. Leon Macon, "The Supreme Court Decision," *Alabama Baptist*, 27 May 1954, 3; Leon Macon, "Georgia Baptists Take Stand on Private School Amendment," *Alabama Baptist*, 4 November 1954, 3; Leon Macon, "Private Schools," *Alabama Baptist*, 9 December 1954, 3.

68. See Gainer E. Bryan Jr., "Baptists Should Speak on School Issue," *Arkansas Baptist*, 27 May 1954, 13. See also "A Negro Speaks," *Arkansas Baptist*, 4 November 1954, 3.

guidance from Christ.[69] The other editorial urged calm once again after the Southern Baptist Convention affirmed the court's decision and reminded the state's Baptist segregationists that "the Convention's action in no way binds any Baptist church."[70] Mississippi's *Baptist Record* did not explicitly oppose the desegregation decision but made clear that Baptist bodies had no business speaking to segregation since it was a political matter. Regarding the Southern Baptist Convention's action supporting *Brown*, the *Baptist Record* argued, "The lowest point in the whole Convention was when the Christian Life Commission went out of its field to dip its finger in politics."[71] Of nine letters to the editor in Mississippi, eight opposed the Supreme Court's decision. None of the letters advocated integration.[72] South Carolina's *Baptist Courier* took no position on the court's ruling but said the South must move slowly if it hoped to reverse a trend as deep-seated as segregation. The *Baptist Courier* also urged "respect for the rights of all people, regardless of race."[73] For this middle group of papers, equal treatment of all people was important, but potentially unsettling reactions to the Supreme Court decision appeared to be more problematic than segregation itself.

Georgia's *Christian Index* and Louisiana's *Baptist Message* comprised the final category of state Baptist papers—those that came out explicitly against the Supreme Court's ruling to desegregate public schools. The positions in these papers resembled those of independent Baptists, who took a harsher stance for segregation than most Southern Baptists.[74] The *Christian Index* called for prayer, thought, and care following the ruling. But in a slap at the Supreme Court, the paper warned: "Public opinion in Georgia and in some of the other states is not ready for non-segregation. When the law gets ahead of public opinion there always is trouble."[75] Along with its opposition to the decision, the *Christian Index* made repeated pleas for calm and brotherly love.[76] The *Baptist Message* said it could not know the full significance

69. "Court Rules on Segregation," *Western Recorder*, 10 June 1954, 5.

70. "Convention Supports Court Ruling," *Western Recorder*, 24 June 1954, 5.

71. A. L. Goodrich, "The SBC Convention," *Baptist Record*, 10 June 1954, 3.

72. See "Letters to the Editor," *Baptist Record*, 24 June 1954, 3–4; "Letters to the Editor," *Baptist Record*, 8 July 1954, 4; "Letters to the Editor," *Baptist Record*, 22 July 1954, 4; "Letters to the Editor," *Baptist Record*, 2 September 1954, 3–4.

73. "Segregation and the Schools," *Baptist Courier*, 3 June 1954, 2.

74. Leonard, *Baptists in America*, 194–97.

75. "Time For Prayer," *Christian Index*, 27 May 1954, 6.

76. See, for example, "Justice, Calmness Keynote Plea of Commission on Racial Issues," *Christian Index*, 25 November 1954, 19, 21; "Baptist Groups Hear Pleas For

of the decision at such an early date but knew with certainty that the ruling was a bad one: "The action of the U. S. Supreme Court in nullifying segregation of the races in the public schools at this time, we believe, was ill advised. Pressure groups in the North, however, have been working to bring to pass this action for many years." Even southern blacks, the paper said, felt integration was unwise.[77] When the annual meeting of Louisiana's state Baptist Student Union approved of the Supreme Court decision, the *Baptist Message* reminded readers that the students' opinion was the opinion of that body only and did not reflect the opinion of any other Baptist group or institution.[78] Like the *Christian Index*, the *Baptist Message* added to its critical message at least one article teaching that people of all races are created equal and should enjoy equal opportunities.[79]

State Baptist papers were not always an accurate gauge of thought within the Southern Baptist Convention as a whole. In their reaction to the Supreme Court's *Brown* decision, however, the near unanimity of the state papers makes two general conclusions possible. First, Southern Baptists felt that brotherhood among the races and some form of equality were important. All the papers, from the most open to the most violently anti-integration, spoke of equality and brotherhood. Further, no letter to the editor, regardless of how opposed to segregation, attempted to justify unkindness toward African Americans. Second, few Southern Baptists dared to denounce segregation. The few denunciations of segregation to appear in 1954 stood out because of their oddity against the backdrop of overwhelming support for the segregated system.

Conclusion

In the 1940s and 1950s Southern Baptists were committed to racial segregation. A handful of leaders promoted racial progress and were working behind the scenes and through the Southern Baptist Convention and state convention social service commissions to reform the denomination. But even the most progressive voices were afraid to speak against segregation as late as the Supreme Court's *Brown* decision of 1954. In the decade

---

Calmness in Segregation Crisis," *Christian Index*, 2 December 1954, 4.

77. "Non-Segregation," *Baptist Message*, 3 June 1954, 2.

78. "B. S. U. on Interracial Issue," *Baptist Message*, 2 December 1954, 2.

79. Wayne Barton, "Jesus Christ and the Racial Question," *Baptist Message*, 24 June 1954, 1, 4.

following World War II conservatives and progressives in the Southern Baptist Convention talked about the equality of all people, but few on either side challenged the segregated system that had dominated the South since the end of Reconstruction.[80]

---

80. Several historians have drawn a similar conclusion regarding Southern Baptist attitudes toward race relations. See, for example, Newman, *Getting Right with God*; Eighmy, *Churches in Cultural Captivity*; Bailey, *Southern White Protestantism in the Twentieth Century*.

Chapter 2

Conservative Theology, Segregation, and Change

BETWEEN 1955 AND 1970, Southern Baptists began to challenge segregation. Historian Mark Newman labeled this period one of reluctant and incremental change, in which Baptists supported the goals but not the tactics of the civil rights movement until 1964 and then repudiated segregation as unchristian in subsequent years.[1] Kenneth Bailey, in his study of white Southern Protestantism, observed that during this period both national and state denominational bodies for the first time affirmed civil rights and racial equality on a large scale.[2]

Scholars have suggested that conservative theology was to blame for this shift. In his groundbreaking study of the civil rights movement, David Chappell argued that leaders in the field of race relations rejected the naïve optimism of liberalism and based their efforts to integrate America on a "prophetic Christian realism" that denounced sin and confronted segregation with coercive action. Segregationists could not overcome the momentum of the civil rights movement, Chappell argued, because they were unable to mount any theological argument to match prophetic Christian realism.[3] More recently, Russell Moore argued that conservative theology led to the overthrow of Jim Crow in the Southern Baptist Convention. The civil rights movement succeeded in the convention,

---

1. Newman, *Getting Right with God*, 22–34.
2. Bailey, *Southern White Protestantism in the Twentieth Century*, 137–45.
3. Chappell, *A Stone of Hope*.

according to Moore, because liberal agents for change used conservative theology to shame churches into changing their views.[4] Because the gospel did not discriminate along racial lines, Southern Baptists realized that they too had no right to discriminate along racial lines, Moore argued.[5] Anecdotally, Charles Marsh supported Moore's claim with his account of how soteriology drove his father, a Southern Baptist pastor, to repudiate segregation. In Mississippi of the late 1960s, "the federal government we could still vilify" but "the rebukes of evangelical leaders like Billy Graham and Carl F. H. Henry, or American missionaries overseas, made my father wince with shame," Marsh said.[6] Such rebukes reminded Southern Baptists that segregation was inconsistent with belief in a salvation indiscriminately offered to all. This belief compelled Southern Baptists to reject segregation. It compelled Marsh's father:

> Billy Graham, to whom my father attributed his own salvation—certainly much more than Bobby Kennedy or Lyndon Johnson—stirred his uneasy conscience into a willingness to change, if not to see change as God-ordained. "The ground at the foot of the cross is level," Graham said. "It touches my heart when I see whites stand shoulder to shoulder with blacks at the foot of the cross."[7]

The doctrines that caused the change were consistent with conservative theology. Southern Baptist theologian Paige Patterson defined a theological conservative as "an ardent teacher of the Scriptures and related themes who retains no reservation at all about the full authority and complete trustworthiness of the Scriptures." A conservative does not question the historicity of biblical accounts of God's supernatural work, Patterson argued.[8] The doctrines that precipitated the racial shift in the

---

4. Moore, "Crucifying Jim Crow," 4.

5. Moore also argued that the doctrine of the church undermined Jim Crow because it called for a community unity in Christ with no racial boundaries. However, historical evidence for his claim regarding the doctrine of the church is noticeably thinner than historical evidence for his claim regarding the doctrine of salvation. Moore even notes, "Conservative Protestants have appropriated the soteriology of racial reconciliation much more easily than they have appropriated the ecclesiology of racial reconciliation." For this reason, the present chapter will treat the doctrine of salvation as it relates to civil rights and not the doctrine of the church. See Moore, "Crucifying Jim Crow," 17.

6. Marsh, *The Last Days*, 254.

7. Marsh, *The Last Days*, 255.

8. Paige Patterson, "My Definition of a Theological Conservative," p. 3, Folder 4, James T. Draper Jr. Papers.

Southern Baptist Convention fit these criteria of conservatism. The idea that God offered salvation to all people took the Bible's teaching at face value and assumed that God imputes Christ's righteousness to believers in a supernatural transaction. The doctrine also assumed the truthfulness of the biblical accounts of Jesus' death and resurrection. Creation in God's image, another important doctrine for precipitating the Southern Baptist shift, likewise took the Bible at face value and assumed that God created humanity in a historical and supernatural manner. American liberalism, in contrast, modified or rejected the Bible's supernatural claims and used empirical reasoning as a test for religious beliefs.[9] Some Southern Baptists were theological liberals. But when it came to race, they spoke in ways consistent with supernatural creation and regeneration.

Yet while conservative theology played a major role in the demise of segregation, another factor was at work too. Southern Baptists might never have reflected on segregation theologically had not the social climate of the 1950s and 1960s driven them to do so. Whereas Southern Baptists formerly saw no tension between preaching a gospel open to all and maintaining a segregated society, mounting social sentiment against segregation called them to a reevaluation. Negative portrayals of segregation in the media forced Southern Baptists to question whether they were participating in an immoral practice.[10] They concluded that they were and that their theology conflicted with their practice of segregation. As the civil rights movement highlighted the tension between theology and social custom, Southern Baptists became more willing to change their social patterns. The social climate created the occasion for considering the racial applications of theology. Together, theology and the social climate moved Southern Baptists toward what historian Fred Hobson called a "racial conversion."[11]

Key leaders in the Southern Baptist Convention underwent this "racial conversion." They were not all theological conservatives. Yet when they progressed toward racial equality, they did so in a manner consistent with conservative theology

---

9. On theological liberalism, see Hutchison, *The Modernist Impulse in American Protestantism*; Turner, *Without God, without Creed*; Mathews, *The Faith of Modernism*.

10. On the civil rights movement and Martin Luther King Jr., see Young, *An Easy Burden*; Chappell, *A Stone of Hope*; Newman, *The Civil Rights Movement*; Branch, *Parting the Waters*; Branch, *Pillar of Fire*; Branch, *At Canaan's Edge*.

11. Hobson, *But Now I See*, 2.

Conservative Theology, Segregation, and Change
W. A. Criswell

W. A. Criswell (1909–2002) served for fifty years as pastor of the First Baptist Church in Dallas, Texas, the largest congregation in the Southern Baptist Convention.[12] He made his initial mark in the area of race relations with an address delivered twice in South Carolina in 1956—first at the state Baptist convention's evangelism conference and then before the state legislature. On February 21, Criswell told attendees at the evangelism conference that they must face a "baptism by fire" if they hoped to be faithful preachers of the gospel. Describing the types of trials they must face, Criswell said he was astonished at ministers "whose forebears and predecessors were martyrs and were burned at the stake" but who themselves refuse to speak about "this thing of integration." Ministers must resist mandatory desegregation as a "denial of all that we believe in," Criswell argued. He also denounced the Supreme Court's 1954 *Brown v. Board of Education* ruling as illegitimate, wrongly forcing integration on the South. Speaking of those who would integrate, he said, "Let them integrate. Let them sit up there in their dirty shirts and make all their fine speeches. But they are all a bunch of infidels, dying from the neck up."[13]

Criswell gave the address with some modifications before the state legislature the next day, where he appeared at the invitation of Governor George Bell Timmerman Jr., a member of the First Baptist Church of Batesburg, South Carolina. Criswell emphasized that while people of all races are of equal worth, forced integration was "a denial of all that we believe in: the cultural life, the social background, the spiritual life . . . to which our families belong."[14] Just like Baptists and Catholics voluntarily segregate for worship, blacks and whites should segregate for worship, Criswell said, because a segregated arrangement is best for all. Perhaps the most dangerous aspect of integration is that it leads to intermarriage, and intermarriage

---

12. On Criswell, see Keith, *W. A. Criswell*; Gregory, *Too Great a Temptation*; Criswell, *Standing on the Promises*.

13. "Dallas Pastor Stirs Controversy with Statements on Integration," *The Baptist Message*, 1 March 1956, 1, 4; "Dallas Pastor Challenges Race Integration in Church," *Dallas Times Herald*, 22 February 1956, 1; "Criswell Rips Integration," *Dallas Morning News*, 23 February 1956, 1.

14. W. A. Criswell, "An Address by Dr. W. A. Criswell, Pastor, First Baptist Church, Dallas, Texas, to the Joint Assembly, State of South Carolina, Wednesday, February 22, 1956, 12:30 P.M.," Box 82, Folder 2, Executive Committee Records.

hurts families and children, he argued. In a free country, no person should be forced to integrate, Criswell concluded:

> Don't force me by law, by statute, by Supreme Court decision, by any way that they can think of, don't force me to cross over in those intimate things where I don't want to go. Let me build my life. Let me have my church. Let me have my school. Let me have my friends. Let me have my home. Let me have my family. And what you give to me, give to every man in America and keep it like our glorious forefathers made it—a land of the free and the home of the brave.[15]

In 1956 Criswell was an ardent segregationist. By 1968, however, he changed his mind. In a sermon at Dallas First Baptist, Criswell declared the church open to anyone of any race who would trust Jesus for salvation and be baptized by immersion: "I declare that the First Baptist Church of Dallas is now and forever a Philadelphian Church of the Open Door. Anybody can come—anybody, and may God bless him and God attend him in the way as he comes."[16] In his 1969 presidential address to the Southern Baptist Convention, Criswell also expressed his new desegregationist view: "Part of the discipleship of Jesus is lifting the destitute out of the gutter, bridging the gulf between races and answering the cries of the helpless."[17]

Two scholars have interpreted Criswell's change as the political maneuver of a power-hungry man who calculated that he had to hide his segregationist feelings if he hoped to be elected to the top leadership post in the Southern Baptist Convention. Curtis W. Freeman, a professor of theology and Baptist studies at Duke University, offered a particularly harsh assessment of Criswell's change: "As a racial conversion narrative the testimony of W. A. Criswell is less than compelling."[18] Freeman questioned the sincerity of Criswell's racial conversion: "Even his professed change at the interpersonal level is left ambiguous due, in part, to uncertainty about how much his unconverted racialized habits of the past continued to be expressed in his speech and behavior after his racial conversion."[19] Criswell's successor in the pulpit of First Baptist Church, Joel Gregory, likewise portrayed Criswell's

15. Criswell, "An Address by Dr. W. A. Criswell."
16. Criswell, "The Church of the Open Door," in Dehoney, *Baptists See Black*, 81–82.
17. Criswell, "The Two-Edged Sword or Christ in Faith and Work," 1969 Presidential Address to the Southern Baptist Convention, SBC Press Kits Collection.
18. Freeman, "'Never Had I Been So Blind,'" 9.
19. Freeman, "'Never Had I Been So Blind,'" 10.

Conservative Theology, Segregation, and Change

shift on the race issue as political calculation. When he wanted to be elected Southern Baptist Convention president, Gregory wrote, "suddenly, Criswell had a change of heart, publicly repented of his segregationist ways, declared the doors of the church opened to everyone, and was shortly thereafter elected president of the Southern Baptist Convention."[20]

Freeman and Gregory failed to account for the importance of theology in Criswell's change. It is undoubtedly true that factors other than theology contributed to the change, but theology was a critical factor. Changing social circumstances drove Criswell to confront inconsistencies between his soteriology and segregation. Theology and sociology combined to produce a real change in Criswell's actions and statements. Even if Criswell had been insincere, his were the public arguments that shaped Southern Baptist opinion. Freeman and Gregory should have acknowledged, at the very least, that through Criswell's arguments conservative theology provoked other Southern Baptists to renounce segregation.

Criswell believed that the gospel involved an invitation offered equally to people of all races and that all people came to faith in Christ on equal footing. Before the South Carolina legislature, he renounced "malice toward anyone" and declared categorically that whites were not any better than African Americans.[21] In a press conference immediately following his election to the Southern Baptist Convention presidency in 1968, Criswell similarly declared that the doctrine of salvation includes every race equally: "God died for us. And that's you, that's me, that's the whole world. And to exclude anyone from it is a negation of the gospel. That's what the gospel is."[22] Touting the multiracial ministry of First Baptist, Criswell told reporters the church had always welcomed professions of faith from people of all races:

> The church is open, and there are colored people in it. And if anyone wants to join that church, it is an open church and always has been. There has never been in our church, which I love as I love my life—there has never been in our church any disposition to turn anyone down who came sincerely, loving the Lord and

---

20. Gregory, *Too Great a Temptation*, 48.
21. Criswell, "An Address by Dr. W. A. Criswell."
22. W. A. Criswell Press Conference at 1968 SBC Annual Meeting in Houston, audio recording.

wanting to join the church. And it still is that way and will always be that way, I think.[23]

Though his claim that First Baptist always had open membership was wrong, Criswell once again highlighted his longstanding belief that the gospel was open to all. In his 1990 autobiography Criswell likewise said he had always sought to reach people of all races with the gospel and recognized any devaluing of any race as sinful. "Never in my life did I believe in separating people on the basis of skin pigmentation," he wrote. "Racism was, is, and always will be an abomination in the eyes of God, and should be in the eyes of God's people."[24] He was wrong about never believing in segregation, but Criswell again highlighted his belief in a gospel for all.

As the civil rights movement drew attention to segregation, Criswell recognized that he had been inconsistent in the application of his soteriology. In 1956, Criswell saw no tension between offering salvation to all races and segregating worship services according to race. By the late 1960s, however, social conditions challenged Criswell's belief that segregation was perfectly consistent with his soteriology. In his sermon, "The Church of the Open Door," Criswell told First Baptist of his conviction that the policy of never rejecting anyone who made a profession of faith needed to be expanded into a policy of officially welcoming people of all races into the congregation's membership. He told of a recent deacons meeting in which he requested an official change in the membership policy: "So I said to those Deacons, that as for me, and my heart, and my life, and my pulpit ministry, I am done with the emptiness of an appeal preached in fear that somebody of a different pigment might accept it and come forward."[25] Criswell spoke of the same situation in his 1970 book, *Look Up, Brother!* First Baptist had always believed that blacks should be accepted as persons for whom Christ died, he said, but recently the church had realized that the doctrine of salvation applied to the social practice of segregation:

> It had been my stated persuasion that we ought to go our separate ways, the colored community and the white community, the colored church and the white church, the black Christian and the white Christian. But as I prayed, searched the Holy Scriptures, preached the gospel, and worked with our people, I came to the profound conclusion that to separate by coercion the body of

23. W. A. Criswell Press Conference at 1968 SBC Annual Meeting in Houston.
24. Criswell, *Standing on the Promises*, 203.
25. Criswell, "The Church of the Open Door," 81.

> Christ on the basis of skin pigmentation was unthinkable, unchristian, and unacceptable to God. When we preach, we ought to address the message to anybody who will listen. When we give the invitation to come to Jesus for salvation, the appeal ought to include everybody.[26]

To the press, he said he had always believed that the solution to the race problem must come by God saving men and changing their hearts. At the same time, he again admitted a change in his own attitude in recent years: "But for my own heart, I have increasingly enlarged my sympathies and my heart toward our colored people."[27] In a September 1968 address to the Southern Baptist Convention's Executive Committee he again spoke of a theological struggle resulting in a change of his opinion regarding integrating churches: "I've never had a battle in my heart, I've never faced one in my life, and I never thought I'd go through it as I have these last several years. Nobody on this earth knew that was going on in my soul. And I came to the firm conclusion that I had to change."[28]

Criswell's evangelical theology apparently did not change. His doctrine of salvation continued to include a general call to salvation for all races. Criswell changed his position on segregation and attributed the change to the biblical doctrine of salvation. Between 1956 and 1968 social pressures apparently drove him to confront the inconsistency between the doctrine and segregation. Social changes played an important role, but Freeman was wrong to claim that the change "may have been more a matter of social decorum than personal conviction."[29] His theology, provoked by social stresses, produced the change.

Herschel Hobbs

Herschel Hobbs (1907–1995) was pastor of the First Baptist Church of Oklahoma City, Oklahoma, from 1949 to 1972. He served as president of the Southern Baptist Convention from 1961 to 1963 and had his sermons broadcast on the weekly radio program *The Baptist Hour*. Like Criswell, Hobbs held a conservative soteriology his entire ministry, arguing that salvation comes

---

26. Criswell, *Look Up, Brother!*, 50.

27. W. A. Criswell Press Conference at 1968 SBC Annual Meeting in Houston.

28. Criswell, "Executive Committee, SBC, Address at Meeting September 17, 1968," audio recording, HC R169t Sou.

29. Freeman, "'Never Had I Been So Blind,'" 11.

only through faith in the risen Christ and that salvation in Christ is offered to all races equally. Theologian Mark Coppenger called Hobbs' devotion to the biblical text "the greatest theological contribution Hobbs made." Hobbs, according to Coppenger, "made it clear that the Bible merits the most careful and extensive attention and devotion we can give" and believed Scripture "is a chief instrument of the lordship of Christ."[30] Also like Criswell, Hobbs did not always see opposing segregation as a necessary corollary of the doctrine of salvation. But between 1960 and 1970, social pressures provoked him to draw a tighter connection between integration and theology. By 1970, Hobbs rejected segregation and argued that integration of the church was a valid application of conservative soteriology.

By the early 1960s, Hobbs had already expressed a conviction that all individuals of all races needed to be saved and that God offered the gospel to all races. At the 1961 annual meeting of the National Baptist Convention, U.S.A., Inc., which Hobbs attended as a fraternal messenger from the Southern Baptist Convention, he preached from Ephesians 2:8–10, a clear statement that he believed salvation "by grace" and "through faith" extended to African Americans.[31] Similarly, he wrote in a 1961 letter that blacks were welcome to come and hear the gospel preached at First Baptist.[32]

Yet Hobbs did not believe in the early 1960s that his soteriology required social integration. At times, he took issue with the civil rights movement and displayed evidence of personal prejudice against African Americans. In a sermon discussing implementation of the Supreme Court's *Brown* decision, Hobbs took issue with civil disobedience aimed at abolishing segregation. Civil disobedience programs, he said, "are a prime cause of the widespread lawlessness and violence which are plaguing our nation today. We are reaping the harvest of civil disobedience."[33] In the same sermon he suggested that police brutality against African-American protesters could be justified. "Sometimes policemen have to be rough with rough people," he said, and "at other times their actions are misconstrued."[34] Racial prejudice appeared in

---

30. Coppenger, "Herschel Hobbs," in *Baptist Theologians*, 446–47.

31. Herschel Hobbs to Porter Routh, 8 September 1961, Box 22, Folder 2, Herschel Hobbs Papers.

32. Herschel Hobbs to Vernon Broom, 4 October 1961, Box 22, Folder 2, Herschel Hobbs Papers.

33. Herschel Hobbs, "The Christian and Law Observance," Box 3, Folder 3, Herschel Hobbs Papers. This sermon has no date, but content referring to the *Brown* decision suggests that the sermon was preached during the late 1950s or early 1960s.

34. Hobbs, "The Christian and Law Observance."

the jokes that Hobbs sometimes told at the expense of blacks.[35] When a fight broke out among the delegates at the National Baptist Convention meeting, Hobbs remarked that the incident "showed that they are just a little above the jungle level when turned loose."[36]

In addition to personal prejudice, Hobbs in the early 1960s seemed to question whether integration—at least immediate integration—was necessary at all. Regarding the 1961 National Baptist Convention, Hobbs remarked that he was glad racial conservative Joseph Jackson was elected over the more progressive Gardner Taylor because Taylor promoted the freedom rides, forced integration, and the work of Martin Luther King Jr.[37] Hobbs agreed with one National Baptist Convention leader who argued that African Americans were "not yet ready for integration as seen by what happened here yesterday [the fight]."[38] When a group of African-American young people led by a white doctor, announced it would picket First Baptist on September 3, 1961, Hobbs told the picket leader that any African American seeking admission to the church's membership would likely receive at least some negative votes.[39] When the picketing occurred, one African-American young man presented himself for membership. The young man received a minimal number of negative votes, but church policy dictated that any candidate for membership receiving at least one negative vote had to appear before a committee of the deacons to state his case for membership. The church eventually voted not to receive the young man because he confessed that he sought membership not because he was

35. Herschel Hobbs to Sterling L. Price, 31 October 1961, Box 22, Folder 2, Herschel Hobbs Papers.

36. Herschel Hobbs to Henry Lyon, 11 September 1961, Box 22, Folder 2, Herschel Hobbs Papers. The fight broke out when a faction of National Baptists supporting progressive Gardner Taylor for president approached the convention's platform while the more moderate president, Joseph H. Jackson was presiding. A scuffle ensued, during which a seventy-four-year-old Detroit minister was pushed off the platform. The minister later died of a head injury sustained in his fall. Martin Luther King Jr. played a key role in the failed effort to elect Gardner to the denomination's top post. See "Negro Minister Accused in Baptist Riot," *Great Bend Daily Tribune*, 10 September 1961, 2.

37. Herschel Hobbs to Porter Routh, 8 September 1961, Box 22, Folder 2, Herschel Hobbs Papers.

38. Herschel Hobbs to Henry Lyon 11 September 1961, Box 22, Folder 2, Herschel Hobbs Papers.

39. Herschel Hobbs to Louie D. Newton, 13 September 1961, Box 22, Folder 2, Herschel Hobbs Papers. See also Herschel Hobbs to Foy Valentine, 4 October 1961, Box 22, Folder 2, Herschel Hobbs Papers; Herschel Hobbs to Vernon Broom, 4 October 1961, Box 22, Folder 2, Herschel Hobbs Papers.

committed to the church, but merely because he wanted to break down a racial barrier.[40] In all of Hobbs's correspondence regarding the picketing at First Baptist, he never expressed opposition to receiving blacks as church members. At the same time, however, he never expressed opposition toward those who wanted a segregated congregation. When he spoke of integration in the early 1960s, Hobbs advocated proceeding with extreme caution and slowness. During a three-day speaking engagement at Golden Gate Baptist Theological Seminary in 1962, he said integration should not be forced any more than childbirth. He termed himself a "gradualist" on integration, though he did come out in favor of applying pressure to groups stubbornly clinging to segregation.[41] At a press conference following his election to the Southern Baptist Convention presidency in 1961, Hobbs came out in favor of integration but wanted the process to slow down. In that press conference he connected his soteriology to his stance on integration and distinguished between the equality that comes through personal salvation and the social process of integration. Recounting his views in 1961, Hobbs said in his autobiography:

> I was/am in favor of integration, but I felt that the current method was moving faster than people on both sides were able to go. You can gain rights by legal means, but the ultimate solution must be found on a person-to-person basis. Jesus never sided with one group or person against another. He preached to both as either sinners saved by grace or outside God's grace due to personal choice.[42]

In the mid-1960s, Hobbs's position remained largely the same, but he began to recognize that the social climate was changing. He still believed that the gospel spoke equally to all people of all races. He also still expressed some opposition to the civil rights movement. Yet circumstances began to force a reevaluation of how Hobbs applied his soteriology to the issue of race. In a 1965 letter to Billy Graham, Hobbs expressed his belief that only the application of the gospel would solve the race problem while also arguing that immediate integration would harm both races.[43] Reiterating

---

40. Herschel Hobbs to J. D. Grey, 10 June 1965, Box 25, Folder 3, Herschel Hobbs Papers. For more on the picketing at First Baptist, see "Negroes Picket 3 Oklahoma City Church Services," *The Lawton Constitution*, 4 September 1961, 17.

41. Bill Rose, "Integration Can't Be Forced," *Oakland Tribune*, 26 October 1962, E13.

42. Hobbs, *My Faith and Message*, 225.

43. Herschel Hobbs to Billy Graham, 20 May 1965, Box 25, Folder 2, Herschel Hobbs

his position that all men are equal under the gospel, he told Leon Macon, editor of the *Alabama Baptist*, that Southern Baptists must preach the good news of Jesus to all races before any progress could occur on the race issue.[44] Nonviolent direct action still drew Hobbs's criticism as he took issue with the civil rights movement. To United States Representative John Buchanan, Hobbs complained that "I think that some people are resisting too strongly and the Civil Rights group is pressing too rapidly. Problems that could have been solved peaceably are being aborted. The result will be to destroy an atmosphere of love and understanding in Alabama that has existed through the years."[45] At times Hobbs drew a contrast between conservative soteriology and the civil rights movement, arguing that both the methods and goals of the movement were at odds with the biblical doctrine of salvation.[46] At other times though, the social strife over civil rights forced him to reconsider the implications of his soteriology. When Hobbs wanted J. D. Grey, pastor of First Baptist Church in New Orleans, to nominate him in 1965 for president of the Baptist World Alliance, he stressed his record of work with African Americans. In addition to entertaining "the Negro and White pastors and evangelists" at First Baptist during a crusade, Hobbs told Grey how he "made the motion in the Board of Trustees at Oklahoma Baptist University that we open the school to Negroes." He also believed that "the Negro pastors in Oklahoma City and I have the very finest relationship." Revisiting the 1961 picketing incident at First Baptist, Hobbs told Grey how he lent personal support to the African-American boy who presented himself for membership.[47] The letter suggested Hobbs knew that in 1965 the Baptist World Alliance would not elect a man president who held anything less than progressive views on integration.

By 1970 he came to recognize that the doctrine of salvation was inconsistent with segregation. Social pressures had increased to a level that forced Hobbs to make a broader application of his conservative

---

Papers.

44. Herschel Hobbs to Leon Macon, 19 April 1965, Box 25, Folder 2, Herschel Hobbs Papers.

45. Herschel Hobbs to John Buchanan, Box 25, Folder 2, Herschel Hobbs Papers. Although no date appears on this letter, both the content of the letter and the dates on other letters in the same folder suggest that Hobbs wrote to Buchanan in 1965.

46. See, for example, Herschel Hobbs to John Buchanan, Box 25, Folder 2, Herschel Hobbs Papers; Herschel Hobbs to Wayne Dehoney, 10 June 1965, Herschel Hobbs Papers.

47. Herschel Hobbs to J. D. Grey, 10 June 1965, Box 25, Folder 2, Herschel Hobbs Papers.

soteriology. In an article from the late 1960s Hobbs repeated the ideas that the gospel should be preached to people of all races and that the gospel was the ultimate solution to the race problem. "A black man plus a white man plus Christ equals two Christian brethren," he said. "This equation, and only this, will solve the racial problem in the United States or elsewhere."[48] But as he articulated that familiar doctrine of salvation, Hobbs leaned toward integration more than ever before. When Hobbs again aspired to the Baptist World Alliance presidency in 1970 he remarked that some "did not think I would be elected because I was from Alabama, and had a brother-in-law down there who was a strong segregationist."[49] According to Hobbs, social pressure shifted so decisively toward integration by 1970 that "insofar as our church is concerned this crisis situation [controversy over integration] is a thing of the past."[50] Whereas, First Baptist of 1961 preached the gospel to all races but was leery of accepting an African American into its fellowship, First Baptist of 1970 had black members and saw Hobbs baptize his first black convert.[51] From his actions and the actions of his church, it appeared that by 1970 Hobbs took the equality of all races under the gospel to mean that African Americans should be integrated and baptized into the local church.

Theology undergirded and informed Hobbs's acceptance of integration. Baptism and church membership were theological.[52] Mounting social pressures led him to apply the theology more consistently. Like Criswell, Hobbs was such a prominent figure that his public arguments shaped Southern Baptist opinion. Based on an evangelical understanding of the Bible, Hobbs led many other Southern Baptists to reject segregation.

48. Herschel Hobbs, "The Bible and Race Relations," Box 3, Folder 3, Herschel Hobbs Papers. Though this article has no date, references in the text to the Detroit race riots of 1967 show that the article was written in the years immediately following 1967.

49. Herschel Hobbs to Louie D. Newton, 10 August 1970, Box 27, Folder 9, Herschel Hobbs Papers.

50. Herschel Hobbs to Norman W. Clapp, 9 October 1970, Box 27, Folder 10, Herschel Hobbs Papers.

51. Herschel Hobbs to J. Norris Palmer, 7 August 1970, Box 27, Folder 9, Herschel Hobbs Papers. Herschel Hobbs to C. R. Daley, 12 October 1970, Box 27, Folder 10, Herschel Hobbs Papers.

52. See, for example, Hobbs' statement to the church on the occasion of its vote to receive the first African American member. While Hobbs did not tell church members how to vote, his analysis was scriptural and theological throughout, rather than pragmatic (Herschel Hobbs, "Statement by Pastor," Box 47, Folder 9, Herschel Hobbs Papers).

Conservative Theology, Segregation, and Change

James Sullivan

A prominent exception to the trend of Southern Baptists changing their position on race was James L. Sullivan (1910–2004). He served as president of the Southern Baptist Sunday School Board, the denomination's Sunday School and publishing entity, from 1953 until his retirement in 1975. He was active in denominational politics beginning during his first pastorate in 1932 and served one term as Southern Baptist Convention president from 1976 to 1977. Between 1955 and 1970 Sullivan hardly shifted his position on race. Unlike other figures, Sullivan also virtually never applied soteriology to the issue of integration. He even said once that race was not a topic that in any way pertained to theology in his way of thinking. Sullivan held much the same position on race at the end of his career as he held at the beginning. While others were drawing connections between their theology and integration, Sullivan kept the two separate. He was one of the few Southern Baptist leaders who failed to reexamine his views in light of conservative theology when social circumstances shifted.

In 1957 Sullivan believed that Christian theology permitted segregation. He revealed his, and the Sunday School Board's, position on race through his response to letters criticizing board publications that appeared to advocate integration. When the Elkdale Baptist Church of Selma, Alabama, complained about integrationist "propaganda" in Vacation Bible School materials, Sullivan replied by appealing to the doctrine of man's creation in God's image. "We have and do ardently believe," he said, "that all men were created in God's image, that they were endowed with divinely given gifts and abilities, and that each should live to his fullest potential in God's sight and in God's services." But Sullivan added that his position dealt with areas of clear biblical teaching and did "not deal with segregation, desegregation, integration, or any other of the inflammatory words which are being used so prevalently."[53] In a letter to Shiloh Baptist Church in Sardis, Alabama, Sullivan argued that the Sunday School Board did not advocate integration, but instead appealed "for a deep Christian attitude toward all men, and a deep Christian love for all fellow-believers."[54] Sullivan advocated the same position in other letters from 1957. God created all men of all races equal, he typically said, but

---

53. James Sullivan to Harry Kirkley, 15 July 1957, Box 3, "Complaints-Segregation" Folder, Records of the Executive Office of the Sunday School Board.

54. James Sullivan to Jack Trammell, 20 December 1957, Box 3, "Complaints-Segregation" Folder, Records of the Executive Office of the Sunday School Board.

the biblical doctrine of the equality of all men does not translate into any specific position on integration or segregation.[55]

In 1963 and 1964, Sullivan maintained his position on race despite mounting social pressures to advocate integration. When the Sunday School Board published a testimony by a Southern Baptist in Kansas celebrating the racial diversity of her church, twelve letters of complaint arrived from the South.[56] In response to the letters Sullivan instructed Gomer Lesch, one of his associates, to reply with the same arguments Sullivan used in 1957. The article "was not published with the intention of advocating integration in any other church," Lesch wrote. The board does not take any position for or against segregation or integration, he added, and teaches merely that "God made mankind in his image and after his likeness and has a divine purpose in each life."[57] Lesch's letters articulated the same arguments again and again. That Lesch's letters reflected Sullivan's position is evident from Sullivan's letters in the same era. In 1963, the First Baptist Church of Picayune, Mississippi, complained about white and black students sleeping in the same dorm at Ridgecrest Baptist Conference Center during a student conference and added that it objected to the advocacy of integration by some speakers at the same conference. Sullivan responded that race mixing at the camp "embarrassed" him and apologized for any speaker coming out in favor of integration. The board, Sullivan repeated, does not support either integration or segregation and does not believe people should be forced to do anything by law regarding the race issue.[58] When churches complained about a Training Union quarterly listing reference books written by Martin Luther King Jr. and other civil rights leaders, Sullivan replied, "The Sunday School Board made a grievous error in listing books by Martin Luther King, James Baldwin, and

55. See, for example, James Sullivan to A. A. Kitchings and W. M. Caskey, 19 June 1957, Box 3, "Complaints-Segregation" Folder, Records of the Executive Office of the Sunday School Board; James Sullivan to J. L. Lum, 9 July 1957, Box 3, "Complaints-Segregation" Folder, Records of the Executive Office of the Sunday School Board; James Sullivan to J. B. Stewart, 25 October 1957, Box 3, "Complaints-Segregation" Folder.

56. See Anderine Farmer, "Red and Yellow, Black and White," *Baptist Training Union Magazine*, September 1963, pp. 8–9, Box 6, Folder 63, Records of the Executive Office of the Sunday School Board. The same box and folder contain the letters of complaint along with Sunday School Board replies.

57. Gomer Lesch to Dee Deason, 24 September 1963, Box 6, Folder 63, Records of the Executive Office of the Sunday School Board.

58. James Sullivan to Wilbur Johnson, 16 July 1963, Box 6, Folder 63, Records of the Executive Office of the Sunday School Board.

John Howard Griffin in the July Young People's Training Union materials. This is an error for which we are extremely sorry, and one which we have taken firm steps to prevent in the future."[59] Sullivan's position was always the same: racism is a fallacy, but racism is a different issue than segregation and the board takes no position on segregation. The reason Sullivan never advocated integration could have been that, unlike some of his contemporaries, he did not regard it as a theological matter.

Sullivan shared his thoughts about race most openly in a 1964 letter to A. A. Kitchings. In that letter Sullivan admitted the existence of powerful biblical arguments in favor of integration. When T. B. Maston submitted a manuscript of his book *The Bible and Race*, for example, Sullivan "could not refute positions he had taken or interpretation without running into conflicts or contradictions which intellectual honesty would forbid." Yet despite the biblical arguments for greater racial openness, Sullivan remained unwilling to endorse integration because, for him, race was not a theological issue. He admitted, "In all honesty, however, I must say that I have had to come to my position on a sociological grounds rather than on a theological basis." How should Southern Baptists solve the problem of racial tensions? "We will find our answers better and quicker by seeking to solve them on a sociological basis without stretching ourselves to find remote religious implications," Sullivan said.[60]

By the early 1970s many Southern Baptists, like Criswell and Hobbs, had shifted their position on race by reconsidering the implications of their theology. But because of his refusal to consider the issue theologically, Sullivan grew increasingly out of step with the thinking of Southern Baptists. A 1971 incident involving a church training quarterly illustrated this reality. In October 1971, Sullivan ordered that 140,000 copies of the quarterly *Becoming* not be distributed because they contained material that "could have been construed as improper promotion on the part of the Sunday School Board of integration in the churches."[61] The questionable material included a

---

59. James Sullivan to James B. Cambron, 7 October 1964, Box 14, Folder 67–64, Records of the Executive Office of the Sunday School Board.

60. James Sullivan to A. A. Kitchings, 8 January 1964, Box 14, Folders 67–64, Records of the Executive Office of the Sunday School Board.

61. "Sullivan Directs Revision of Printed Quarterly," *Baptist Press*, 28 October 1971, Box 50, Records of the Executive Office of the Sunday School Board. Box 50 contains several folders all labeled "Becoming Incident" and without numbers to distinguish them. Therefore, in all notes of material on the Becoming Incident, only the box number will be given.

photograph of an African-American boy in conversation with two white girls, which, along with some textual material, "was subject to misinterpretation."[62] In Sullivan's view, the recalling of the materials was an appropriate application of the board's position on race—which was still to promote love for all people but not take any specific stand to promote either integration or segregation.[63] But reaction to the recall was not what Sullivan expected. In the four months following the incident, the Sunday School Board received more than 475 letters opposing the recall and only 205 supportive letters.[64] More than twenty Baptist groups passed resolutions condemning the recall as inappropriate.[65] Though many in the Southern Baptist mainstream had rejected segregation on theological grounds, Sullivan appeared perplexed by the flood of negative reaction, blaming the "extreme left" and the press for blowing an episode out of proportion when he was merely attempting to carry out what he thought was the will of Southern Baptists.[66] In reality, however, Sullivan simply fell out of step with Southern Baptists because many were approaching the race issue theologically and reformulating their positions as social pressures forced a reconsideration of how soteriology applied to integration. Sullivan was an exception to the trend of changed attitudes in the Southern Baptist Convention. His case suggested that failure to derive racial attitudes from conservative theology doomed one to grow out of touch with the Southern Baptist mainstream.

Clifton Allen

Others at the Sunday School Board shared Sullivan's position. Clifton J. Allen (1901–1986), for example, came to the Sunday School Board in 1937 as associate editorial secretary and became editorial secretary in 1945. His long

---

62. "Sullivan Directs Revision of Printed Quarterly."

63. "Dealing With Race in the Board's Publishing Program," Box 50, Records of the Executive Office of the Sunday School Board. See also, "Position Paper: The Sunday School Board and Race Relations," Box 50, Records of the Executive Office of the Sunday School Board.

64. "Total Response via Mail," Box 50, Records of the Executive Office of the Sunday School Board.

65. Jim Newton, "Reaction Roundup: Revision of Becoming Prompts Record Response toward BSSB," *Baptist Press*, 24 November 1971, Box 50, Records of the Executive Office of the Sunday School Board.

66. "Remarks by Dr. James L. Sullivan," Box 50, Records of the Executive Office of the Sunday School Board.

ministry in Southern Baptist life included a weekly radio program, in which he taught the week's Sunday School lesson, and extensive writing and editing of denominational publications. Like Sullivan, Allen failed to oppose segregation. But more than Sullivan, Allen opposed racial prejudice.

He based his opposition of prejudice on theology. Allen connected race relations with the doctrines of creation and salvation. In 1956 Allen told a Sunday School teacher from Tennessee, "I believe the Bible is absolutely clear in teaching that in the sight of God or in the feeling and attitude of God there is absolutely no distinction between races." Doctrinally, Christians should view "every man as a person made in the image of God and... remember that Christ tasted death for every man."[67] That same year, Allen penned a statement entitled "An Appeal for a Christian Spirit in Race Relations." Twenty-eight Southern Baptist leaders signed the statement, which cited seven theological truths as applicable to race relations. Creation of every man in God's image, the death of Christ for all men, Christ's call to love all men, and the brotherhood of all true Christians were among the doctrines Allen applied to race. The statement confessed that improper behavior in race relations often results from "failing to face the full implications of our discipleship at this point."[68]

In addition to seeing the theological side of the race issue, Allen possessed by the late 1950s an awareness of mounting social pressures against segregation. Allen's extensive collection of news reports, government documents, and materials from other denominations testified to that reality.[69] He spoke of the 1954 Supreme Court ruling on school desegregation as causing a "crisis" in America and recognized continuing tension regarding the Supreme Court's decision in the years that followed.[70] In 1955, Allen faced social pressure from within the Sunday School Board when other employees criticized a statement he wrote for failing to promote

---

67. Clifton Allen to John S. Counts, 9 February 1956, Box 59, Folder 17, Clifton J. Allen Papers.

68. Clifton Allen, "An Appeal for a Christian Spirit in Race Relations," Box 59, Folder 11, Clifton J. Allen Papers.

69. See, for example, Box 15, Folder 42 and Box 59, Folders 10–11, Clifton J. Allen Papers, for a sampling of Allen's news reports, government documents, and materials from other denominations dealing with race.

70. See "Concerning the Problems Arising from the Current Situation About Race Relations: A Statement for Editors and Writers," 15 October 1957, Box 59, Folder 11, Clifton J. Allen Papers; Edward P. Colson to Clifton Allen, 5 May 1955, Box 59, Folder 16, Clifton J. Allen Papers.

integration.⁷¹ Allen also felt pressure to integrate from the Foreign Mission Board. "Dr. [Grady] Cauthen [president of the Foreign Mission Board] has said that our missionaries are facing difficult questions and serious problems on the mission fields," Allen wrote in 1956 about the consequences of segregation.⁷²

Yet Allen did not oppose segregation. He tended to distinguish between prejudice and segregation.⁷³ He wrote in a 1955 editorial policy, "We do not believe that the inherent equality of races in the sight of God argues against the validity of voluntary segregation."⁷⁴ In 1956, Allen made one of his only favorable statements about integration on record. He confessed that "we have inherited a great deal of prejudice" and blacks had been mistreated. He also criticized those southerners who argued that integration of schools would lead to amalgamation of the races. "It is highly important for us to realize that social changes take place slowly," he wrote, but whites must not fight against school integration.⁷⁵

Allen and Sullivan both had poor records when it came to opposing segregation. But the differences between Allen and Sullivan suggested that theology was a factor in Southern Baptists' handling of racial injustice. Sullivan, with his atheological approach to race relations, never advocated integration as many Southern Baptists rushed ahead of him. Allen, however, with his more theological approach to race relations, opposed prejudice more aggressively. Sullivan highlighted the difference between himself and Allen when Allen asked him to sign the 1956 "Appeal for a Christian Spirit in Race Relations." Though Allen was willing to sign, Sullivan refused, fearing the statement's negative political consequences. If the people of the South interpreted the statement as sanctioning integration of the public schools, Sullivan wrote to Allen, "there could be more damage done than good accomplished as far as the Sunday School Board is concerned."⁷⁶ Applying evangelical theology to race drove Allen to denounce prejudice publicly. His influence, through radio Sunday School lessons and printed

---

71. See Box 59, Folder 16, Clifton J. Allen Papers.

72. "Race Relations: Editorial Policy," Box 59, Folder 16, Clifton J. Allen Papers.

73. Clifton Allen to Mrs. John W. Outlaw, 16 May 1956, Clifton J. Allen Papers.

74. Clifton Allen to Mrs. John W. Outlaw, 16 May 1956, Clifton J. Allen Papers.

75. Clifton Allen to John S. Counts, 9 February 1956, Box 59, Folder 17, Clifton J. Allen Papers.

76. James Sullivan to Clifton Allen, 3 April 1956, Box 59, Folder 18, Clifton J. Allen Papers.

publications, carried his arguments to thousands and shaped opinion in the Southern Baptist Convention.

Other Southern Baptists on Race

Two additional denominational leaders of the 1960s, K. Owen White and Franklin Paschall, also advanced racial justice in a manner consistent with conservative theology. Both served as Southern Baptist Convention president, and though they differed in their overall degree of adherence to conservative theology, both rejected segregation under the influence of such theology.

White (1902–1985) served as Southern Baptist Convention president from 1963 to 1964 and pastored the First Baptist Church of Houston, Texas, from 1953 to 1965. He was a strong conservative who believed integration was desirable, but only integration fueled by application of the gospel rather than by the liberal social gospel.[77] During his term as convention president, White opposed civil rights proposals when he believed they did not stem from a Christian worldview. In several 1964 letters, White expressed his opposition to the civil rights bill making its way through Congress. His opposition was not to the "general principles" of the bill but to "very objectionable features which appear in it."[78] Even in his own church, White opposed integration efforts when he felt they did not stem from the gospel. On the first Sunday after White was elected Southern Baptist Convention president, a young black man came forward during the invitation at First Baptist expressing a desire to join the church. Because of racial tensions in the city, White opted to counsel the young man before the church voted on him. When White learned that the young man came forward only to test the membership policy of the church and not to seek fellowship with likeminded believers, he recommended to the church that it reject the candidate's request for membership. The church followed its pastor.[79] White

---

77. For an example of White's theological conservatism, see K. Owen White, "Death in the Pot," *Baptist Standard*, 10 January 1962, 6.

78. K. Owen White to G. R. Schettler, 27 March 1964, Box 1, Folder 7, K. Owen White Papers. See also, K. Owen White to Mrs. K. G. Reed, 1 April 1964, Box 1, Folder 7, K. Owen White Papers; K. Owen White to Mr. And Mrs. H. H. Harrell, 1 April 1964, Box 1, Folder 7, K. Owen White Papers; K. Owen White to Mack P. Stewart, 1 April 1964, Box 1, Folder 7, K. Owen White Papers.

79. K. Owen White, "Statement by Pastor of Houston Church," *Baptist Standard*, 19 June 1963, 11; "Negro Fails in Membership Bid at First Church, Houston," *Baptist*

explained in 1964 that approaching the race issue without a theological perspective was futile:

> I have been saying all over the convention territory that we are desperately in need of revival which would change our whole way of living. However, I do not think that dealing with the race issue alone is going to be the answer to all our problems.[80]

Protests occurred at First Baptist in the months following the rejection of the black man's membership request, but White did not yield to the pressure to integrate until he saw an opportunity for integration that did not compromise the Bible's standards of church membership.[81] Such an opportunity came in 1965 when an African-American woman, who White felt was sincere, expressed a desire for gospel fellowship as a member of First Baptist. Despite White's recommendation to accept the woman, the church voted in secret ballot April 21, 1965, not to receive any blacks into its membership.[82] When the result was read publicly, White told the church he was disappointed in the vote.[83] One day later White resigned from First Baptist to become metropolitan missions coordinator with the California Southern Baptist Convention. He told both friends and the media that his move had nothing to do with the vote.[84] Regardless of White's motive for the move to California, one fact was certain: he advocated integration. His position of influence meant that he spread his views on race to thousands of other Southern Baptists.

Paschall (1922–2009), president of the Southern Baptist Convention from 1966 to 1968 and pastor of the First Baptist Church in Nashville, Tennessee, also advanced racial justice in a manner consistent with conservative theology. He said the doctrine of salvation was the key to race relations. "I sincerely believe that the gospel of Christ in the heart of a Negro and the gospel of Christ in the heart of a white man will reconcile the two, so making

---

Standard, 19 June 1963, 11.

80. K. Owen White to Aileen Henderson, 29 April 1964, Box 1, Folder 7, K. Owen White Papers.

81. For information on continuing protests, see "Baptist Church in Houston," *Big Spring Herald*, 29 July 1963, 3A.

82. "Houston Church Won't Integrate," *San Antonio Express/News*, 25 April 1965, 9B.

83. "Houston Church Won't Integrate."

84. "Texas Pastor Quits; Denies Race Cause," *Press-Telegram*, 14 April 1965, A4. K. Owen White to Wayne Dehoney, Box 22, Folder 21, Wayne Dehoney Papers.

peace," he said.[85] He argued that the struggle for social justice was based on God's supernatural work in the hearts of regenerate believers in Christ.[86] Like Criswell, Hobbs, Allen, and White, Paschall approached the issue of race with a theological mindset. Like some of his contemporaries, he took a significant stand for race when social pressures mounted. At the 1968 Southern Baptist Convention annual meeting, Paschall presided as the denomination adopted a landmark statement on racial reconciliation.[87]

More than some of his contemporaries, however, Paschall hesitated to support integration. At a press conference following his election to the Southern Baptist Convention presidency in 1966, he avoided endorsement of integration by telling reporters that "integration is a matter for local churches."[88] He also exchanged letters in 1967 with a church member who felt distressed over the fact that First Baptist refused to baptize two twins of a minority race (the specific race is unclear from the correspondence) when they made professions of faith in Christ during a worship service. Paschall explained the situation by saying the "Sunday evening service was not nearly as bad as it seemed" and that "the spirit of the people after the service during the fellowship period was great."[89] Despite Paschall's timidity to push integration, he still fell within the trend—he advocated racial justice in a manner consistent with conservative theology when social pressure heightened.

Conclusion

Between 1955 and 1970 conservative theology drove Southern Baptists to reevaluate their stands on segregation and integration. Doctrines that stemmed from a traditional evangelical interpretation of the Bible and a belief in the supernatural convinced them that segregation was wrong. Social pressures played a role in the shift by creating the occasion for

---

85. Franklin Paschall to William N. Blansitt, 13 June 1968, Box 14, Folder 457, Henry Franklin Paschall Papers.

86. Franklin Paschall to Mr. and Mrs. L. E. Powell, 31 May 1968, Box 14, Folder 457, Henry Franklin Paschall Papers.

87. "Southern Baptists Face Issue of Racial Equality," *The Press-Courier*, 8 June 1968, 5; "Baptists Pick Dr. Criswell as President," *Big Spring Herald*, 6 June 1968, 3A.

88. "Baptists Keep Hands off Social Issues," *Chronicle-Telegram*, 28 May 1966, 7.

89. Franklin Paschall to George Leiby, 15 February 1967, Box 14, Folder 457, Henry Franklin Paschall Papers.

Southern Baptist leaders to rethink their stands on race. As they rethought, many Southern Baptists drew new applications from their conservative theology. Criswell, Hobbs, and White all represented this trend. Allen and Paschall advocated racial justice in a manner consistent with conservative theology even though they failed to oppose segregation. Sullivan, who approached segregation from a professed atheological viewpoint, was an exception. Conservative theology was so important for Southern Baptists on the issue of race that we will see next how the doctrines of salvation and creation played a role even in the Southern Baptist Convention's left-leaning Christian Life Commission.

Chapter 3

Foy Valentine and the Christian Life Commission Vision

IN THE EARLY 1960S, Southern Baptist denominational leaders feared that the Christian Life Commission's aggressive program of advocating racial equality would alienate white churches in the Deep South and thus decrease support of the Southern Baptist Convention's Cooperative Program. As a result of this fear, Foy Valentine, executive director of the Christian Life Commission, often found himself on the receiving end of rebukes from uneasy leaders. In 1961, for example, Owen Cooper, a Mississippi Baptist layman and member of the Executive Committee, told Valentine, "I think the greatest contribution I can make to the life of Southern Baptists is to keep you from getting another dime."[1] Valentine explained that though Cooper's rebuke stemmed from the commission's stand on race, Cooper and other leaders "didn't intend to be racists." They "just didn't want trouble stirred up" and sought to "keep the money coming in for the Cooperative Program."[2]

Yet during the remaining twenty-five years of Cooper's life, a remarkable transformation occurred that illustrated a larger trend in Southern Baptist life. Valentine maintained contact with Cooper, and by his death in 1986 the Mississippi leader and two-time Southern Baptist Convention president

---

1. *Oral Memoirs of Foy Dan Valentine*, vol. 2, interview by Thomas L. Charlton, 30 May 1989, Texas Baptist Project, Baylor University Institute for Oral History, 2004, 62.
2. *Oral Memoirs of Foy Dan Valentine*, vol. 2, 63.

became an advocate for racial justice and equality.[3] Once a staunch opponent of Christian social activism, Cooper even won the Christian Life Commission's Distinguished Service Award in 1986 for advocacy of Christian social causes.[4] During the same period, hundreds of thousands of other Southern Baptists underwent a similar transformation. Valentine and the Christian Life Commission played an important role.[5]

Valentine was the key leader of a stream of Southern Baptists involved with the Christian Life Commission who, between the mid-1950s and the mid-1980s, convinced their denomination that racism was incompatible with the Bible. These leaders were liberals in their theology, but Valentine and his cohorts knew that Southern Baptists responded best to arguments consistent with conservative theology. Even more important, they appropriated conservative evangelical concepts in matters of race and applied the Bible's message of free salvation to race relations. Southern Baptist racial progressives worked during the same time period as the leaders of the civil rights movement, but they were distinct from the civil rights movement. Valentine and others in his stream shared many beliefs with the leaders of the civil rights movement yet diverged from the movement by seeking to advance racial justice through education rather than nonviolent direct action.

Valentine and the "Genealogy of Dissent"

Born July 3, 1923, in Edgewood, Texas, Valentine attended Baylor University in Waco, Texas, in the early 1940s before earning two degrees from Southwestern Baptist Theological Seminary in Fort Worth. Valentine's early life, beginning with the Baylor years, felt the influence of what historian David Stricklin called the "genealogy of dissent"—a group of liberal Southern Baptists whose progressive social and theological views took them beyond the comfort zone of rank-and-file Southern Baptists.[6] Though this group did

---

3. *Oral Memoirs of Foy Dan Valentine*, vol. 2, interview by Thomas L. Charlton, 30 May 1989, Texas Baptist Project, Baylor University Institute for Oral History, 2004, 63.

4. "Christian Life Commission" (1986), p. 2, Box 4, Folder 6, Christian Life Commission Minutes.

5. For helpful surveys of Southern Baptists and social issues, see Hankins, *Uneasy in Babylon*; Spain, *At Ease in Zion*; Eighmy, *Churches in Cultural Captivity*; Sutton, *A Matter of Conviction*; Harper, *The Quality of Mercy*; Manis, *Southern Civil Religions in Conflict*.

6. Stricklin, *A Genealogy of Dissent*.

not wield significant influence over most Southern Baptists, they influenced Valentine, who in turn brought their social progressivism to the Texas and Southern Baptist Convention Christian Life Commissions.

In the twentieth century, Stricklin argued, there was a small group of Southern Baptists who unapologetically dissented from the denominational status quo on issues of social justice and equality. Members of this group all descended from Walter Nathan Johnson (1875–1952), a pioneer integrationist in the 1920s and 1930s, and his students Clarence Jordan and Martin England.[7] Jordan and England influenced such notable dissenters as Ken Sehested, founder of the North American Baptist Peace Fellowship; Will D. Campbell, publisher of the liberal journal *Katallagete*; and Perry and Patricia Perkins, co-laborers with leftwing evangelical leader Jim Wallis.[8] Especially in the area of racial integration, the dissenters displayed far more aggression in righting injustice than Southern Baptists generally.[9] While most Southern Baptists either were silent or spoke for segregation during the era of Jim Crow, Jordan, England, and Texas preacher Carlyle Marney drove one stream of dissenters to reassess the South's traditional view of race.[10] From Jordan and England, Valentine felt the influence of the genealogy of dissent.[11]

Valentine's first contact with Jordan occurred while Valentine studied at Baylor. Campus minister Bob Denny brought in several speakers with more liberal perspectives than students were accustomed to hearing, and those speakers affirmed Valentine's developing conviction that the gospel applied to the social issues of everyday life in addition to personal regeneration.[12] Of the speakers Valentine heard on campus, he recalled, "the most meaningful ones to me were Charles Wells and Clarence Jordan."[13] After his initial contact with Jordan in Waco, Valentine encountered him again

---

7. Stricklin, *A Genealogy of Dissent*, 19–20, 39.

8. Stricklin, *A Genealogy of Dissent*, 41–44.

9. Stricklin, *A Genealogy of Dissent*, 49–81.

10. Stricklin, *A Genealogy of Dissent*, 66–74.

11. Stricklin, *A Genealogy of Dissent*, 74–75. Stricklin noted that Valentine and the Home Mission Board's Victor Glass were the only two students of Jordan, England, and Marney who entered the Southern Baptist Convention's official agencies and leadership mechanisms.

12. *Oral Memoirs of Foy Dan Valentine*, vol. 1, interview by Daniel B. McGee, 19 February 1976, Texas Baptist Oral History Consortium, Baylor University Institute for Oral History, 1990, 68.

13. *Oral Memoirs of Foy Dan Valentine*, vol. 1, 66.

during a meeting at Southern Baptists' Ridgecrest conference center in 1944. At that meeting, Jordan invited Valentine to spend the summer at Koinonia Farm, an interracial Christian community founded by Jordan and England in southwest Georgia.[14] Valentine spent ten weeks at Koinonia Farm experiencing his most extensive exposure to date to the liberal social gospel tradition and living alongside African Americans.[15]

During the period of Valentine's stay at the farm, Koinonians built their ideology from both traditional southern Protestantism and the liberal social gospel tradition.[16] Koinonia Farm offered an interracial community where blacks and whites shared Christian fellowship and agricultural training.[17] Though Koinonia later cooperated with the civil rights movement in various ways, Jordan's farm differed from the civil rights movement in its ideology at an important point—a difference present in seed form even during Valentine's era on the farm. While the civil rights movement of the 1950s and 1960s aimed for integration in general, Koinonia Farm sought specifically Christian community and advocated a more communal vision of society than did the civil rights movement.[18]

The ideas of Koinonia Farm and its founders made a lasting impression upon Valentine. More than forty years after his summer at Koinonia, Valentine remarked of his stay with Jordan, "It was a very profoundly moving relationship that was deepened, to my great, everlasting, spiritual profit, with Clarence Jordan there."[19] Regular correspondence with Jordan and England following Valentine's departure revealed the depth of their friendship.[20] During Valentine's seminary days, Jordan gave him a blank check to use if he ever needed it.[21] Jordan apparently referred to the blank check in a 1944 letter when he wrote, "When you use the other check, and don't

---

14. *Oral Memoirs of Foy Dan Valentine*, vol. 1, 71.

15. *Oral Memoirs of Foy Dan Valentine*, vol. 1, 71, 74.

16. K'Meyer, *Interracialism and Christian Community in the Postwar South*, 16–23.

17. K'Meyer, *Interracialism and Christian Community in the Postwar South*, 42–62.

18. K'Meyer, *Interracialism and Christian Community in the Postwar South*, 145–64.

19. *Oral Memoirs of Foy Dan Valentine*, vol. 2, interview by Thomas L. Charlton and David Stricklin, 4 December 1989, Texas Baptist Project, Baylor University Institute for Oral History, 2004, 182.

20. See correspondence with Clarence Jordan and Martin England, Box 2A6, Folders 1–10, Foy Valentine Papers.

21. *Oral Memoirs of Foy Dan Valentine*, vol. 2, interview by Thomas L. Charlton and David Stricklin, 4 December 1989, Texas Baptist Project, Baylor University Institute for Oral History, 2004, 182.

hesitate to do so, drop us a line and we'll send you another 'spare.'"[22] The relationship persisted throughout Jordan's life, with periodic contact and correspondence between the two for decades.[23]

Jordan fell in the theological tradition historian Kenneth Cauthen labeled "evangelical liberalism." Evangelical liberals were convinced of the truth of historic Christianity but adjusted it to the demands of the modern era. Evangelical liberals believed in special revelation, but reasonableness was the fundamental test of any truth claim for them. At times evangelical liberals revised historic Christian truths to fit reason. Walter Rauschenbusch was a prominent evangelical liberal with his emphasis on the social gospel, as was Baptist preacher Harry Emerson Fosdick.[24] Jordan fell within this tradition because he simultaneously believed in the truth of Christianity and rejected historic doctrines. He read the Bible as an authoritative guide for life and salvation. Yet he rejected the virgin birth and believed the Bible is not always accurate in its reporting of historical details or scientific facts.[25] Similar to Rauschenbusch, Jordan conceived the kingdom of God in very earthly terms. The kingdom, Jordan said, is a group of people working for Christ's goals and caring for one another.[26]

Valentine felt a spiritual kinship with England also. He consulted England when he thought God might be calling him to missions in the Orient.[27] Twenty years after Valentine's stay at Koinonia Farm, England wrote a note of encouragement when Valentine lost an important vote related to race at the 1964 Southern Baptist Convention annual meeting.[28] England was an evangelical liberal like Jordan. Often he articulated his theological concerns in ways akin to Rauschenbusch, the father of the social gospel.[29] England steered away from preoccupation with the afterlife and materialism, which he believed turned the gospel into a philosophy of

---

22. Clarence Jordan to Foy Valentine, 26 October 1944, Box 2A6, Folder 4, Foy Valentine Papers.

23. Clarence Jordan to Foy Valentine, 26 October 1944, Box 2A6, Folder 4, Foy Valentine Papers.

24. Cuathen, *The Impact of American Religious Liberalism*, 27–29.

25. Snider, "The 'Cotton Patch' Gospel," 59, 89.

26. Snider, "The 'Cotton Patch' Gospel," 68.

27. Martin England to Foy Valentine, 8 January 1945, Box 2A6, Folder 10, Foy Valentine Papers.

28. Martin England to Foy Valentine, 29 May 1964, Box 2A103, "Post-Convention Letters Answered" Folder, Foy Valentine Papers.

29. See Rauschenbusch, *A Theology for the Social Gospel*.

self-help.[30] England held that "to ignore the concerns of suffering humanity in the face of Jesus' preoccupation with them was and is faithless."[31] Christians ought to alleviate human suffering, England believed, and not focus on being saved from sin.[32]

After his summer with Jordan and England, Valentine stood within the tradition of evangelical liberalism for the rest of his life. He associated with noted social gospel advocates like Carlyle Marney, Victor Glass, Will Campbell, William Finlator, Warren Carr, and Bob Seymour.[33] Valentine was careful not to deny historic Christian doctrines and offend mainstream Southern Baptists, but he formulated his theology in a manner akin to Rauschenbusch. Valentine's articles and speeches used traditional Christian language, but often without referring to anything otherworldly or supernatural. He believed, like Rauschenbusch, that a central aspect of his ministry was showing Southern Baptists "that the gospel has relevance in everyday life."[34] The gospel meant identifying with the poor, Valentine said, and he located himself in the theological stream of Jordan and Southwestern Baptist Theological Seminary social gospeler T. B. Maston.[35] In the political sphere Valentine spoke openly about his liberalism. He stated that he "never voted for a Republican under any circumstances for any office on earth and never intend[ed] to."[36]

Valentine at times criticized his friends in the tradition of evangelical liberalism, but not concerning their theology. Valentine's most significant criticism of Jordan and the other dissenters was that they failed to earn a

30. Stricklin, "Clarence Jordan (1912–1969), Jasper Martin England (1901–1989), and Millard Fuller (1935–): Koinonia Farm: Epicenter for Social Change," in McSwain, *Twentieth-Century Shapers of Baptist Social Ethics*, 179–80.

31. Stricklin, "Clarence Jordan (1912–1969)," 182.

32. Stricklin, "Clarence Jordan (1912–1969)," 182.

33. *Oral Memoirs of Foy Dan Valentine*, vol. 2, interview by Thomas L. Charlton and David Stricklin, 4 December 1989, Texas Baptist Project, Baylor University Institute for Oral History, 2004, 182–87.

34. *Oral Memoirs of Foy Dan Valentine*, vol. 2, interview by Thomas L. Charlton and David Stricklin, 30 May 1989, Texas Baptist Project, Baylor University Institute for Oral History, 2004, 58.

35. *Oral Memoirs of Foy Dan Valentine*, vol. 2, interview by Thomas L. Charlton and David Stricklin, 30 May 1989, Texas Baptist Project, Baylor University Institute for Oral History, 2004, 67, 79.

36. *Oral Memoirs of Foy Dan Valentine*, vol. 2, interview by Thomas L. Charlton and David Stricklin, 4 December 1989, Texas Baptist Project, Baylor University Institute for Oral History, 2004, 178.

hearing among mainstream Southern Baptists. Regarding such progressives as Jordan, England, Campbell, Finlator, Carr, Marney, and Seymour, Valentine said:

> They just hadn't opted to get into places of power and to earn places of respect, where they would be heard.... They have a bit of a superiority complex from having gone to school in the North, and come back and wonder why everybody doesn't give them places of leadership. We've got to earn a place of leadership, wherever you go to school. And even, if in a case of Clarence Jordan or Carlyle Marney, you went to school and talked with the right accent, have the right credentials—you still got to pay a certain amount of dues in order, when you stand up, to be heard.... The outsider who yaps at the outside, never going to church, drinking a little whiskey, and privately just doing his own thing—they have some influence, to be sure, but it's really pretty peripheral.[37]

Valentine preferred the tactics of people like Maston, who worked within the Southern Baptist Convention's denominational structure to create opportunities to speak in favor of social progressivism.[38] Yet ideologically, Valentine was an evangelical liberal throughout his career in Southern Baptist leadership.

Valentine and the Texas Christian Life Commission

While still working toward his master of theology and doctor of theology degrees at Southwestern Seminary, Valentine showed deep interest in social concerns, particularly race relations. In 1949, he completed his doctoral dissertation under Maston, entitled "A Historical Study of Southern Baptists and Race Relations, 1917–1947." Under Maston, Valentine also gained an introduction to the Urban League and the National Association for the Advancement of Colored People.[39] During his student days,

---

37. *Oral Memoirs of Foy Dan Valentine*, vol. 2, interview by Thomas L. Charlton and David Stricklin, 4 December 1989, Texas Baptist Project, Baylor University Institute for Oral History, 2004, 187.

38. *Oral Memoirs of Foy Dan Valentine*, vol. 2, interview by Thomas L. Charlton and David Stricklin, 4 December 1989, Texas Baptist Project, Baylor University Institute for Oral History, 2004, 187. See also Valentine, *T. B. Maston*.

39. *Oral Memoirs of Foy Dan Valentine*, vol. 1, interview by Daniel B. McGee, 19 February 1976, Texas Baptist Oral History Consortium, Baylor University Institute for Oral History, Baptist General Convention of Texas, 1990, 77–78.

he additionally served as a special representative in race relations for the Baptist General Convention of Texas and conducted an interracial youth revival in Brownwood, Texas, in 1948. Valentine said of his seminary years, "I majored in ethics with Dr. Maston and continued through all those five years of graduate study my interest in race relations."[40] After graduation from Southwestern, Valentine moved to Gonzales, Texas, in 1950 to pastor the First Baptist Church.[41]

Contemporaneous with Valentine's move to Gonzales, another move was afoot in Texas Baptist life, a move to bring social gospel concerns into the mainstream. In 1949 the state convention's executive, J. Howard Williams, appointed a committee consisting of Maston, A. C. Miller, and Baylor President William R. White to study the most effective way for Texas Baptists to deal with social problems. That committee added four members to become the "Committee of Seven" and, after several preliminary meetings, called for the formation of an agency to focus denominational attention on social matters.[42] Discussion of the possible new agency increased as the 1950 annual meeting of the Baptist General Convention of Texas approached, but the Committee of Seven still lacked a name for the agency on the day the meeting opened. Providentially, an evangelist attempted to warn the convention that the agenda of the new agency differed from the agenda of conservative evangelicalism. He said Texas Baptists must not neglect evangelism in the interest of supporting this "commission on the Christian life." Upon hearing the evangelist's words, Miller leaned over to Maston, who was sitting next to him, and said, "That's the name, the Christian Life Commission."[43] The two leaders proposed the name, and the convention voted to form the Christian Life Commission with Miller as the first executive secretary.[44]

40. *Oral Memoirs of Foy Dan Valentine*, vol. 1, interview by Daniel B. McGee, 19 February 1976, Texas Baptist Oral History Consortium, Baylor University Institute for Oral History, Baptist General Convention of Texas, 1990, 77.

41. Dwayne Hastings, "Foy Valentine, Dead at 82, Led SBC Moral Concerns Arm 27 Years," *Baptist Press*, 9 January 2006.

42. Storey, "That's Our Name," 16–17.

43. *Oral Memoir of Acker C. Miller*, interview by Rufus B. Spain, 13 August 1971, Religion and Culture Project, Baylor University Program for Oral History, 1972, 70–71.

44. *Oral Memoir of Acker C. Miller*, interview by Rufus B. Spain, 2 January 1972, Religion and Culture Project, Baylor University Program for Oral History, 1972, 86–88. The Committee of Seven suggested that the commission initially be composed of Stewart A. Newman, George Steward, Grady Metcalf, T. B. Maston, A. B. Rutledge, Herbert Howard, W. R. White, Joseph Stiles, and Carl Bates.

Foy Valentine and the Christian Life Commission Vision

From 1950 until 1952, Miller led Texas Baptists to address the social concerns important to evangelical liberals. But he packaged the work in a manner that resonated with more conservative Baptists who held a high view of Scripture. The desire not to alarm conservatives factored into Texas Baptists' decision to name their agency the Christian Life Commission rather than follow the Southern Baptist Convention's lead and call it the Social Service Commission. Miller reflected, "We felt here in Texas that we should change from that emphasis on 'social' because of the way that Baptists felt about social issues. That was one reason that we named it the Christian Life Commission so as to join it up with and make it be affiliated with the idea of the Christian life."[45] Though admitting influence from the social gospel tradition, Miller was adamant that a Christian Life Commission had biblical warrant:

> This press which the Christian Life Commission is now making did not begin in 1950, nor yet with Rauschenbusch, nor yet with the doctrine of humanism, not even with the emphasis which the modern democratic movement made on the value of man. This emphasis is boldly proclaimed throughout the Bible, that is, the attitude we've assumed all the way along and that we took to the Southern Baptist Convention and its commission.[46]

When Miller resigned his post in Texas to become general director of the Southern Baptist Convention's Social Service Commission in 1953, Valentine was named director of the Texas commission and continued the tradition of a social gospel approach packaged to satisfy conservatives.

Valentine's career with the Texas Christian Life Commission began slowly. He rejected the initial offer of employment and forced J. Howard Williams to approach at least two other men about the job before returning to Valentine. When the directorship was offered to Valentine a second time, he accepted.[47] Yet his reluctance to assume the office did not translate into timidity on the job. He considered race to be a critical issue during his tenure at the Texas Christian Life Commission, and he addressed it with boldness. Three months after the Supreme Court's decision outlawing racial segregation in public schools, Valentine wrote an editorial in the

---

45. *Oral Memoir of Acker C. Miller*, interview by Rufus B. Spain, 2 January 1972, Religion and Culture Project, Baylor University Program for Oral History, 1972, 104.

46. *Oral Memoir of Acker C. Miller*, interview by Rufus B. Spain, 2 January 1972, Religion and Culture Project, Baylor University Program for Oral History, 1972, 105.

47. Storey, "That's Our Name," 24.

Baptist Standard calling on all prejudiced Texas Baptists to change their attitudes. He wrote:

> Many have recently been hoping that the Supreme Court in its consideration of the "separate but equal" doctrine would not come up with anything unusual or unpleasant. Whatever else may be said about these attitudes, they cannot be justified by the New Testament or by the spirit and teachings of Jesus Christ.[48]

Valentine went on to support the Southern Baptist Convention's endorsement of the Supreme Court's decision and called on Texas Baptists to heed the advice of other anti-segregation editorials.[49] In addition to his writing efforts, Valentine led the commission to lobby at the Texas state capital against "some of the racist legislation that the legislators put through or tried to put through for public consumption so they could be seen as voting for the preservation of segregation."[50] Valentine recalled that while west and south Texas did not share the extreme racism of the Deep South, there was still a significant racist element in Texas Baptist life that objected to the Christian Life Commission's advocacy of racial justice.[51]

In spite of such opposition, Valentine diagnosed the race problem with precise language and offered a realistic assessment of the consequences Texas would face if it failed to improve the situation. In a 1957 address to the faculty of Southwestern Seminary, in the spirit of Rauschenbusch, Valentine presented a social interpretation of Christianity that he believed would help solve racial problems. He argued that the black-versus-white race problem in America influenced economics, education, and religion in the South.[52] Slavery, racial segregation, attitudes of white supremacy, isolationism from other races and cultures, physical differences between the races, and the recent Supreme Court decision all contributed to the

---

48. Foy Valentine, "A Christian Solution," *Baptist Standard*, 8 July 1954, 2.

49. Foy Valentine, "A Christian Solution," *Baptist Standard*, 8 July 1954, 2.

50. *Oral Memoirs of Foy Dan Valentine*, vol. 1, interview by Daniel B. McGee, 1 May 1976, Texas Baptist Oral History Consortium, Baylor University Institute for Oral History, Baptist General Convention of Texas, 1990, 106.

51. *Oral Memoirs of Foy Dan Valentine*, vol. 1, interview by Daniel B. McGee, 1 May 1976, Texas Baptist Oral History Consortium, Baylor University Institute for Oral History, Baptist General Convention of Texas, 1990, 100, 111.

52. Foy Valentine, "An Evaluation of the Racial Situation in the South (Integration—Progress and Problems Among Southern Baptists)," pp. 3–4, Box 2A32, Folder 130, Foy Valentine Papers.

racial crisis, Valentine said.[53] Out of the racial crisis emerged both conflict and progress, he said. The most disturbing conflict was "the conflict which exists between Christian doctrine and doing." Many churches shamefully shunned the absolute truth of racial equality, he added, in the name of preserving fellowship.[54] Though Baptists should have preached the Bible to alleviate racial prejudice, Valentine indicted Baptists for "failing to communicate the gospel at this point." He continued, "We could hardly have failed at a more significant or crucial point."[55] Preachers who believed the Bible spoke against race prejudice but failed to communicate that truth to their congregations had "no redemptive influence at all at this point on the people to whom they [were] responsible for mediating the gospel."[56] He concluded that Christians needed to integrate quickly based on their convictions about the gospel.[57]

Baptist historian John Storey aptly summarized the thinking of Valentine and his Christian Life Commission colleagues in Texas when he called them both "genuinely committed to personal regeneration" and "determined to address serious social problems and to proclaim forcefully what fellow Baptists ought to be doing." For Valentine, a Christianity that did not move beyond individual regeneration was an irrelevant Christianity. "There was something different about those Texas Baptists who fashioned the CLC," Storey wrote.[58] The difference was the application of the social gospel to racism in a manner that did not offend conservatives.

Valentine and the SBC Christian Life Commission

On June 1, 1960, Valentine took a new step in his career of advocating racial justice as he became executive secretary of the Southern Baptist Convention's Christian Life Commission in Nashville.[59] In that position he continued to advance the cause of racial equality with social gospel theology packaged in the language of conservative evangelicalism. Reflecting

53. Valentine, "An Evaluation of the Racial Situation in the South," 4–8.
54. Valentine, "An Evaluation of the Racial Situation in the South," 11.
55. Valentine, "An Evaluation of the Racial Situation in the South," 17.
56. Valentine, "An Evaluation of the Racial Situation in the South," 18.
57. Valentine, "An Evaluation of the Racial Situation in the South," 22–23.
58. Storey, "That's Our Name," 2.
59. "Christian Life Commission Annual Meeting, Nashville, Tennessee, February 29–March 1, 1960," Box 1, Folder 17, Christian Life Commission Minutes.

on his move to Nashville, Valentine said his goal was to show Southern Baptists that the Christian gospel applied to life in general and not merely to eternal salvation. In particular, he sought to show Southern Baptists that the gospel applied to the race issue.[60] Without appealing to the civil rights movement directly, Valentine argued to Southern Baptists that the concerns of the movement should also be concerns for any Christian who took the Bible seriously. He knew that most civil rights leaders would not gain a serious hearing among Southern Baptists, so Valentine used Bible-based language to spread the message of the civil rights movement to his fellow southerners.[61]

Despite his determination to advance racial justice among Southern Baptists, Valentine knew he faced serious obstacles. Denominational leaders, Valentine said, feared speaking against prejudice or segregation because doing so ran the risk of curbing gifts to the Cooperative Program, Southern Baptists' cooperative mechanism for funding denominational programs and missions.[62] Overt racism in many churches combined with institutional racism among leaders like Owen Cooper and Executive Committee executive secretary Porter Routh. Valentine summarized:

> No, you wouldn't want to call Owen Cooper really a racist. Or a Porter Routh, who tried to kill the Christian Life Commission with his committee of fifteen a few years later, or the state secretaries who refused to start an ethics agency in their state territory; they didn't intend to be racists, they just didn't want trouble stirred up. Just don't make trouble, don't rock the boat. Let's keep the money coming in for the Cooperative Program.[63]

---

60. *Oral Memoirs of Foy Dan Valentine*, vol. 2, interview by Thomas L. Charlton and David Stricklin, 30 May 1989, Texas Baptist Project, Baylor University Institute for Oral History, 2004, 58.

61. *Oral Memoirs of Foy Dan Valentine*, vol. 2, interview by Thomas L. Charlton and David Stricklin, 30 May 1989, Texas Baptist Project, Baylor University Institute for Oral History, 2004, 70–71.

62. *Oral Memoirs of Foy Dan Valentine*, vol. 2, interview by Thomas L. Charlton and David Stricklin, 30 May 1989, Texas Baptist Project, Baylor University Institute for Oral History, 2004, 61.

63. *Oral Memoirs of Foy Dan Valentine*, vol. 2, interview by Thomas L. Charlton and David Stricklin, 30 May 1989, Texas Baptist Project, Baylor University Institute for Oral History, 2004, 63.

Some Baptist state conventions feared upsetting the racial status quo so much that they refused to start ethics agencies as late as the late 1980s.[64] Southern Baptist opposition to racial progressivism resulted in motions from the floor of the convention to oppose and even abolish the Christian Life Commission throughout the 1960s. Such opposition made it difficult for Valentine to raise funds to continue the commission's work. Frequently he raised money in the North among non-Southern Baptists because, in his view, Southern Baptists were not willing to support the cause of racial justice.[65]

In spite of such opposition, between 1960 and his retirement in 1987 Valentine carefully presented social gospel theology with conservative evangelical language and moved Southern Baptists toward increased racial inclusiveness. In retirement, Valentine said of his career with the Christian Life Commission, "I expect the most important work I did was one of consciousness raising. And by that I mean helping Baptists to see that the gospel has meaning with regard to race."[66]

Christian Life Commission in the 1960s

From the start Valentine drew on Rauschenbusch-like liberalism. In his first spoken report to the Southern Baptist Convention, he referenced sin as a social reality rather than an individual reality. He called racism "the number one social-political-moral problem in the world today" and condemned Southern Baptists for taking official stands against racism but continuing to disobey the biblical mandate to reconcile the races.[67] Valentine urged Christians to combat social evil with their collective influence:

---

64. *Oral Memoirs of Foy Dan Valentine*, vol. 2, interview by Thomas L. Charlton and David Stricklin, 30 May 1989, Texas Baptist Project, Baylor University Institute for Oral History, 2004, 66. Valentine cited Alabama and South Carolina as states that resisted ethics agencies up to 1989, when this interview was conducted.

65. *Oral Memoirs of Foy Dan Valentine*, vol. 1, interview by Daniel B. McGee, 18 November 1976, Texas Baptist Oral History Consortium, Baylor University Institute for Oral History, Baptist General Convention of Texas, 1990, 131–32.

66. *Oral Memoirs of Foy Dan Valentine*, vol. 2, interview by Thomas L. Charlton and David Stricklin, 30 May 1989, Texas Baptist Project, Baylor University Institute for Oral History, 2004, 73.

67. Foy Valentine, "The Philistines Be upon Us," spoken report of the Christian Life Commission to the Southern Baptist Convention, St. Louis, Missouri, May 25, 1961, pp. 3–4, Box 2, Folder 1, Christian Life Commission Minutes.

> We Christians can not call all the plays in this kind of world but we can, with the help of God, call enough of them to change the current pattern of tense, bitter, fruitless, antagonistic, sinful relationships between Negroes and whites to a pattern of positive Christian love and genuine Christian brotherhood. We can be the salt of the earth in a world where racial pride and prejudice have become an awful stench in the nostrils of God. We can be the light of the world in a social order hamstrung by segregation and afflicted by caste where the lights are dim and even the stars are prone to wander.[68]

Like Rauschenbusch and Fosdick, Valentine mixed traditional evangelical language of the atonement with his calls for social change. In addition to the law of the land requiring racial desegregation in public institutions, Valentine said, all professed Christians were bound by the higher law of Christ, "who, when He died at Calvary broke down the middle wall of partition, the dividing wall of hostility, between men."[69] In another sermon Valentine delivered during his first year in office, he again employed the language of the atonement along with a call for amelioration of social evils. He called embracing the gospel the only adequate solution to the race problem. "God has given the only adequate solution to it in Jesus Christ," Valentine said, "who died, not against race prejudice, but for us all. It is in such a dark areas as race relations that Christ's call to make religion relevant by being the light of the world takes on its clearest meaning."[70] That first year, Valentine additionally suggested to the Southern Baptist Convention the possibility of using an African American on the program of the denomination's annual meeting and mentioned race as an area of concern in the Christian Life Commission's written annual report.[71]

The following year, Valentine continued his opposition to racism and segregation, and gave Southern Baptists an explicit reminder of his liberal theological influences. In his 1962 spoken report to the Southern Baptist Convention, Valentine argued that by reacting violently "to the extremes of some leaders of the social gospel movement," Southern Baptists

---

68. Valentine, "The Philistines Be upon Us," 4.

69. Valentine, "The Philistines Be upon Us," 4.

70. Foy Valentine, "Relevant Religion," p. 4, Box 2, Folder 1, Christian Life Commission Minutes.

71. "Minutes of the Christian Life Commission, Annual Business Meeting, February 27-28, 1961," p. 7, Box 2, Folder 1, Christian Life Commission Minutes; *1961 Southern Baptist Convention Annual*, 248-50, in "SBC Annuals."

"vented our wrath not only on their erroneous views but also on their valid insights."[72] Most denominations wrongly reflected the culture rather than the Word of God, Valentine said, and Southern Baptists fell into that pattern when they carried on the racist values of slavery. As a remedy, he called on Southern Baptists to embrace the socially transforming power of the gospel message.[73]

Again in 1963, Valentine stressed social salvation. But this time he used the evangelical language of individual regeneration. He argued in his spoken report to the Southern Baptist Convention that Southern Baptists needed to abolish racial discrimination not merely because law required it, but because "it is a sin against almighty God and a rejection of the precious blood of Jesus Christ, his only begotten son."[74] Persisting in racism does violence to the gospel, he said:

> To pretend that our prejudice in maintaining the walls of racial segregation, class consciousness, economic exclusiveness, and social snobbery does no violence to the gospel of Jesus Christ our Lord and the altar of God, Savior, is to close our eyes to the real purpose of the life and death of Christ.[75]

In an article for *Home Missions* magazine that same year Valentine argued the gospel was so intertwined with the race issue that failing to improve race relations made it appear to unbelievers that the gospel was untrue, since racist lives did not line up with the message of Christ.[76] When Southern Baptists responded to Valentine's message on race, he was not surprised. He knew it was because they took the Bible seriously and heeded appeals using its terms and concepts.[77]

---

72. Foy Valentine, "Believe and Behave," oral report to the 1962 Southern Baptist Convention in San Francisco, p. 2, Box 2, Folder 2, Christian Life Commission Minutes.

73. Foy Valentine, "The World in the Church and the Church in the World," pp. 1, 6, Box 2, Folder 2, Christian Life Commission Minutes.

74. Foy Valentine, "You Can't Go Home Again," spoken report to the Southern Baptist Convention in Kansas City, May 9, 1963, p. 2, Box 2, Folder 3, Christian Life Commission Minutes.

75. Valentine, "You Can't Go Home Again."

76. Foy Valentine, "Missions and Confusion," Box 2, Folder 3, Christian Life Commission Minutes.

77. *Oral Memoirs of Foy Dan Valentine*, vol. 2, interview by Thomas L. Charlton and David Stricklin, 30 May 1989, Texas Baptist Project, Baylor University Institute for Oral History, 2004, 60.

Many Southern Baptists resisted the Christian Life Commission's advocacy of desegregation and Valentine's advocacy of Christianity as a social force. In 1964, as in previous years under Valentine, the commission emphasized the gospel as a solution to "racial strife" in its written annual report. It also chided Southern Baptists, whose "thunderous silence in the face of oppressive injustice for American Negroes has amounted to a serious complicity in the problem."[78] In addition to its report, the commission presented the convention with a recommendation concerning race relations. The recommendation called the denomination to several courses of action including approving of churches with open-door policies for all races, pledging support for civil rights laws, and helping to defeat racism.[79] When time came to vote on the recommendation, James W. Middleton, pastor of the Shreveport, Louisiana, First Baptist Church, offered a substitute motion. Both Middleton and Vernon Simpson of Theodore, Alabama, urged messengers to pass the substitute to avoid dividing the convention on a controversial issue.[80] The substitute motion declared that every human possessed dignity before God, commended Southern Baptists for their previous stands on race, and urged "every Southern Baptist church to earnestly pray and work that peaceful Christian solutions may be found in all of the racial relationships facing the world today."[81] Middleton's motion failed to pledge support for any civil rights legislation, however, and did not commend desegregation of churches or agencies. Some messengers from the Deep South protested that the Christian Life Commission's recommendation improperly implied that churches were not in good standing with the denomination if they failed to integrate.[82] Undoubtedly, part of the motivation for the substitute motion was racist, but it also emphasized Christianity as a force among individuals and churches rather than society.[83] Many supporters of the substitute believed that the commission's emphasis on social Christianity was too liberal and failed to understand the gospel properly. Though the substitute motion was declared defeated initially on a standing vote by messengers, the convention took a ballot vote because the margin appeared

78. *1964 Southern Baptist Convention Annual*, 229, in "SBC Annuals."

79. *1964 Southern Baptist Convention Annual*, 73.

80. "Convention Amends and Adopts Recommendations," *Baptist Courier*, 4 June 1964, 12.

81. *1964 Southern Baptist Convention Annual*, 74.

82. "Convention Amends and Adopts Recommendations," 12.

83. Leon Macon, "More about the Convention," *Alabama Baptist*, 4 June 1964, 3.

slim. On the ballot vote, the substitute motion was adopted and the Christian Life Commission's race recommendation was set aside.[84] Valentine saw the action as a major defeat for the cause of racial equality.[85] Messengers saw Valentine's recommendations as unhelpful attempts to solve local problems with sweeping social pronouncements.

Also in 1964, two conferences were watershed events in the Christian Life Commission's battle to ameliorate racism. The conferences, held at the Ridgecrest and Glorieta Southern Baptist conference centers, addressed the topic of "Christianity and Race Relations." Some speakers were open about their evangelical liberalism and advocacy of the social gospel. For example, Southwestern Seminary's T. B. Maston and Southern Seminary's Henlee Barnette were both on the Southern Baptist Convention's theological left and appeared on the programs. Barnette identified himself as a disciple of Rauschenbusch.[86] Yet all the speakers addressed race with a theologically conservative vocabulary, appealing to Scripture and longstanding Southern Baptist convictions. C. E. Autrey, director of the Home Mission Board's division of evangelism and missions, argued in his presentation that racism was a sin impeding evangelism at home and abroad. The church needed to repent of racism, Autrey said, if it hoped to win people of other races to faith in Christ.[87] Barnette argued that in creation, in the church, and in heaven there is only one race before God—the race of humanity.[88] One of Maston's presentations argued that all races have a common origin and need not be kept separate, according to the Bible. We must love people of other races, Maston said.[89] Other addresses condemned racism as a disorder and a sin and even urged Southern whites to consider joining the nonviolent protest movement to eradicate Jim Crow laws. C. A. Roberts, pastor of First Baptist Church in Tallahassee, Florida, told conference attendees how he accepted the call to his church unaware of its staunch segregationist tendencies but was working to change racist attitudes.[90]

84. *1964 Southern Baptist Convention Annual*, 72.

85. See Box 2A103, "Post-Convention Letters Answered" Folder, Foy Valentine Papers.

86. Barnette, *A Pilgrimage of Faith*, 131–32.

87. *Christianity and Race Relations: Addresses from Conferences at Glorieta and Ridgecrest Sponsored by the Christian Life Commission, August 1964*, pp. 173–78, Box 17, Folder 533, Henry Franklin Paschall Papers.

88. *Christianity and Race Relations*, 178–81.

89. *Christianity and Race Relations*, 181–85.

90. *Christianity and Race Relations*, 185–91.

Many Southern Baptists attended the conferences. Valentine reported in 1965 that the aggregate attendance of 3,290 at the two 1964 conferences was by far the largest in the history of Christian Life Commission conferences. He also reported that the commission reproduced 1,500 copies of the conference addresses for distribution among Southern Baptists.[91] The success was notable, especially given the strong rebukes speakers gave the denomination.[92] For Valentine, the conferences, along with advances in both the convention and the culture, made 1964 a key year for racial justice. By July the Civil Rights Act of 1964 took effect, banning discrimination in all public places and federal programs. In the fall Martin Luther King Jr. received the Nobel Peace Prize for his leadership in the civil rights movement. Americans backed President Lyndon Johnson's civil rights advocacy by reelecting him over Republican Barry Goldwater by a margin of 486 to 52 in the Electoral College.[93] Such public focus on civil rights made Southern Baptists more likely to reexamine their own views on race. Valentine believed the commission was in step with the times more than any other Southern Baptists:

> The fact is that in 1964, there was a new wave of interest in civil rights matters; the civil rights legislation came on strong with the help of Lyndon Johnson and was passed, and it was the most important move forward for blacks in a hundred years. The Commission again was at the blue point of the flame, with regard for social concern, because there wasn't anybody else in Southern Baptist life that was doing much open talking about this subject of civil rights and race relations.[94]

Again in 1965 racists and opponents of social Christianity opposed Valentine's report to the Southern Baptist Convention. Valentine argued in his report that the disciplines of missions, evangelism, and New Testament studies all provided strong reasons to oppose racism and segregation. "Our most thoughtful New Testament scholars," he said, "have unequivocally declared that the racial pride which spawns segregation and discrimination

91. *1965 Southern Baptist Convention Annual*, 244, in "SBC Annuals."

92. Religion News Service, "Apply Christianity to Race, Southern Baptists Urged," *Alabama Baptist*, 10 September 1964, 7; Baptist Press, "Challenge to Improve Race Relations," *Religious Herald*, 3 September 1964, 11.

93. Sutton, *A Matter of Conviction*, 172–74.

94. *Oral Memoirs of Foy Dan Valentine*, vol. 1, interview by Daniel B. McGee, 18 November 1976, Texas Baptist Oral History Consortium, Baylor University Institute for Oral History, Baptist General Convention of Texas, 1990, 141.

is an offense to the gospel, does violence to the altar of God, and is rightly understood as a sin against God and humanity."[95] Resistance to Valentine's challenge came when the convention voted to add a paragraph emphasizing local church autonomy and the spirituality of the church. In an obvious effort to blunt the force of the Christian Life Commission's admonitions, messengers amended the report to "recognize that our main task is to support and promote our programs of world missions and evangelism."[96] The amendment expressed the same sentiments as the amendment in 1964. It both upheld segregation and expressed the belief that Christianity should center on individual regeneration rather than social salvation.[97]

Opposition to Valentine's program of racial advocacy, however, did not deter him from continuing to press the issue with Southern Baptists. In 1967 and again in 1968, the Christian Life Commission emphasized the gospel mandate to see people of all races as united in Christ. Though the 1967 annual report made no mention of race, the commission drafted a pamphlet that year attempting to give biblical answers to the problem of race relations. Valentine likely omitted race from the report because he wanted to focus his remarks on the Vietnam War without arousing opposition from segregationists. Amid heavy resistance to the commission's stance against the war, Valentine invited Senator Mark Hatfield, a leading peace advocate, to address the convention during the Christian Life Commission report. "Victory in Vietnam" messengers were not pleased with Hatfield's presence, and Valentine knew he could not afford to offend messengers on two fronts during the same convention.[98] The commission's 1967 race pamphlet, citing the Pauline epistles, argued that Christ broke down racial divides and that the church could not reinforce society's racism and still follow Jesus:

> The clear and consistent teaching of the New Testament is that when men come into relationship with Christ, they are brothers and are united with one another. Whatever may have divided them before, "here there cannot be Greek and Jew, circumcised and uncircumcised, barbarian, Scythian, slave, free man, but Christ is all and in all" (Colossians 3:11). When people are united

---

95. *1965 Southern Baptist Convention Annual*, 247.
96. *1965 Southern Baptist Convention Annual*, 247.
97. Leon Macon, "A Look at the Convention," *Alabama Baptist*, 17 June 1965, 3.
98. Sutton, *A Matter of Conviction*, 181.

in Christ, all of the categories that the world uses to divide them become secondary.[99]

Valentine's 1968 spoken report to the Southern Baptist Convention underscored the same point. After defining and explaining the problem of racism, he argued that "there is no way out of the mire of prejudice except by the hard road of a moral ministry that demonstrates repentance. There is no cure for racism but Christian brothering."[100] Valentine received sustained applause upon completing his report, although some messengers sat noticeably still in their seats.[101] In an effort to put its money behind its arguments, the Christian Life Commission in December 1968 voted to deposit $2,000 with "an appropriate Negro financial institution" (the equivalent of about $15,000 in 2020). By so doing the commission hoped to encourage other Southern Baptists to conduct business with African-American companies.[102] The Southern Baptist Convention presented perhaps its most significant treatment of race relations to date in 1968 when it adopted the "Statement Concerning the Crisis in Our Nation." A group of convention leaders, including Valentine, drafted the statement. The statement opposed racism with conservative theological ideas and vowed to "personally accept every Christian as a brother beloved in the Lord and welcome to the fellowship of faith and worship every person irrespective of race or class."[103] Current events were evidence, according to the statement, that there was indeed a crisis in America. Riots in more than sixty American cities, poverty, and slum housing were just some of the crisis situations, the statement argued.[104] In addition to those events, other crises were on the minds of messengers. On April 4, Martin Luther King Jr. was assassinated on the balcony of the Lorraine Motel in Memphis, Tennessee. Then on the opening day of the convention's annual meeting, presidential candidate Robert Kennedy was assassinated by disgruntled Palestinian immigrant Sirhan

---

99. "Issues and Answers: Race Relations," p. 2, Box 2, Folder 7, Christian Life Commission Minutes.

100. Foy Valentine, "Words and Deeds," address to the 1968 annual meeting of the Southern Baptist Convention, Box 2, Folder 8, Christian Life Commission Minutes.

101. Sutton, *A Matter of Conviction*, 185.

102. "Minutes of the Meeting of the Christian Life Commission of the Southern Baptist Convention, December 3–5, 1968," Box 2, Folder 8, Christian Life Commission Minutes.

103. *1968 Southern Baptist Convention Annual*, 67–69, in "SBC Annuals."

104. *1968 Southern Baptist Convention Annual*, 67–69.

Sirhan.[105] Southern Baptists sent expressions of shock and sympathy to the Kennedy family and held a special prayer time for all families involved in the tragic situation.[106] In the wake of the turmoil messengers adopted the crisis statement by a 5,687—2,119 vote.[107] Racist elements still existed in the convention, but the statement was a sign Southern Baptists were willing to oppose racism theologically. They said Jesus' death on the cross "is the miraculous redemption for every individual" regardless of race. They also declared their intention to proclaim the gospel to persons of every race and minister to human needs. The lordship of Christ, the statement said, affects a Christian's conduct in every human relationship.[108] The "Statement Concerning the Crisis in our Nation" was not Valentine's social gospel vision of Christianity. Yet with the statement Southern Baptists moved closer to Valentine by applying their theology to race.

In 1969, Valentine and the commission criticized a conservative approach to race. Messengers to the Southern Baptist Convention's annual meeting rejected the critique. The commission issued warnings against "extremism" and presented for the convention's adoption twelve recommendations on extremism. The convention accepted the commission's report without adopting the recommendations.[109] Messengers likely rejected the recommendations because they believed Valentine was making a veiled attack against theological conservatives. The statement on extremism criticized both modernistic liberals and conservatives who believed personal regeneration was the only way to advance the kingdom of God. It implied that evangelical liberals were the only group that approached social crises properly. Messengers agreed with the condemnation of the far left. They passed a resolution calling the claims of black nationalists "outrageous" and expressed disapproval of the movement's tactics.[110] Condemnation of the right, however, appeared to be aimed at people within the denomination and did not sit as well with messengers. Extremists "of the right," the statement said, "declare that the church's concern is only for men's soul and seek

---

105. Sutton, *A Matter of Conviction*, 183–84.

106. Jack Brymer, "SBC Messengers Adopt Record Budget, Veto Name Change, Approve Manifesto," *Alabama Baptist*, 13 June 1968, 1.

107. *1968 Southern Baptist Convention Annual*, 73.

108. *1968 Southern Baptist Convention Annual*, 67–69.

109. *1969 Southern Baptist Convention Annual*, 77–78.

110. Baptist Press, "Baptist Take Dim View of Objectors, Militants at New Orleans Conv.," *Alabama Baptist*, 19 June 1969, 8.

to force every member into a rigid adherence to the Bible as they see it, while ignoring the strong pervasive emphasis of our Lord upon a costly discipline which places moral and ethical demands upon every Christian in all personal and social relationships."[111] In an address to the Christian Life Commission's December 1969 meeting, Ashville, North Carolina, pastor Cecil Sherman explicitly applied the commission's warnings on extremism to race. He took aim at the far left though, and so did not incur the same resistance Valentine faced during the summer. Sherman warned that those who desired to work on the cutting edge of race relations would have to work with inappropriately militant black leaders. Being biblical on race, he said, did not necessarily translate into participating in the radical activities of Stokley Carmichael and Malcolm X.[112]

During the 1960s Valentine and the Christian Life Commission pushed Southern Baptists toward racial advance with a social gospel theology cloaked in the language of evangelical theology. Some of Southern Baptists' resistance to the commission was due to racism. But theology also played a role. When messengers to the denomination's annual meetings detected the liberalism, they fought—as in 1964 and 1969. When they had opportunity, however, Southern Baptists passed statements condemning racism using conservative language and ideas. That happened in 1968 and signaled things to come.

Christian Life Commission in the 1970s

In the 1970s, Valentine continued to press for an end to racial prejudice. Rank-and-file Southern Baptists responded positively when Valentine used terms and concepts familiar to conservatives. But increasingly Valentine and the commission revealed that their beliefs were more liberal than Southern Baptists generally. Advocating abortion and entertaining discussion about permissive views of human sexuality incited some of the greatest outcries from Southern Baptists.

In the early 1970s the commission pressed for racial equality in its reports and meetings, though not as forcefully as in the 1960s. The 1970 annual report to the Southern Baptist Convention mentioned race as a

111. Baptist Press, "SBC Deletes Recommendations from Extremism Statement," *Alabama Baptist*, 26 June 1969, 6.

112. Cecil Sherman, "Incident in Ashville: An Address Delivered by Cecil Sherman at the Annual Meeting of the Christian Life Commission, December 2, 1969, Nashville, Tennessee," Box 2, Folder 9, Christian Life Commission Minutes.

concern but did not discuss the issue at all.[113] During that same year, commission staff member Bill Pinson argued that the commission should stop attacking blatant individual prejudice and focus its efforts against more subtle institutional racism.[114] The shift to focusing on institutional racism though, did not shift Valentine's method of argument. He still advocated Christianity as a social force to change the contemporary racial climate. He argued that those in the Southern Baptist Convention who objected to pressing for social change "want the Bible preached in the truncated form to which they have become accustomed in the cultural religion of our established church."[115] The true Christian, Valentine said, had no choice but to confront both individual and social sins, such as militarism, poverty, crime, and white racism.[116] Again in 1971 the commission's annual report mentioned race without discussing it extensively, but one of its publications offered an explanation of institutional racism.[117] A Christian Life Commission insert in the April 1971 issue of *Home Missions* magazine labeled institutional racism a central piece of the urban crisis in America:

> Though blacks do not constitute all of the urban poor, they do make up the bulk of this group. Racial prejudice has helped seal them into the endless cycle of poverty. Without quality education, better jobs cannot be found. Without improved living conditions and mental appetites more finely whetted for learning, urban education is not likely to improve. Without increased incomes, general conditions cannot be improved ... and so goes the endless not-so-merry carousel.[118]

Also in 1971, the commission drafted a resolution which made clear that even though the type of racism in America had shifted, Christianity still presented the only solution. After chronicling the continuing problem of racism in America, the resolution affirmed the commission's desire to

113. *1970 Southern Baptist Convention Annual*, 204–05, in "SBC Annuals."
114. "Memo from Bill Pinson, Memphis CLC Staff Meeting, January 4–5, 1970," Box 2, Folder 10, Christian Life Commission Minutes.
115. Foy Valentine, "The Christian Life Commission—Agenda: Engagement," address to the Christian Life Commission, p. 3, 8 December 1970, Box 2, Folder 10, Christian Life Commission Minutes.
116. Valentine, "The Christian Life Commission," 7.
117. *1971 Southern Baptist Convention Annual*, 208–10, in "SBC Annuals."
118. "A Christian Life Commission Resource Paper: Urban Crisis, An Insert in the April 1971 Issue of Home Missions," Box 3, Folder 1, Christian Life Commission Minutes.

"witness to a reconciling love which puts out the flames of racial animosity and fear."[119] The early 1970s additionally brought increased promotion by the commission of Race Relations Sunday, a day on the denominational calendar to focus on the issue of race. In 1971 materials for Race Relations Sunday went to more than fifty thousand pastors and Baptist leaders.[120] The following year Race Relations Sunday again marked a significant promotion for the commission, although it only distributed materials to 40,000 pastors and leaders.[121] There was no count of how many churches participated in Race Relations Sunday, but the widespread distribution of literature suggested widespread participation. In addition, the commission hosted a second summer conference on race at Ridgecrest in 1973 entitled, "Race: New Directions for a New Day."[122] Valentine repeated in 1973 that "institutional racism" had become a major concern for him.[123] Using the language of conservative theology once again, the commission stressed that only the Word of God could alleviate the racism entwined in the American way of life. The gospel not only struck at the heart of racist people, but also racist schemes and institutions, according to the commission. "To withhold the Word of God in this important arena of race relations is to court disaster," a pamphlet said.[124]

The early 1970s brought trouble for the Christian Life Commission when it departed from conservative values and theology during a 1970 seminar entitled "Toward Authentic Morality for Modern Man." The seminar, held in Atlanta, featured a debate in which leading proponents of unbiblical ethical systems addressed participants followed by a Christian response. Two of the speakers were Joseph Fletcher, the founder of situational ethics, and Anson Mount, manager of public affairs for *Playboy* magazine. Mount argued that *Playboy* did a better job than the church of influencing the culture and offered a kind of substitute religion that redefined sexual norms

---

119. "Tentative Resolution on the Continuing Racial Crisis," Box 3, Folder 1, Christian Life Commission Minutes.

120. *1972 Southern Baptist Convention Annual*, 221, in "SBC Annuals."

121. *1973 Southern Baptist Convention Annual*, 208, in "SBC Annuals."

122. "Christian Life Conferences, Glorieta and Ridgecrest," Box 3, Folder 6, Christian Life Commission Minutes.

123. Foy Valentine, "Remarks Concerning the Christian Life Commission," p. 2, Box 3, Folder 3, Christian Life Commission Minutes.

124. "Share the Word Now in Race Relations," p. 1, Box 3, Folder 3, Christian Life Commission Minutes.

and advocated a healthy love of life.[125] The presentations scandalized many Southern Baptists and brought repercussions on the commission. In the months following the seminar, more than a dozen Baptist state papers and news outlets editorialized on the event.[126] The South Carolina state paper, for example, argued that "nothing was accomplished by having Mount and Fletcher as participants. They drew attention away from a dozen able speakers. They attracted embarrassing and adverse publicity. They revealed nothing new."[127] Virginia's *Religious Herald* reported that before the seminar began more than one hundred letters and at least two editorials in Baptist state papers criticized the commission for sponsoring the event.[128] At the 1970 Southern Baptist Convention annual meeting, messengers introduced four motions proposing drastic action against the commission because of its Atlanta seminar. A motion to strike the commission's $200,000 Cooperative Program allocation was defeated along with a motion "that the Convention call for the resignation of the elected staff of the CLC."[129] A motion that the commission explain its motives for the Atlanta seminar and a motion that the commission be abolished were both tabled after a group of convention leaders issued a statement asking for forgiveness, understanding, and prayer.[130] Both votes to table were too close to be decided on standing votes and required ballot votes.[131] The *Baptist Courier* editorialized that the "closeness of some of the votes amounted to a stern reprimand" of the commission. The *Courier* added that many of the actions at the convention "came from fundamental elements determined to right what they saw as liberal trends in the Southern Baptist Convention."[132] Although the commission survived these attacks, the presence of such negative sentiment reflected an underlying distrust that had simmered during the 1960s and began to expand in the 1970s. Valentine

---

125. Proceedings of the 1970 Christian Life Commission Seminar, "Toward Authentic Morality for Modern Man," Atlanta, Georgia, March 16–18, 1970. See also Sutton, *A Matter of Conviction*, 190–91.

126. "Resume of Developments," Box 2, Folder 9, Christian Life Commission Minutes.

127. "Two Speakers Who Were Not Needed," *Baptist Courier*, 26 March 1970, 3.

128. Baptist Press, "Letters, Editorials Protest Seminar on 'Authentic Morality,'" *Religious Herald*, 19 March 1970, 4.

129. *1970 Southern Baptist Convention Annual*, 57, 60, 67, 76–77, in "SBC Annuals."

130. *1970 Southern Baptist Convention Annual*, 68, 76–77.

131. "SBC Messengers Table Motions to Abolish Christian Life Commission," *Baptist Courier*, 11 June 1970, 8.

132. "Convention Holds Close to Center Course," *Baptist Courier*, 11 June 1970, 3.

remarked in September 1970 that there had been "some predictable fallout from the Atlanta seminar"—predictable because Southern Baptists had little tolerance of liberal social or theological mores.[133]

The mid-1970s brought continued application of Christianity to race, but also continued undermining of racial justice efforts by the commission's liberal social views. The 1974 Christian Life Commission annual report lamented the "retrenched and solidified racism in the middle 1970s" and said the only solution was to break down racial barriers by believing the gospel. "Christians have an obligation to press for justice, brotherhood, reconciliation, and unity in Christ across racial lines," the report said.[134] One messenger proposed amending the report's section on race, but his effort was defeated after some debate.[135] In addition to its report, the commission presented for the convention's adoption a recommendation concerning race relations. The recommendation urged the convention to be open to cooperation across races in order to "bear witness to Jesus Christ, who has broken down the middle wall of partition between races and who calls us into unity with each other and with him."[136] The convention adopted the recommendation.[137] Messengers did not embrace all Christian Life Commission recommendations though. They slapped down a recommendation that SBC agencies and churches elect "women to positions of leadership for which God's gifts and the Holy Spirit's calling equip them." Some saw it as a subtle endorsement of women deacons and pastors.[138] The commission fought against prejudice again in its 1975 and 1976 annual reports and even included in its 1976 consultation on public school education a presentation on the pros and cons of busing to achieve school integration. The commission recommended that Southern Baptists vote for political candidates based, in part, on their positions regarding race.[139]

---

133. "Minutes, Advisory Committee of the Christian Life Commission, September 25, 1970," Box 2, Folder 10, Christian Life Commission Minutes.

134. *1974 Southern Baptist Convention Annual*, 208, in "SBC Annuals."

135. "CLC Statement on Race Is Approved," *Religious Herald*, 20 June 1974, 5.

136. *1974 Southern Baptist Convention Annual*, 210.

137. *1974 Southern Baptist Convention Annual*, 81.

138. "SBC Discusses Women's Rights, Elects Black," *Baptist Courier*, 20 June 1974, 6.

139. "Christian Life Commission Consultation on Public School Education, Southern Baptist Convention Building, Room 330, April 20, 1976" and "Minutes of the Meeting of the Christian Life Commission of the Southern Baptist Convention," p. 5, Box 3, Folder 6, Christian Life Commission Minutes.

The commission again undermined its efforts when a speaker at its September 1976 meeting coupled the agency's stance on race with a permissive view of therapeutic abortion. James Dunn, executive director of the Texas Christian Life Commission, argued to the commission that "right-wing extremism" was unhelpful and that too many Christians were susceptible to such extremism because they "are suckers for anyone quoting Scripture."[140] Echoing African-American scholars Howard Thurman and James Cone, Dunn argued that Jesus always took the side of those who suffered.[141] Dunn said born-again faith was not enough; believers also needed a born-again ethic.[142] When Christians adopt the ethic of Jesus, they "begin to see the structures and systems of society more from the vantage point of the victim," Dunn said. He added that "we will realize the ethic of Jesus Christ only as we identify with those who suffer as He did."[143] When he mentioned race, Dunn argued that a compassionate Christian minister should support busing for many of the same reasons he should support therapeutic abortion. "It is hard for me to conceive of Martin Luther King, Jr., supporting a blanket prohibition of busing to achieve racial balance," Dunn said. "It is impossible for me to see any compassionate pastor ruling out all therapeutic abortion."[144] A speaker at another Christian Life Commission event in 1976 advocated a similar view on abortion. Paul Simmons, associate professor of Christian ethics at Southern Seminary, said caring Christians should not steer women away from abortion. He also said men should not have a say in the abortion debate.[145] Because of such social and theological ideas, which were considerably to the left of rank-and-file Southern Baptists, Valentine faced consistent pressure in 1976 to silence the Christian Life Commission, abolish it, or subsume it under another Southern Baptist agency.[146]

140. James M. Dunn, "Southern Baptists and Christian Ethics: The Challenge of a New Day," p. 3, Box 3, Folder 6, Christian Life Commission Minutes.

141. See Thurman, *Jesus and the Disinherited*; Cone, *For My People*.

142. Baptist Press, "SBC Ethical Concepts Also Need to Be 'Born Again,'" *Alabama Baptist*, 23 September 1976, 1.

143. James M. Dunn, "Southern Baptists and Christian Ethics: The Challenge of a New Day," p. 6, Box 3, Folder 6, Christian Life Commission Minutes.

144. Dunn, "Southern Baptists and Christian Ethics," 4.

145. Baptist Press, "Abortion Issue Has Shifted to Churches, Theologian Says," *Alabama Baptist*, 9 September 1976, 13.

146. *Oral Memoirs of Foy Dan Valentine*, vol. 1, interview by Daniel B. McGee, 19 November 1976, Texas Baptist Oral History Consortium, Baylor University Institute for

In the late 1970s, the commission continued to address race relations. Despite statements like Dunn's, at times it spoke almost exclusively in conservative terms and concepts. Beginning in 1977, the commission drafted a statement of social principles that the Southern Baptist Convention adopted in 1979. Southwestern Seminary's T. B. Maston wrote the initial draft of the document, which supported racial equality with the traditional doctrines of creation and redemption:

> Men and women are created in the image of God (Gen. 1:26–27). This and the fact that Christ died for all men gives to men and women their value and worth: an individual person is worth more than all things material (Matt. 16:26). The preceding means that no man or woman, boy or girl, regardless of color, culture, or condition of life should ever be treated as a mere means.[147]

Race prejudice was inherently unchristian, the document said, and while voluntary separation of the races was permissible in churches and society, "there should be no segregation, maintained by law or pressure."[148] The document even argued that Christian principles required believers to accept interracial marriages and resist the social trend of white flight from the inner city areas into which African Americans had begun to move.[149] Refusing to back down on the race issue, the Christian Life Commission in 1978 decided to publish a new series of literature that dealt with topics such as "Race," "Race: Affirmative Action," "How to Stabilize a Racially Changing Community," "Jobs for Black Young People," and "A Primer on Race."[150] At decade's end, the commission continued to promote Race Relations Sunday annually and offer to churches two printed pieces on race—a pamphlet entitled "The Bible Speaks on Race" and a resource paper designed to help Christians make informed decisions on the issue of busing.[151] Recalling the 1970s from his perspective in 1989, Valentine said

---

Oral History, Baptist General Convention of Texas, 1990, 168–70.

147. T. B. Maston, "Principles of Christian Social Concern and Action," p. 4, Box 3, Folder 7, Christian Life Commission Minutes.

148. Maston, "Principles of Christian Social Concern and Action," 14.

149. Maston, "Principles of Christian Social Concern and Action," 14–15.

150. "Christian Life Commission Literature Consultation Proceedings, Nashville, SBC Building, Room 330, April 13, 1978," Box 3, Folder 8, Christian Life Commission Minutes.

151. "Race Relations: 'Let Us Not Be Weary . . . ,'" Box 3, Folder 8, Christian Life Commission Minutes.

he used the decade to encourage Baptist institutions to take down "whites only" and "for colored" signs and hold seminars with African-American speakers invited to participate.[152]

Christian Life Commission in the 1980s

In the 1980s Valentine and the commission continued to express concern regarding racial justice, but clear applications of evangelical theology to the issue were few. Southern Baptists therefore refused to follow the commission's lead. As the Southern Baptist Convention's conservative resurgence gained momentum, Valentine spent a significant portion of his time embattled in conflict with conservatives and comparatively little of his time appropriating their theology to advocate racial justice. Consequently, by Valentine's retirement in 1987 the commission lost the convention's ear and found itself on the receiving end of a hostile takeover designed to reestablish the conservative theological position that Valentine had appropriated during the previous two decades to press Southern Baptists to new levels of racial inclusiveness.

In Christian Life Commission meetings and seminars, race emerged as a topic of concern with some frequency in the early 1980s. In September 1980, the commission's Program Committee recommended

> that the Christian Life Commission concentrate its efforts to serve Christ and Southern Baptists at the cutting edge of racial concerns warning against overt and subtle forms of racism in our churches and in our national life, and actively encouraging Southern Baptists to promote racial and ethnic harmony and bring about racial and ethnic justice.[153]

The full commission adopted the recommendation, which the Program Committee felt necessary due to the resurgence of the Ku Klux Klan, the economic gap between black and white Americans, and the growing influx of other racial minorities.[154] The recommendation went largely unnoticed

---

152. *Oral Memoirs of Foy Dan Valentine*, vol. 2, interview by Thomas L. Charlton and David Stricklin, 30 May 1989, Texas Baptist Project, Baylor University Institute for Oral History, 2004, 76.

153. "Minutes of the Annual Meeting of the Christian Life Commission of the Southern Baptist Convention, September 16–17, 1980," p. 3, Box 3, Folder 10, Christian Life Commission Minutes.

154. "Expanded Agenda, Program Committee, Conference Room 330, SBC Building," Box 3, Folder 10, Christian Life Commission Minutes.

by Baptist state papers, which focused on the developing conservative resurgence. The following year the commission again expressed concern over the race issue, authorizing the production of a video on race relations and a new series of initiatives to "help Southern Baptists deal redemptively with the current challenge related to race."[155] In addition to listing race relations consistently as a concern in its annual reports, the commission held a consultation on Hispanics, a Ridgecrest conference on race, and a one-day workshop on race during the first half of the 1980s.[156]

Despite the commission's feeling that race was a major issue for the 1980s, up to Valentine's retirement, the decade was dominated by concerns over the agency's perceived liberalism rather than its application of Christianity to racial justice. Hints of liberalism were present from the first commission meeting of the decade, when Donald Shriver, president of Union Theological Seminary in New York, traditionally a bastion of theological liberalism, presented an address to the trustees.[157] In 1982, the commission presented its Distinguished Service Award to Jimmy and Rosalyn Carter, the former President of the United States against whom Southern Baptist conservatives turned in the 1980 election for his perceived liberalism on social issues.[158] In 1984 and again in 1986 motions from the floor of the Southern Baptist Convention annual meetings, attacked the commission and Valentine for liberal stands on abortion that were contrary to the recorded position of the convention.[159] Baptist state newspapers viewed the 1984 motions as part of a wave of conservatism taking over the convention. In 1984 conservatives showed their strength by electing a president from their party for the fifth consecutive year. They showed their rejection of Valentine's brand of Christianity by passing resolutions opposing abortion

---

155. "Minutes of the annual meeting of the Christian Life Commission of the Southern Baptist Convention, September 15–16, 1981," Box 4, Folder 1, Christian Life Commission Minutes.

156. "Minutes of the Program Committee, Christian Life Commission of the Southern Baptist Convention," Box 3, Folder 10; "Christian Life Commission" (1982), p. 2, Box 4, Folder 2; "Minutes of the Annual Meeting of the Christian Life Commission of the Southern Baptist Convention, September 14–15, 1982," p. 7, Box 4, Folder 3, Christian Life Commission Minutes.

157. "Christian Life Commission" (1980), p. 1, Box 3, Folder 10, Christian Life Commission Minutes.

158. See Carter, *Keeping the Faith*, 561–62.

159. *1984 Southern Baptist Convention Annual*, 30–31, 34, 53, 56, 58, 67–68, in "SBC Annuals"; *1986 Southern Baptist Convention Annual*, 69, 72, 76–77, in "SBC Annuals."

and the ordination of women.[160] The 1986 motion on the Christian Life Commission recommended

> that the 1986 Southern Baptist Convention request the trustees of the Christian Life Commission, upon the next vacancy for the position of executive director of the Commission to fill that position with someone whose record and confession demonstrates convictions concerning the sanctity of unborn life in accordance with the sentiments expressed in the 1980, 1982, and 1984 resolutions opposing abortion.[161]

The motion reflected the convention's conservative shift. The *Baptist Courier* editorialized that "the fundamental conservatives have for many years warned against 'creeping liberalism' in Southern Baptist ranks. They wanted none of it in the teaching of seminary professors or in literature produced by the agencies." In the quest to expel liberalism, the Christian Life Commission was one of the agencies "of primary interest" for conservatives.[162] Through the turmoil, Valentine persisted in arguing for a more permissive view of abortion than messengers to annual meetings expressed.[163] Though Valentine announced his retirement in April 1986, the commission continued to travel the trajectory he charted on abortion. In September of that year, trustees narrowly rejected binding the agency's literature on abortion to the Southern Baptist Convention's pro-life position—an obvious gesture of defiance against the conservative moving convention.[164]

Valentine made no secret of his dislike for conservatives. He devoted much of his attention to opposing the more conservative element in the denomination, whom he labeled "fundamentalists." Beginning in 1981, conservative Southern Baptist Convention committees on nomination placed conservative trustees on Valentine's board without consulting

---

160. "Conservatives Solidify Grip; Win Most Key SBC votes," *Baptist Courier*, 21 June 1984, 6–8. Iva Jewel Tucker, "Messengers Elect Stanley President, Discourage Ordination of Women," *Alabama Baptist*, 21 June 1984, 1, 6.

161. *1986 Southern Baptist Convention Annual*, 69.

162. John E. Roberts, "Convention Clearly Intends to Remain Conservative," *Baptist Courier*, 19 June 1986, 3.

163. Ray Waddle, "Baptist Moderates Win Vote," *The Tennessean*, September 18, 1986, 1A, 2A.

164. David Wilkinson, "CLC Trustees Reject Move to Narrow Abortion Stance," Christian Life Commission News Release, 18 September 1986, Box 4, Folder 6, Christian Life Commission Minutes.

him.[165] Such moves angered Valentine. Fundamentalists, Valentine said, "are not historically true Baptists." The fundamentalists taking control of the Southern Baptist Convention "are Khomeini-type fundamentalists with a lock set in their mind," he said. Like the Pharisees, fundamentalists lock themselves "into a mindset . . . where they have the truth rather than for the truth to have them, and recognize that the Holy Spirit may very well, like the wind, blow where it listeth, and produce different opinions in different times, and different ways."[166] When Valentine retired in 1987, he claimed to have done so for health reasons. He took note, however, that 1987 marked the last year he could retire and still hope for a moderate successor, because the commission's board looked as though it would shift to a conservative majority in 1988.[167]

After Valentine's retirement, feuding between moderate and conservative board members continued. A moderate search committee recommended as executive director N. Larry Baker, a dean and professor of ethics at Midwestern Baptist Theological Seminary. Baker was elected by a margin of 16 to 13. The opposition reflected concerns on the part of conservatives regarding his positions on abortion, capital punishment, and women in ministry.[168] Though the commission mentioned race in its 1987 annual report, prepared by Valentine before his retirement, the battles over perceived liberalism overshadowed efforts at promoting racial justice. Conservatives on the commission board made a motion in 1987 to fire Baker due to his stands on social issues, but the motion failed by virtue of a 15—15 tie in the vote.[169] Baker eventually resigned in June 1988, facing certain termination as conservatives gained a wider majority on the board.[170]

---

165. *Oral Memoirs of Foy Dan Valentine*, vol. 2, interviewed by Thomas L. Charlton, 22 May 1989, Texas Baptist Project, Baylor University Institute for Oral History, 2004, 25–26.

166. *Oral Memoirs of Foy Dan Valentine*, vol. 2, interview by Thomas L. Charlton, 10 August 1989, Texas Baptist Project, Baylor University Institute for Oral History, 2004, 144.

167. *Oral Memoirs of Foy Dan Valentine*, vol. 2, interview by Thomas L. Charlton and David Stricklin, 4 December 1989, Texas Baptist Project, Baylor University Institute for Oral History, 2004, 197–98.

168. "Christian Life Commission" (1986), p. 2, Box 4, Folder 6, Christian Life Commission Minutes; "Minutes of the Annua Meeting of the Christian Life Commission of the Southern Baptist Convention, September 15–16, 1987," Box 4, Folder 7, Christian Life Commission Minutes.

169. "Minutes of the Annual Meeting of the Christian Life Commission of the Southern Baptist Convention, September 15–16, 1987," Box 4, Folder 7, Christian Life Commission Minutes.

170. "Christian Life Commission" (1987), p. 3, Box 4, Folder 7, Christian Life

Foy Valentine and the Christian Life Commission Vision

During the early 1980s, the commission's influence waned among Southern Baptists. Virtually absent from the commission's records from that period is any application of the traditional doctrines of creation or redemption to race. Instead, Valentine and his colleagues used much of their energy to advocate positions most Southern Baptists viewed as liberal. With increased liberalism came decreased influence in the convention, and the stage was set for a new Christian Life Commission head who would advance racial justice by returning to conservative principles.

Conclusion

Over more than thirty years, Valentine influenced Southern Baptists in Texas and nationwide to adopt a more progressive view of racial equality and integration. He succeeded when he spoke in a manner consistent with conservative theology. But when he showed social gospel influences, Southern Baptists did not follow. Valentine was an evangelical liberal. Yet he moved Southern Baptists on race because often he did not sound like a liberal. Rather, he voiced his arguments using the language of conservative theology, particularly the doctrines of creation and redemption. When he stuck with conservative arguments, Southern Baptists lent their ear to Valentine, though sometimes reluctantly. When he appeared to Southern Baptists to identify with liberal social and theological views however, Valentine's influence decreased until he faced the possibility of termination by the mid-1980s. Valentine aptly summarized the success of his ministry when he said in 1989 that "it would have been counterproductive" for him to identify his own efforts at racial equality with those of the liberal leaders of the civil rights movement. "It's better for me," he said, "to just get it right out of the Bible and do it as something that God expected them to do right about."[171] As with leaders like Criswell and Hobbs, Valentine spoke to race using the language of conservative theology.

Commission Minutes. See also Ray Waddle, "Besieged Baptist Director Sought as Pastor," *The Tennessean*, 12 May 1988, 1B, 3B.

171. *Oral Memoirs of Foy Dan Valentine*, vol. 2, interview by Thomas L. Charlton and David Stricklin, 4 December 1989, Texas Baptist Project, Baylor University Institute for Oral History, 2004, 155.

Chapter 4

The Experience of Southern Baptist Seminaries and Colleges

SOUTHERN BAPTISTS LISTENED TO appeals to Scripture but either tuned out or turned hostile when leaders appealed to social science or liberal theology. In a letter to the Home Mission Board's Emmanuel McCall, Southwestern Baptist Theological Seminary Professor T. B. Maston remarked in 1970, "As you know, there isn't anything more convicting to Baptists, black and white, than 'Thus saith the Bible.'"[1] Maston encapsulated the principle that Southern Baptist seminaries had used for thirty years to spur their denomination to greater acceptance of racial integration.

Maston's situation was a microcosm of what occurred in the larger world of Southern Baptist seminaries and colleges between the 1940s and the 1990s. Social pressures created opportune moments for considering the topic of race relations. Those opportune moments resulted in advances for racial equality when the schools appealed to their constituencies using ideas consistent with conservative theology. Generally, Southern Baptist seminary professors were not conservatives. They addressed social concerns because they were committed to the social gospel. But they appealed to conservative commitments to move the Southern Baptist masses. In fact, Southern Baptists reacted negatively when they detected anything other than conservative theology from their college and seminary professors.[2]

1. T. B. Maston to Emmanuel McCall, 23 January 1970, Folder 721, T. B. Maston Papers.

2. On racial integration in Southern Baptist Colleges and seminaries, see Newman, *Getting Right with God*; and *Southern Baptist Educator* (newspaper), 1950–1970.

Southern Baptist Seminaries and Colleges

Southwestern Baptist Theological Seminary in Fort Worth, Texas, and the Southern Baptist Theological Seminary in Louisville, Kentucky, were the two most influential schools in race relations for the latter part of the twentieth century. Those institutions established the pattern that repeated at smaller seminaries and Southern Baptist colleges. By focusing on Southwestern and Southern seminaries then tracing in broad strokes similar patterns at other institutions, one can see how a theologically informed social conscience combined with social movements to change the face of Southern Baptist ministerial education.

Southwestern Seminary

The impulse for racial justice at Southwestern Baptist Theological Seminary originated with the school's early interest in social gospel concerns. Southwestern offered courses in ethics and social Christianity as early as 1910, when the campus moved from Waco to Fort Worth.[3] The interest in social Christianity arose at Southwestern largely due to the influence of the social gospel movement in the early twentieth century.[4] Maston became the most influential advocate for racial justice at Southwestern by mid-century, and his theology continued the liberal tradition. Charles Franklin McCullough has shown that Maston held neoorthodox views and objected to the doctrine of biblical inerrancy. Walter Rauschenbusch, H. Richard Niebuhr, Reinhold Niebuhr, and Emil Brunner all influenced Maston.[5] Regarding Scripture, Maston said the Bible might have inaccuracies in geography, history, or science.[6] He insisted that the Bible could not be equated with the Living Word of God and that its words were not the believer's final authority.[7] In his courses, Maston at times drew from social sciences more than the Bible. The economics of race, a psychological study of race, and the contributions of blacks to American life were all lecture topics in Maston's courses.[8] In lecture notes for one course on race, Maston said, "The

---

3. *Oral Memoirs of T. B. Maston*, interview by Rufus B. Spain, 30 August 1973, Religion and Culture Project, Baylor University, Program for Oral History, 1973, 108.

4. *Oral Memoirs of T. B. Maston*, interview by Rufus B. Spain, 30 August 1973, Religion and Culture Project, Baylor University, Program for Oral History, 1973, 110.

5. McCullough, "An Evaluation of the Biblical Hermeneutic of T. B. Maston," 25–37.

6. McCullough, "An Evaluation of the Biblical Hermeneutic of T. B. Maston," 67.

7. McCullough, "An Evaluation of the Biblical Hermeneutic of T. B. Maston," 76.

8. See Folders 2343–2345, T. B. Maston Papers.

emphasis throughout will be on the broader social problems. We will seek to interpret these problems from the religious viewpoint, but we leave the strictly religious approach to the Department of Missions."[9] Representatives from the National Association for the Advancement of Colored People addressed Maston's classes as did representatives from the Home Mission Board's department in charge of work with National Baptists.[10]

Yet when it came to addressing the Southern Baptist masses, Maston knew the social gospel or any other brand of theological liberalism would be ineffective. Maston explained that one could not convince Southern Baptists with purely social arguments:

> I've told the fellows a lot of times through the years that instead of going out and preaching social salvation and so forth, what they needed to do is just preach the application of the Gospel to everyday life. It's the same thing. But to avoid the word "social" which arouses some opposition on the part of some people to what you're trying to do.[11]

So Maston used traditional exegesis to present the Bible's teachings.

In public discussions of race, he appealed to traditional evangelical doctrines such as creation in the image of God, the death of Christ for all, and the unity of the church.[12] In a speech to the 1956 annual meeting of the Southern Baptist Convention, Maston challenged messengers to apply to segregation the principle of Christian equality—a truth Maston emphasized in his courses repeatedly.[13] Biblical principles that apply to the issue of race included, Maston said, the doctrine of creation in the image of God, the church's status as the family of God and siblings in Christ, the universal atonement of Christ, and the Golden Rule.[14] When understood correctly, these doctrines would change churches, according to Maston. He said that "God's message to his churches, if delivered tactfully but fearlessly, will

---

9. T. B. Maston, "The Race Problem," course lecture notes, p. 1, Folder 2364, T. B. Maston Papers.

10. See Folder 109, T. B. Maston Papers.

11. *Oral Memoirs of T. B. Maston*, interview by Rufus B. Spain, 30 August 1973, Religion and Culture Project, Baylor University, Program for Oral History, 1973, 113.

12. McCullough, "An Evaluation of the Biblical Hermeneutic of T. B. Maston," 149–54.

13. "Baptists Told Equality Key in Racial Issue," *Associated Press*, 31 May 1956, Folder 2448, T. B. Maston Papers.

14. T. B. Maston, "Southern Baptists and the Negro," pp. 4–5, Folder 2448, T. B. Maston Papers.

challenge the community and will lift the world toward God's ideal for the world."[15] Among the courses in which Maston shared such teachings were "Social Teachings of the Bible," "Christianity and Contemporary World Issues," "Basic Ethics," and "The Church and Race Relations."[16]

Maston said in a 1965 address that Southern Baptists must live up to their claims of being people of the Bible by obeying its teachings on race. He called failing to live out the Bible's teaching on race "practical atheism" and said, citing James 2:1, "Entirely too many of our people who claim to be 'a people of the Book' continue to show partiality as they 'hold the faith of our Lord Jesus Christ.'"[17] In two undated writings on race relations, Maston again appealed to biblical doctrines to alleviate racial tension. He cited God's sovereignty, God's fatherhood, God's love, God's requirement of obedience, and God's command to help the weak as biblical teachings encouraging kindness toward racial minorities.[18] Maston also argued:

> To live as Christ would have us live in relation to those of other races, we must recognize the relevance of certain biblical ideals and ideas to the contemporary racial situation. Some of those ideas or ideals are that we are "of one" or from one source (Acts 17:26), that God created man in his own image (Gen. 1:26), and that Christ died for all men.[19]

God's revelation to Peter in Acts 10 also is an important biblical passage on race, Maston added, teaching that God is no respecter of persons.[20] Maston taught those same biblical principles in his courses during the 1960s. He cited in a 1968 class Acts 17:26, creation in God's image, the universal atonement, and the value of an individual person.[21] Maston identified the Bible as the tool most likely to move Southern Baptists on the issue of race. "Nothing will point up our failure more and yet nothing will challenge our

15. T. B. Maston, "Southern Baptists and the Negro," pp. 5, Folder 2448, T. B. Maston Papers

16. See Folders 1303, 2364, 905, 2341, 2342, T. B. Maston Papers.

17. T. B. Maston, "Southern Baptists and the Negro," pp. 1–3, 18, Folder 1282, T. B. Maston Papers.

18. T. B. Maston, *The Christian and Race Relations*, pp. 4–7, Folder 1295, T. B. Maston Papers.

19. T. B. Maston, "What Is the Christian's Approach to Race Relations?," p. 3, Folder 1424, T. B. Maston Papers.

20. Maston, "What is the Christian's Approach to Race Relations?," 3.

21. T. B. Maston, "The Role of the Christian Leader in the Racial Crisis," p. 6, Folder 1425, T. B. Maston Papers.

people more than a review and an underscoring of basic biblical concepts that relate to the whole area of race and race relations," he said.[22]

Social gospel theology did not always translate into action against prejudice and segregation. Through the 1920s Southwestern's faculty did not promote the gospel's full implications for the issue of race. According to Maston, several faculty members were members of the Ku Klux Klan at that time and only later concluded that the organization's racism was at odds with the biblical notion of faithfulness to God. Maston himself attended a Klan meeting in the 1920s at the invitation of theology professor W. T. Conner. Maston explained:

> I don't mind saying that I once attended one meeting of the Klan over in—they had a hall over in North Ft. Worth. And I attended that at the invitation of Dr. W. T. Conner. So it [the Klan] did have some influence at least in that sense that some got involved in it. But so far as I know, none stayed in it.[23]

Conner's participation in the Klan illustrated how little the early social ethics courses at Southwestern caused students and faculty to examine critically the prevailing assumptions about race. They could endorse integration but at the same time reinforce negative racial stereotypes. J. Howard Williams, Southwestern's president from 1953 to 1958, argued for integration by invoking the Declaration of Independence's claim that all men are created equal. "The American people need to re-examine these great concepts," Williams argued, "recognizing that all mankind has a common heritage in creation."[24] Christians had remained wrongly silent on the question of race, he continued, and the world can "point an accusing finger at us because we offer so few constructive suggestions on this problem."[25] Yet Williams' assessment of the race problem was not entirely progressive. Showing some paternalism, he argued that the African American "brought with him certain social customs and moral concepts which are deep-rooted and will not be changed overnight—his free-and-easy way of life, which does not think too much of tomorrow, his lack of physical cleanliness, his concepts of morals, his low standards in the

---

22. Maston, "The Role of the Christian Leader in the Racial Crisis," 6.

23. *Oral Memoirs of T. B. Maston*, interview by Rufus B. Spain, 23 August 1972, Religion and Culture Project, Baylor University, Program for Oral History, 1973, 57.

24. J. Howard Williams, "Concerning Integration," *Southwestern News*, December 1957, Folder 104, J. Howard Williams Papers.

25. Williams, "Concerning Integration."

realm of sex."[26] For Williams, part of the solution to the race problem was for African Americans to be patient, improve their hygiene and morals, and wait for society to achieve the Christian ideal.[27]

Despite such hints of prejudice, Southwestern educated blacks on its campus well before the integration of public institutions became the law. During the 1930s, the seminary granted diploma credit for work done at Bishop College, a Baptist-oriented school in Dallas for African Americans. On May 6, 1941, however, the Southwestern faculty voted that the program with Bishop College be discontinued and that night classes for black preachers be offered on the seminary campus instead.[28] Between 1942 and 1953, the seminary offered night classes and extension work for blacks on the diploma level only. Upon completion of their coursework, black students graduated in a special evening graduation service, separate from the white graduates. Until 1953, Southwestern offered extension courses for African Americans in Austin, Waco, Beaumont, Mexia, Mission, and Dallas.[29] In November 1950, the trustees unanimously passed a motion to "approve the admission of negro graduates of senior colleges, who have received definite calls from the Lord to definite religious work, as regular students in Southwestern Baptist Theological Seminary" and to invite sister seminaries to consider a similar action.[30] By 1955, the first two African-American graduates of the seminary earned their degrees. Leon Hardee received the bachelor of divinity while Marvin C. Griffin received the master of religious education.[31] Dormitories continued to be segregated by race until 1956, when trustees eliminated housing discrimination at the urging of students and faculty.[32]

The number of black students and faculty at Southwestern during the 1950s and 1960s suggested mixed success in the seminary's quest to break down racial barriers. In 1959, nearly twenty years after the seminary first allowed African Americans to study on its campus, Maston lamented that there were only twenty-one total black students in all six Southern Baptist

26. Williams, "Concerning Integration."
27. Williams, "Concerning Integration."
28. Baker, *Tell the Generations Following*, 269.
29. Baker, *Tell the Generations Following*, 313.
30. Baker, *Tell the Generations Following*, 313.
31. Baker, *Tell the Generations Following*, 353.
32. Baker, *Tell the Generations Following*, 354.

seminaries combined.[33] In one 1963 survey, the numbers remained low for Southwestern. Despite its status as a leader in the push for integration, Southwestern was the only Southern Baptist seminary not to have a single African American enrolled that year, according to the survey. Along with its report of black enrollment, the seminary commented:

> We do not make any "special" effort to recruit Negro students. We try to treat all students and prospective students alike without regard to race. A "special" effort to recruit Negro students would be a violation of this principle of equality. We do have scholarships available for graduates of Bishop College (a Negro college now in Dallas). This is made possible through a gift to the seminary a number of years ago.[34]

Another report from the same era showed a slightly different picture, suggesting either that 1963 was an off year for African-American enrollment or that the aforementioned count of black students in 1963 was inaccurate. A 1961 report indicated that Southwestern had more than 26 black students enrolled—the highest total of any Southern Baptist seminary. Southwestern also had three African-American graduates by 1961.[35] But a significant number of white students still harbored racist viewpoints despite the teaching in ethics and theology courses. Maston reported in 1958, "We are finding that we have a good many students who are very definitely segregationalists in their whole perspective."[36] Maston added that "a few faculty members" also held segregationist views, "but not many."[37] In 1967, Maston called unsuccessfully for the hiring of the first black professor at Southwestern.[38]

In the 1970s and 1980s Southwestern trained students for ministry to racial minorities and increased the presence of minorities on campus. In 1972, the seminary issued a proposal to open an urban study center

33. T. B. Maston to Guy Bellamy, 13 March 1959, Folder 109, T. B. Maston Papers.

34. "Negroes in Southern Baptist Convention Seminaries, Spring 1963," Folder 1285, T. B. Maston Papers.

35. Untitled document listing years Southern Baptist Colleges and seminaries were integrated, Folder 1288, T. B. Maston Papers.

36. T. B. Maston to Ralph A. Phelps, 22 October 1958, Folder 905, T. B. Maston Papers.

37. T. B. Maston to Ralph A. Phelps, 22 October 1958, Folder 905, T. B. Maston Papers.

38. Jim Jones, "A Seminary Issue in Black and White," *Fort Worth Star-Telegram*, 21 March 1967, Folder 956, T. B. Maston Papers.

in Washington, DC, in conjunction with Southeastern Baptist Theological Seminary in Wake Forest, North Carolina. Especially for doctor of ministry students, the center was designed to provide opportunities for the study of ministry to ethnic minorities. "Since we are clearly going to have to do an effective job both evangelizing and ministering among eth[n]ic and cultural minorities, this would be an ideal setting for such a study," the proposal said of Washington.[39] In the mid-1970s, Maston wrote a significant portion of the Home Mission Board study, "Ministering in Changing Ethnic Patterns."[40] By the 1980s, a sufficient number of African-American students attended Southwestern to establish a National Baptist Student Fellowship on Campus. Maston remarked in 1983 that black students increasingly had become a "vital part of our life" on campus and increased to a "considerable number."[41]

Yet Southwestern's attitude about race was still a mixed bag. Intermarriage was sufficiently controversial in 1982 to provoke a letter from Maston to Emmanuel McCall seeking advice when a black male student developed a romantic interest in a white female student. Maston argued that while not immoral, intermarriage was unwise given the social climate of the day.[42] McCall replied that the couple should consider the significant social difficulties they would face. He cited interracial seminary couples he knew as examples of the fact that interracial marriage could hinder a Baptist's ministry in the 1980s.[43] Even in the late 1980s, all the racial progress on campus did not totally eliminate racial tension. In 1989, four Korean-American students charged racial discrimination when security officers treated them with what they deemed to be excessive rudeness and suspicion. Both the students and security officers involved acknowledged a racial dynamic in the incident.[44]

Along with building better race relations on campus, the success of Southwestern's push for racial justice evidenced itself in the influence of seminary graduates. Foy Valentine was perhaps the most visible

---

39. "Proposal for Urban Study Center, Washington, D.C.," Drawer 16, "Urban Strategy" Folder, Robert E. Naylor Papers.

40. Emmanuel McCall to T. B. Maston, 4 March 1974, Folder 721, T. B. Maston Papers.

41. T. B. Maston to James W. Culp Sr., 22 April 1983, Folder 839, T. B. Maston Papers; T. B. Maston to Emmanuel McCall, 16 March 1983, Folder 721, T. B. Maston Papers.

42. T. B. Maston to Emmanuel McCall, 24 June 1982, Folder 721, T. B. Maston Papers.

43. Emmanuel McCall to T. B. Maston, 7 July 1982, Folder 721, T. B. Maston Papers.

44. See Folder 695, James Leo Garrett Papers.

Southwestern graduate pressing for racial equality, but a cohort of others testified to the seminary's influence on their ministries of racial reconciliation as well.[45] For example, in 1953 Bob Taylor, pastor of the Southside Baptist Church in Baton Rouge, Louisiana, said Maston's influence led him to hold a joint worship service with his church and a black Baptist church. "I shall never forget in class what you said one day about being true to the Bible," Taylor wrote to Maston about his teaching on race.[46] In 1956 Maston reported that a number of Southwestern alumni had been fired from pastorates because of their integrationist teachings on race.[47] Lee Porter, a Maston doctoral graduate, reported in 1961 that he pressed local ministers and churches to desegregate public schools and nearly lost his position as pastor of Windbourne Avenue Baptist Church in Baton Rouge as a result.[48] Later in the 1960s, Ralph Phelps, president of Ouachita Baptist College in Arkadelphia, Arkansas, and a Southwestern doctoral graduate, reported that the seminary influenced heavily his efforts to oppose segregation.[49] Maston students ascended to positions of convention leadership in the 1970s. Maston student and racial progressive, Jimmy Allen, was elected Southern Baptist Convention president in 1977. The same year, two other Maston students, Lee Porter and Olan Runnels, were elected convention officers.[50] William M. Pinson, later president of Golden Gate Baptist Theological Seminary and a notable Southwestern graduate himself, called the 1977 convention "a T. B. Maston convention." Pinson wrote, "With Jimmy [Allen] and Olan [Runnels] being elected president and first vice-president and Lee Porter another one of the officers you almost had a clean sweep. You were pretty well represented in the speakers also."[51]

Southwestern steadily increased its advocacy of racial justice through the twentieth century. Liberal theology influenced Maston to lead the seminary toward racial justice. But so many Maston protégées and their churches followed Maston's lead because he pressed them with conservative biblical arguments. Yet during the same era another Southern Baptist

---

45. See Tillman, "T. B. Maston."
46. Bob Taylor to T. B. Maston, 26 January 1953, Folder 956, T. B. Maston Papers.
47. T. B. Maston to Emanuel Rish, 9 November 1956, Folder 956, T. B. Maston Papers.
48. Lee Porter to T. B. Maston, 15 May 1961, Folder 930, T. B. Maston Papers.
49. Ralph A. Phelps to T. B. Maston, 12 May 1968, Folder 904, T. B. Maston Papers.
50. Jimmy Allen to T. B. Maston, 20 June 1977, Folder 23, T. B. Maston Papers.
51. William M. Pinson Jr. to T. B. Maston, 23 June 1977, Folder 915, T. B. Maston Papers.

seminary competed with Southwestern for the distinction of having the greatest influence over Southern Baptists in race relations.[52]

Southern Seminary

At Southern Seminary professors advocated social Christianity beginning in the early twentieth century.[53] In 1918, Southern Professor Charles S. Gardiner offered the first course on race relations at any Southern Baptist seminary. Gardiner's successor, Jesse B. Weatherspoon, continued teaching on race, including material on race in his introductory Christian ethics courses and offering a graduate-level course devoted entirely to race relations. Weatherspoon taught both courses from 1929 to 1942.[54]

The seminary's instruction of African Americans extended back nearly as far as its interest in race relations. President John R. Sampey reported to the trustees in 1936 on the necessity of helping black preachers obtain theological training. After hearing Sampey, the trustees voted to appropriate funds for two graduate students to provide "theological training to colored pastors and theological students in their own building in Louisville, Ky."[55] The program of instructing black theological students continued until 1940, when a trustee subcommittee recommended that the board establish "an extension department of the Seminary for the training of Negro preachers."[56] Receiving African-American students into the seminary as regular students was out of the question because of Kentucky's Day

---

52. For a sense of the rivalry between Southwestern and Southern Seminaries on the race question, see T. B. Maston to Mrs. J. D. Sapp, 26 April 1958, Folder 2649, T. B. Maston Papers. Maston wrote, "On page eleven you imply that the Southern Seminary trustees were the first ones to vote to admit Negro students. I believe that actually you will find that Southwestern took action before Southern."

53. For a summary of Southern Seminary's early dealings with race relations, see Barnette, "The Southern Baptist Theological Seminary and the Civil Rights Movement: From 1859–1952. Part One."

54. Barnette, "The Southern Baptist Theological Seminary and the Civil Rights Movement: From 1859–1952," 535–36.

55. "Excerpt from Trustee Minutes of May 12, 1936, p. 113," Folder 15-2-A4b, Duke McCall Papers.

56. "Excerpt from Trustee Minutes of June 11, 1940, p. 142," Folder 15-2-A4b, Duke McCall Papers.

Law, which prohibited educational institutions from receiving both white and African-American students as pupils.[57]

Instruction of African Americans at the seminary campus began in 1942 with the Negro Extension department's admission of Garland Offutt and four other students. In 1946, B. J. Miller, J. V. Bottoms, and Claude Taylor also enrolled as students in the Negro Extension department.[58] The black students initially received instruction from professors and graduate students in vacant faculty offices, since Kentucky's attorney general said such a practice did not violate the Day Law.[59] Offutt quietly continued his course of study until 1944, when he earned the number of credits necessary for the master of theology degree. With the faculty's approval, Offutt became Southern's first black graduate in May 1944.[60] The graduation also marked Offutt as the first black graduate of any Southern Baptist seminary. Offutt continued at Southern, pursuing the doctor of theology until he graduated a second time in 1948.[61] Sometime after Offutt's first graduation, in the mid-1940s (1946, according to the recollection of Professor John J. Owens), the seminary began allowing black students to sit in classrooms with white students in violation of the Day Law.[62] Some professors and administrators recalled that violating the law was not a moral stand as much as it was a practical matter. Owens, for example, said of the biracial teaching, "I wasn't trying to be an agent of change. . . . [H]ere are some fellas that wanted to learn, and more power to them. I'll be glad to meet in class with them."[63] Duke McCall, Southern's president beginning in 1951,

---

57. Barnette, "The Southern Baptist Theological Seminary and the Civil Rights Movement: From 1859–1952," 537.

58. Barnette, "The Southern Baptist Theological Seminary and the Civil Rights Movement: From 1859–1952," 538–39.

59. "Excerpts from Faculty Minutes," "Theology Faculty, September 9, 1941, p. 51, Bk. 11," Folder 15-2-A4b, Duke McCall Papers.

60. "Excerpts from Faculty Minutes," "Theology Faculty, March 16, 1944, p. 167, Bk. 11," Folder 15-2-A4b, Duke McCall Papers.

61. "Excerpts from Faculty Minutes," "Theology Faculty, September 13, 1948 (p. 48, Br. 12)," Folder 15-2-A4b, Duke McCall Papers. See also Mueller, *A History of Southern Baptist Theological Seminary*, 237.

62. *Oral History Interview of Estill Jones, John J. Owens, Henry Turlington, and Wayne Ward*, 7. Barnette dated the beginning of biracial education in 1947 or 1948 (Barnette, "The Southern Baptist Theological Seminary and the Civil Rights Movement: From 1859–1952," 539–40).

63. *Oral History Interview of Estill, John J. Owens, Henry Turlington, and Wayne Ward*, 9.

agreed, saying Offutt "took his classes in the professor's office until the professor got tired of covering the same material twice and invited him to sit in the back of the room during the regular class."[64] But Wayne Ward, a Southern professor who began teaching African Americans in 1947 or 1948, felt that it was a matter of principle. According to Ward, by teaching blacks and whites in the same classrooms, "We were practicing passive resistance, and we'd already prayed about it—both the blacks who were also subject to arrest and those of us who were teaching them, and we were committed to go to prison if we had to."[65] Ward recalled an incident when a police officer arrived at his class to issue a warning about violating the Day Law. When the officer showed some hesitation to enter the class, Ward told him God would punish him if he arrested anyone. Ward said of the incident, "You just had to confront people with the fact that they were being called upon to enforce a law that was immoral and for those who believe the Bible and were Christians, it was also a violation of everything as a Christian you need to be."[66]

White seminary students and Negro Extension Department students continued studying in the same classrooms until 1951, when trustees voted to admit black students to the seminary provided they met the same admission standards required of whites. The only restriction the black students faced was to be denied access to the dormitories.[67] McCall said fighting to admit black students was the first decision he made as Southern's president, precipitated by the director of admissions asking him what to do about African-American students.[68] Though the Day Law remained in effect until 1954, by 1951 seminary officials felt certain they could win any legal challenges. McCall explained:

> My memory is that we decided to ignore the law. We thought we had moral ground—and probably the legal ground as well—to ignore it. We didn't think the authorities were going to challenge the seminary over the admission of black students. We thought if anybody did, and got into a federal court, it probably would get

---

64. McCall, *Duke McCall*, 142.

65. *Oral History Interview of Estill Jones, John J. Owens, Henry Turlington, and Wayne Ward*, 15.

66. *Oral History Interview of Estill Jones, John J. Owens, Henry Turlington, and Wayne Ward*, 15.

67. Excerpt from Trustee Minutes, SBTS, March 13, 1951," Folder 15-2-A4b, Duke McCall Papers.

68. McCall, *Duke McCall*, 141–42.

thrown out. The faculty of the seminary had voted to admit blacks during the preceding year.[69]

The faculty embraced the idea of integration by 1951. Ethics professor Henlee Barnette recalled the words of President Ellis A. Fuller when the faculty considered a motion to recommend the admission of black students. Fuller said, "If we admit these students, I want to ask you how many of you will be willing to have them in your home when you have students for a meal. I don't want a show of hands. I want each of you whose answer is 'Yes' to stand." When the entire faculty stood, Fuller said, "Well, then, I will join you and will propose it to the Board of Trustees."[70] By 1957 seventeen black students, five of whom were Nigerians, were admitted.[71]

Southern administrators and students pressed for integration. Quietly the seminary hired Emanuel A. Dahunsi, a black Nigerian, to teach New Testament in the late 1950s.[72] The students took a stand for integration when, in 1950, a survey of students revealed that 94.7 percent favored admitting "a few qualified Negro College graduates."[73] The same year, five student representatives met with Southern's trustees requesting that black students be admitted.[74]

Theology helped motivate such racially progressive stands. The arguments of three professors—J. B. Weatherspoon, Edward A. McDowell, and Wayne Ward—illustrated the point. Weatherspoon was one of the first professors to teach black students in the 1940s and advocated racial equality to the faculty.[75] Though a doubter of the verbal inspiration of Scripture and

---

69. McCall, *Duke McCall*, 141.

70. Barnette, "The Southern Baptist Theological Seminary and the Civil Rights Movement: From 1859–1952," 545.

71. "Negro Students up to 1957," Folder 15-2-A4b, Duke McCall Papers.

72. Duke McCall, "Statement to Deans Council," 23 September 1968, Folder 2-6-N1, Duke McCall Papers. Resolution of sympathy for the death of Emanuel A. Dahunsi, 13 February 1979, Folder 03-5-N2, Duke McCall Papers.

73. Ira De A. Reid, "The Negro Baptist Ministry: An Analysis of Its Profession, Preparation and Practices," pp. 259–63, "Bellamy, Black Church Extension Division" Box, "Reports, Surveys, Black Church Relations Dept., Missions Ministries div." Folder, Unprocessed Home Mission Board Records. See also Barnette, "The Southern Baptist Theological Seminary and the Civil Rights Movement: From 1859–1952," 541.

74. Reid, "The Negro Baptist Ministry," 259–63. Barnette, "The Southern Baptist Theological Seminary and the Civil Rights Movement: From 1859–1952," 543.

75. *Oral History Interview of Estill Jones, John J. Owens, Henry Turlington, and Wayne Ward*, 5; "Excerpts from Faculty Minutes," Folder 15-2-A4b, Duke McCall Papers.

holding a progressive view of Christian missions, Weatherspoon turned to evangelical doctrine when he argued for racial justice.[76] In a pamphlet entitled *Why All the World*, Weatherspoon argued that the doctrines of creation and salvation demanded taking the gospel to people of all races. He wrote:

> We are very slow to realize that humanity is one, that we are all His offspring, that He made of one every nation of men, that He ordained the time and habitation of all nations. Whether men be white or black or red or brown they are all akin. . . . Only through the gospel of Christ can men find brotherhood and see the Kingdom of God on earth.[77]

In 1947, the Southern Baptist Convention's Committee on Race Relations, chaired by Weatherspoon, argued that the doctrines of the lordship of Christ, the Holy Spirit, the Bible as the Word of God, the dignity and worth of each individual man, the fellowship of believers, and democracy in government all pushed Baptists toward a more just attitude regarding other races.[78] Again in 1954, Weatherspoon argued that it was impossible for Southern Baptists to move "forward in Jesus Christ" unless they affirmed the Supreme Court's school desegregation decision and pursued equal justice.[79]

McDowell was another Southern professor who used theology to press for racial justice. Professors Estill Jones, Henry Turlington, John J. Owens, and Wayne Ward all cited McDowell as instrumental in pushing the faculty to begin instruction of black students.[80] Jones recalled that McDowell "was an inspiration to all of us on the campus with respect to racial relationships in the south." McDowell also brought up the subject of race "at every opportunity possible in teaching New Testament."[81] McDowell cited Philemon and the "teachings of Jesus Christ" to argue that Christian doctrine was the reason the world first developed a conscience concerning race relations. "The development of a conscience concerning man's

---

76. Roberts, "Jesse Burton Weatherspoon," 41–43, 67–108.

77. J. B. Weatherspoon, *Why All the World?* (Richmond: Foreign Mission Board, n. d.), 7, Box 3, Folder 15, J. B. Weatherspoon Papers.

78. 1947 Report of the Committee on Race Relations, Box 1, Folder 14, Race Relations Collection.

79. Weatherspoon floor speech, Box 1, Folder 19, Race Relations Collection.

80. *Oral History Interview of Estill Jones, John J. Owens, Henry Turlington, and Wayne Ward*.

81. *Oral History Interview of Estill Jones, John J. Owens, Henry Turlington, and Wayne Ward*, 3.

treatment of man was one of the first fruits of Christianity's impact upon the Graeco-Roman world," he wrote.[82]

Ward likewise pushed for racial equality at Southern because of his belief that to do so was consistent with the Bible's teaching. Ward called racial discrimination "a violation of everything Christian you need to be."[83] He said the reason professors risked legal prosecution to teach black students was their belief that to do so was consistent with Scripture's plain teachings. He said of the faculty, "We were just stumbling along, trying to find out how to be a little more consistent."[84]

In the 1960s, Southern Seminary continued a forward progression in the area of racial equality. Yet the most notable event of the decade, which occurred in 1961, demonstrated that when seminary faculty did not appeal to conservative doctrine to support their actions, neither rank-and-file Southern Baptists nor trustees went along with them.

On April 19, 1961, civil rights leader Martin Luther King Jr. delivered the Julius Brown Gay lectures at Southern. Originally, the faculty's Visiting Lecturers Committee—comprising Charles McGlon, James Leo Garrett, and Allen W. Graves—invited King to be part of a panel also consisting of Brooks Hays, Howard Butt, and George Meany. However, when none of the other panelists could come, King was left to address the seminary community alone.[85] While on the campus, King spoke in chapel to approximately 1,400 people and later participated in a question-and-answer session before 500 people in a combined session of the seminary's ethics classes.[86] In chapel, King argued that the world was moving from an old age of colonialism and segregation to a new age of freedom and dignity. He said the church should play a prominent role in such a time of societal transition by helping to uproot prejudice and show segregation to be a moral evil:

---

82. Edward A. McDowell, "Southern Churches and the Negroes," n. d., Folder 2, Box 3, Series 4, J. B. Weatherspoon Papers.

83. *Oral History Interview of Estill Jones, John J. Owens, Henry Turlington, and Wayne Ward*, 15.

84. *Oral History Interview of Estill Jones, John J. Owens, Henry Turlington, and Wayne Ward*, 16.

85. Visiting Lecturers Committee to Southern Seminary trustees, 1 May 1961, Folder 14-4-K1, Duke McCall Papers.

86. Ora Spaid, "Dr. King Says 'Segregation Is Dead,'" *The Courier-Journal*, 20 April 1961, Folder 14-4-K1a, Duke McCall Papers. For a summary of King's visit, see Barnette, "The Southern Baptist Theological Seminary and the Civil Rights Movement: The Visit of Martin Luther King Jr."

Southern Baptist Seminaries and Colleges

> The church must make it clear that if we are to be true witnesses of Jesus Christ, we can no longer give our allegiance to a system of segregation. Segregation is wrong because it substitutes an I-It relationship for the I-Thou relationship. Segregation is wrong because it relegates persons to the status of things. Segregation is wrong because it does something to the personality; it damages the soul. It often gives the segregator a false sense of superiority, and it gives the segregated a false sense of inferiority.[87]

King went on to explain the goals of African Americans, attack segregation in the church, explain his philosophy of "soul force," and encourage faith in man's ability to solve the problem of racism.[88] Absent from the sermon, however, were scriptural arguments or appeals to the doctrines of traditional, orthodox Christianity to support his program of integration. The sermon closed with what sounded more like theological liberalism than what one would expect to hear in a Southern Baptist pulpit. "We will be a part of that creative minority that will stand firm on an issue," King said, "will help us bring into being the Kingdom of God knowing that in the process, God struggles with us."[89] In the session with the seminary's ethics classes, King delivered a speech arguing for nonviolent resistance to evil and subsequently dialogued with students about subjects including breaking unjust laws, the NAACP, the legal requirement that businesses serve people of all races and religions, and the need for churches to integrate.[90]

In response to King's visit, Southern Baptists in general, and even the seminary's trustees, expressed alarm. McCall had all of his speaking engagements in Mississippi cancelled in the wake of King's appearance, and one man in Dothan, Alabama, said he planned to devote $40,000 to getting McCall fired.[91] McCall's wife and children received "nasty" phone calls because of the incident, and other faculty members who defended the seminary's invitation of King became targets of attacks too.[92] Many Southern Baptists sent the seminary letters of complaint, which attempted to make arguments from

---

87. "Address Given by Dr. Martin Luther King Jr., as one of the Gay Lectures, Southern Baptist Theological Seminary, April 19, 1961 (Mimeographed copy taken from a taped recording)," Folder 14-4-K1, Duke McCall Papers.

88. "Address Given by Dr. Martin Luther King Jr."

89. "Address Given by Dr. Martin Luther King Jr."

90. Barnette, "The Southern Baptist Theological Seminary and the Civil Rights Movement: The Visit of Martin Luther King Jr.," 83–85.

91. McCall, *Duke McCall*, 224.

92. McCall, *Duke McCall*, 224.

Scripture against King and his tactics.[93] One organization, known as the Alabama Baptist Laymen, expressed particularly strong anti-King sentiments, equating the civil rights leader with liberalism and the National Council of Churches. The group wrote that "hundreds of congregations throughout the South do not care for Martin Luther Kingism or one worldism of the National Council of Churches who King says have promised their full support and financial resources backing him."[94] So strong was negative sentiment that the letters of complaint continued for three years.

Three months after King's visit, Southern's trustees issued two letters distancing the institution from King and his positions—one to concerned Southern Baptists and the other to seminary faculty members. In the letter to concerned Southern Baptists, Ernest L. Honts, chairman of the trustee executive committee, spoke of the seminary's "primary desire to place the advancement of the cause of Christ through our beloved denomination above any force which might attempt to divide us." He went on to express what sounded like an apology:

> Realizing that the Southern Baptist Theological Seminary is an agency of the Southern Baptist Convention and that it must serve the entire denomination in which varying opinions exist, the Executive Committee of the Board of Trustees, together with President Duke K. McCall, wishes to express regret for any offense caused by the recent visit of the Reverend Martin Luther King, Jr., to the campus of the Seminary.[95]

To the faculty, trustees issued an assurance that no one was in trouble, but cast doubt on the faculty's judgment in inviting King as a guest lecturer. The trustee executive committee wrote: "We would suggest that in the future before an invitation is issued to a person currently involved in a public controversy that such invitation be considered by the appropriate faculty committee with a committee from the Board of Trustees."[96]

One reason for the negative reaction was racism. At the same time, rank-and-file Southern Baptists perceived the seminary faculty and King

---

93. See Folders 14-4-K1, 14-4-K1b, Duke McCall Papers.

94. Telegram from Dean Fleming to Duke McCall, 15 May 1961, Folder 14-4-K1b, Duke McCall Papers.

95. "Copy (Letter to be sent to all persons who have written the Seminary protesting visit of Martin Luther King)," 27 July 1961, Folder 14-4-K1, Duke McCall Papers.

96. "Executive Committee Minutes," 27 July 1961, p. 8, Folder 14-4-K1, Duke McCall Papers.

to be out of step with orthodox, evangelical theology. Louisville's *Courier-Journal* reported that several seminary professors emerged from King's chapel sermon, which lacked a single scriptural reference, saying, "That was the gospel."[97] One of King's most prominent faculty supporters, Henlee Barnette, placed King in a category with famed liberal Walter Rauschenbusch as one of the three great prophets America had produced. The third such prophet, Barnette said, was Abraham Lincoln.[98] Barnette never shied away from announcing his theologically liberal views, calling the doctrine of biblical inerrancy "itself a heresy."[99] One week after King's visit to campus, the faculty, led by Barnette, adopted a resolution supporting McCall and the Guest Lecturer's Committee for inviting King to campus.[100] In addition to the faculty's self-identification with liberal views, *Redbook Magazine* published an article in its August 1961 issue suggesting Southern Seminary students questioned the doctrines of the virgin birth, creation as described in Genesis, a literal heaven, and a literal hell.[101] Though the *Redbook* article contained obvious methodological flaws, some Southern Baptists lumped it together with King's visit as evidence that the seminary had departed from conservative theology.[102] Ernest S. Waite, pastor of the First Baptist Church of Warrensburg, Missouri, wrote a letter in August 1961 warning McCall, "The lay people of this area are beginning to take note of all of this unfavorable publicity to Southern Seminary." The distress in Missouri apparently included both King and the *Redbook* article.[103] The First Baptist Church in Greenville, Mississippi, also pointed to both the *Redbook* article and the King visit as symptomatic of the same problem. Representatives of the church wrote a letter that prompted McCall to respond with a

97. Ora Spaid, "Dr. King Says 'Segregation Is Dead,'" *The Courier-Journal*, 20 April 1961, Folder 14-4-K1a, Duke McCall Papers.

98. Barnette, *A Pilgrimage of Faith*, 131–32.

99. Barnette, *A Pilgrimage of Faith*, 148.

100. "Resolution (Adopted by the Joint Faculty – April 27, 1961)," Folder 14-4-K1, Duke McCall Papers. Barnette, "The Southern Baptist Theological Seminary and the Civil Rights Movement: The Visit of Martin Luther King Jr.," 86.

101. Jhan Robbins and June Robbins, "The Surprising Beliefs of Our Future Ministers," *Redbook*, August 1961, 36–37, 107–10.

102. The *Redbook* article did not specifically survey the doctrinal beliefs of Southern Seminary students, but took a combined survey of students at several schools, including Southern, Yale Divinity School, New York's Union Theological Seminary, and Augsburg College Seminary.

103. Ernest S. Waite to Duke K. McCall, 29 August 1961, Folder 14-4-K1b, Duke McCall Papers.

defense of both Southern's theological orthodoxy and its invitation of King to lecture.[104] Though many of the critics of King's visit argued exclusively on racial grounds, the letters linking King and the *Redbook* article demonstrated that some Southern Baptists objected to perceived theological liberalism, not just racial progressivism. While faculty members may have felt King's theology was the gospel, many Southern Baptists failed to go along because they reached an opposite conclusion—Southern Seminary, along with Martin Luther King, challenged the gospel. Six churches in Alabama went so far as to withhold the share of their Cooperative Program gifts that would have supported Southern.[105]

No event from the 1960s or 1970s touched Southern Baptist sensitivities related to race as much as King's visit, but the seminary faculty continued to press for racial justice. Beginning in the mid-1960s, the seminary undertook a concerted effort to recruit black students. Southern hired retired military chaplain Col. Robert Herndon to work full-time recruiting black students. At a salary of $4,000 per year, Herndon travelled the country promoting Southern Seminary in particular and Southern Baptist seminaries in general.[106] The effort, which lasted two years, increased Southern's black student population "from about twelve or fifteen to twenty-five or thirty," according to McCall.[107] Southern could not increase its black student population more, McCall said, because northern seminaries and divinity schools such as Harvard, Yale, Princeton, and Columbia offered full scholarships for all eligible black students while Southern merely offered admission on the same basis as white students.[108] In addition to recruiting African-American students, some professors pushed to recruit black faculty in 1968. The push resulted in the dean of the School of Theology recommending a black scholar to the trustees for a faculty position. While the proposed scholar was not hired, the episode prompted McCall to declare that any person of any race should be added to the faculty if he was the most qualified candidate for the job.[109] Recruitment of African-American

104. Duke McCall to Mrs. B. E. Smith, 31 July 1961, Folder 14-4-K1b, Duke McCall Papers.

105. "Six Baptist Churches Withhold Seminary Funds," Folder 14-4-K1a, Duke McCall Papers.

106. McCall, *Duke McCall*, 264. Letters from McCall to various pastors and Baptist leaders, December 1966, Folder 13-5-N1, Duke McCall Papers.

107. McCall, *Duke McCall*, 264.

108. McCall, *Duke McCall*, 264.

109. Duke McCall, "Statement to Deans Council," 23 September 1968, Folder

faculty members was only one of many racial advances some on campus wanted. Barnette in 1968 listed nine goals "some of us here at Southern propose": (1) to integrate the faculty; (2) to integrate the administrative staff in positions above the menial level; (3) to integrate the board of trustees; (4) to train more black students for denominational positions, foreign missions, and service in white churches; (5) to provide scholarships for African Americans; (6) to develop inner-city ministry programs for students; (7) to develop an integrated community ministry; (8) to develop tutorial services at the seminary; and (9) to modify the curriculum to help students face problems challenging the church.[110] Also in 1968, Barnette delivered a chapel address eulogizing King after his assassination.[111]

In the 1970s administrators consciously attempted to diversify the campus. When the administration founded the Clarence Jordan Lectureship in 1970 in honor of the late advocate of interracial brotherhood, African-American clergyman Benjamin Mays was recommended to serve as a member of the steering committee.[112] A 1974 luncheon for black pastors brought Emmanuel McCall, Garland Offutt, W. H. Goatley, and several other African-American leaders to campus.[113] Despite the lack of success in black student recruitment efforts a decade earlier, Southern initiated another push for black student recruitment in 1975, visiting historically black college campuses and hosting conferences on the seminary campus in Louisville.[114] But perhaps the most important action related to race in the 1970s was the establishment of a black church studies program. Beginning in 1967, Emmanuel McCall delivered guest lectures in church history, missions, and ethics classes. By 1969 the administration began discussions with McCall about establishing courses dedicated to black church studies, and in 1970 McCall was named visiting professor of black church studies and assigned to teach a course each January. Three years later, McCall agreed to coordinate all black church studies classes and established a five-class rotation: the

---

02-6-N1, Duke McCall Papers.

110. Henlee Barnette, "Southern Seminary Report," in *Crisis Report*, 15 August 1968, Folder 03-2-H17, Duke McCall Papers.

111. Barnette, *A Pilgrimage of Faith*, 131–32.

112. Allen W. Graves to McCall, Dillard, and Hull, "Inter-Office Correspondence, The Southern Baptist Theological Seminary," 11 February 1970, Folder 14-2-J2, Duke McCall Papers.

113. List of attendees, Folder 13-8-L4, Duke McCall Papers.

114. See Folder 15-8-B2, Duke McCall Papers.

Black Church, Black Theology, Black Church History, Worship in the Black Church, and the Black Church and Social Justice.[115]

By the late 1970s and early 1980s, the black church studies program blossomed and word spread among African-American Baptists that Southern Seminary was the "largest black seminary in the country" because it had more black students than any of the historically black seminaries in America.[116] The reputation was incorrect, but Southern did have more than fifty black students during the 1980–81 academic year.[117] Along with the increase in African-American students, in 1986 Southern hired T. Vaughn Walker as its first black faculty member. The hiring also marked the first time any Southern Baptist seminary hired an African American to be a faculty member.[118] Black enrollment remained strong through 1995 but experienced some decrease in the early 1990s due to the cutting of a scholarship program for African-American seminarians by the Home Mission Board and perceptions in the African-American community that conservative seminary administrators might be racist.[119]

Although various cultural factors influenced the persistence of racial diversity at Southern, the most successful integration efforts were consistent with conservative theology. In fact, Walker remarked that before the campus transitioned to conservative control under the administration of R. Albert Mohler Jr., he perceived himself to be the most theologically conservative person on campus.[120]

115. Emmanuel L. McCall, "A Case for Black Studies," *Southern Baptist Educator*, May–June 1974, 14–15.

116. T. Vaughn Walker, interview by author, digital recording, Louisville, Kentucky, 17 April 2008.

117. *Thirtieth Annual Report to the Board of Trustees of the Southern Baptist Theological Seminary*, Student Statistical Report Fall 1971–Spring 1981, C-50, Archives, Southern Baptist Theological Seminary, Louisville, Kentucky. Two of the largest historical black seminaries in America, the Virginia Union University Divinity School and the Howard University Divinity School, both had more total students in 1980–81 than Southern Seminary had black students (Association of Theological Schools in the United States and Canada, *Fact Book on Theological Education 1980–1981*, 53, 56).

118. "Southern Seminary Names First Black Professor," *Ethnicity*, July/August 1986, 7.

119. Walker, interview by author, 17 April 2008. Emmanuel McCall, interview by author, digital recording, telephone conversation with McCall in Atlanta, Georgia, 24 April 2008. For additional discussion of African-American perceptions of Southern Baptist Convention seminaries, see chapter 5 below.

120. T. Vaughn Walker, interview by author, author's notes, Louisville, Kentucky, 17 April 2008.

Southern Baptist Seminaries and Colleges
Race at Other Southern Baptist Seminaries

Race relations at New Orleans, Southeastern, Golden Gate, and Midwestern Baptist Theological Seminaries followed similar patterns. Social pressures mounted over time, and the institutions looked to theology as a catalyst for racial progress. But when seminary faculties turned for inspiration to more liberal theology than was comfortable for rank-and-file Southern Baptists, constituents were less willing to follow the lead of their seminaries.

Official integration came during the 1940s and 1950s for all four of the convention's smaller seminaries. Golden Gate integrated in 1947, and was thus fully open to all races when it became a Southern Baptist Convention institution in 1950. New Orleans followed with official integration in 1954, and Southeastern and Midwestern both in 1958.[121] By 1963, the African American enrollment grew to eight at Southeastern, seven at Golden Gate, two at New Orleans, and one at Midwestern.[122] Along with their 1963 black student enrollment figures, each seminary offered a comment on the status of race relations on its campus. New Orleans and Midwestern both said they welcomed all students but did not make special efforts to recruit African Americans. Southeastern, while it had no plan for black student recruitment, hoped the Southern Baptist Advisory Council on Work with Negroes would "communicate to us any helpful ideas they may have about the recruitment or placement of Negro students."[123] Golden Gate was the only seminary to set as policy the intentional recruitment of African Americans:

> We do some things to promote the recruitment of Negro students. We keep pretty close contact with a number of the pastors in this area; we visit, of course, with them on various campuses in the South where they are students; occasionally, through summer mission work, we will touch some who come this way; and we have done some correspondence with students on Negro college campuses.[124]

---

121. List of year all Southern Baptist Convention seminaries and colleges integrated, Folder 1288, T. B. Maston Papers.

122. "Negroes in Southern Baptist Convention Seminaries, Spring 1963," Folder 1285, T. B. Maston Papers.

123. "Negroes in Southern Baptist Convention Seminaries, Spring 1963."

124. "Negroes in Southern Baptist Convention Seminaries, Spring 1963."

Five years later, Golden Gate, Southeastern, and Midwestern Seminaries reported additional progress when the Home Mission Board compiled reports on how each Southern Baptist agency was addressing the subject of race. Olin Binkley, Southeastern's president, reported that all seminary facilities and resources were open to all students. A faculty committee regularly issued suggestions as to ways the seminary could improve local race relations. In addition, black pastors were invited to speak on the campus and a course on the church and contemporary issues included a study of race relations.[125] Midwestern president Millard J. Berquist similarly reported African Americans speaking in chapel and other campus venues. Midwestern also sought to establish scholarships for African-American students and work more closely with black institutions in its area. Berquist bragged that Charles Briscoe, a black Midwestern graduate, "is right in the middle" of civil rights activities and "leading the Negro people."[126] Once again, Golden Gate issued a glowing report, boasting that the seminary had more black students than any other seminary on the west coast and more foreign students than all other west coast seminaries combined. An evening class organized by the Home Mission Board involved whites and blacks discussing race relations in an urban setting, and Urban Church Institutes for pastors dealt with race issues as well. President Harold K. Graves remarked, "We have always had many students of the various races involved in the seminary."[127]

According to Graves, Golden Gate's success on the race issue stemmed in part from the school's cultural setting and in part from the biblical convictions of its students and faculty. Before the seminary affiliated with the Southern Baptist Convention, the diversity of northern California was reflected in the student body. During its first semester as a convention agency, Golden Gate had 177 students from twenty-five states and four foreign countries.[128] By the 1956–1957 academic year, students established regular missionary work among Chinese and Italian people in the San Francisco Bay area, and the first graduation at the seminary's Strawberry Point campus in 1960 saw a black student receive the master

---

125. "Crisis Report," Southeastern Seminary report, Folder 03-2-H17, Duke McCall Papers.
   126. "Crisis Report."
   127. "Crisis Report."
   128. Graves, *Into the Wind*, 105.

of religious education degree.[129] When the civil rights movement took the national spotlight in 1965, Golden Gate students and faculty responded in overwhelming agreement. Teachers and students donated funds to help Louisiana student Anthony Vos attend the Selma March in Alabama. The student body also unanimously approved pro-civil rights telegrams to be sent to Martin Luther King Jr. and Alabama's governor, George Wallace.[130] In response to concerned Southern Baptists, Graves explained that theology and the social climate of California combined to produce the students' reaction. He wrote to a friend:

> Many Christians feel that the Scriptures have much to say concerning the worth of individual people in God's sight. In light of this truth, it is easy for people in this area to feel that a great host of people are being denied their rights and to want to speak out against it.

In the same letter he added that in the students' minds, speaking out in favor of civil rights was a matter of Christian witness:

> A witness to basic principles of rights to American citizens, as seen by people here, was called for as the students saw it. As a matter of fact, they felt their witness in an effective way to much of the California scene was at stake. It was in that regard, of course, a judgment of a situation that it has been impossible for them to explain or justify.[131]

A theologically informed social conscience likewise existed at Southeastern Seminary. Though the seminary was founded as a progressive institution and contended with liberalism among its faculty for the first forty years of its existence, many of Southeastern's racial advances drew from theology shared by most Southern Baptists.[132] Trustees voted in 1957 to admit qualified black students, and by 1959 professor Edward A. McDowell, formerly of Southern Seminary, reported that African Americans had enrolled in both the master of theology and bachelor of divinity programs.[133]

129. Graves, *Into the Wind*, 168, 209.
130. Graves, *Into the Wind*, 254–55.
131. Graves, *Into the Wind*, 256–57.
132. For information on Southeastern Seminary's progressive beginning and liberal faculty, see Bland, *Servant Songs*; Harper and McKinion, *Then and Now*.
133. Edward A. McDowell to Carlyle Marney, 19 September 1959, Box 32, Carlyle Marney Papers. On Southeastern trustees' vote to admit black students, see S. L. Morgan Sr., "Southeastern Seminary to Admit Negroes," *Biblical Recorder*, 3 August 1957, 14.

As at Southern, McDowell advanced race relations on campus with theological arguments starting in 1952, when he was hired to teach New Testament. Weatherspoon also brought his theology of race to Southeastern as a professor from 1959 until 1963.[134] A third example of a Southeastern professor applying theology to the race issue came in a pamphlet written by Stewart A. Newman entitled *The Christian's Obligation to All Races*. Newman, who came to the seminary from Southwestern in 1952, argued that the doctrines of human equality in Christ and the universal human need for the gospel should compel Southern Baptists to conduct themselves kindly toward people of other races. To claim the name of Christ created a moral mandate to solve the race problem, he said: "Christianity must furnish the spirit of good will which alleviates fear and which generates toleration and patience among members of the human race."[135] The era of Newman, McDowell, and Weatherspoon ushered in a steady stream of racial progress as Baptists bought into their arguments from Scripture.

An analogous situation unfolded at New Orleans Seminary as New Testament professor Frank Stagg called for increased racial justice based on the exegesis of Scripture. In the 1940s, professor J. W. Shepherd accompanied students on mission projects to teach Bible and theology to African-American ministers.[136] Then under the presidential administration of H. Leo Eddleman (1959–1970), the seminary welcomed black chapel speakers including Charles Boddie of the American Baptist Theological Seminary in Nashville and Joseph H. Jackson, president of the National Baptist Convention U.S.A., Inc.[137] During this period, Stagg pushed forward the advance with New Testament exegesis, arguing that the most sure way to defeat segregation was to take the Bible seriously. He said at a 1962 conference on race that arguing for segregation or discrimination from the Bible was a gross misuse of the scriptural text.[138] Stagg drew from Jesus, Acts, and the epistles to argue that segregation was diametrically opposed to the work of

---

134. Bland, *Servant Songs*, 10, 19.

135. Stewart A. Newman, *The Christian's Obligation to All Races* (Nashville: The Christian Life Commission of the Southern Baptist Convention, n. d.), "Race Relations" Folder, Baptist History File.

136. Howe, *Seventy-Five Years of Providence and Prayer*, 82–83.

137. Mueller, *The School of Providence and Prayer*, 132.

138. Frank Stagg, "The Bible and Race," in *Christianity and Race Relations: Messages from the Sixth Annual Christian Life Workshop*, Southwestern Baptist Theological Seminary, Fort Worth, Texas, March 12–13, 1962, 2, Christian Life Commission Resources Files.

Christ.[139] "Taken seriously," he said, "the Bible undercuts racial prejudice and discrimination. By biblical standards racial prejudice and discrimination are as evil as adultery or murder."[140]

Southern Baptist Colleges

Many differences existed between the situation at Southern Baptist seminaries and that at Southern Baptist colleges affiliated with Baptist state conventions. Yet integration at Baptist colleges occurred during the same period, and arguments from Baptists involved in the integration hinted that conservative theology played a role at colleges too.

Wayland Baptist College in Plainview, Texas, was among the first Southern Baptist colleges to integrate when it admitted its first African-American student in 1951. Integration occurred when a west Texas black school teacher asked whether she could attend Wayland to meet continuing education requirements for teacher certification. The teacher's reasoning was practical rather than theological. If Wayland, located thirty-five miles from her home, would not admit her, she would have been forced to travel to Waco for education approximately 350 miles away. Students, faculty, and trustees all approved of admitting blacks, so trustees made the action official in the spring of 1951. Soon Wayland became a hub for Nigerian students seeking to train for leadership in mission work. The college's president, James W. Marshall, a former personnel director at the Foreign Mission Board, welcomed the Nigerians because opportunities for training at other Southern Baptist colleges were closed. By 1957, Wayland graduated five Nigerian students and enrolled six to eight black students each semester in addition to the Nigerians. Black Colombian students likewise attended Wayland in the 1950s, and white and black students roomed together with only one complaint from a white parent between 1951 and 1957.[141] A student editorial from 1955 reported Christian convictions as a motive for integration at Wayland: "American democracy was at its best when faculty, students, and trustees voted to admit Negroes because 'it is the Christian thing to do.'"[142]

139. Stagg, "The Bible and Race," 6.
140. Stagg, "The Bible and Race," 1.
141. Handwritten notes dated 1957, Box 1, Folder 22, Race Relations Collection.
142. "Wayland Wins Freedoms Foundation Honor Medal," *Southern Baptist Educator*, April 1956, 9.

Several other Southern Baptist Colleges followed suit in the 1950s. Kentucky's Georgetown College and Missouri's Hannibal LaGrange College both integrated in 1955.[143] A 1957 report in the *Southern Baptist Educator*, a publication of the Southern Baptist Education Commission, reported that "approximately half a dozen of our colleges ... have opened their doors to Negro students." It added, however, that "most of our colleges are still caught in the struggle. Their ultimate course is yet to be determined."[144] Four years later, the list of Southern Baptist colleges to integrate had expanded, including Hardin-Simmons University, the University of Corpus Christi, Oklahoma Baptist University, William Jewell College, and Mars Hill College.[145]

Along with integration efforts, the 1950s saw racial tension on Baptist college campuses. One instance of racial tension occurred at Ouachita Baptist College in Arkadelphia, Arkansas. Because of the school desegregation crisis in Little Rock, public schools did not open in the fall of 1958. College president Ralph Phelps, a former doctoral student of T. B. Maston, led Ouachita to open a segregated private school to educate white children while the public schools remained closed. Though Phelps discussed a desegregated school with trustees, they did not think establishing an interracial school was wise. Phelps remarked, "I am convinced that if we tried to open an integrated school, the church in which we held classes would be bombed or attacked by mob."[146] The school opened with five hundred students enrolled, and Phelps insisted that no money from the Cooperative Program was used for the venture.[147] The president said the new school was "not an experiment in integration or segregation but is an adventure in education."[148] Phelps also argued that Ouachita was not free to desegregate any of its ventures until so instructed by Arkansas Baptists.[149] Maston and

143. Untitled document listing year various colleges and seminaries integrated, Folder 1288, T. B. Maston Papers.

144. G. Earl Guinn, "The Southern Baptist College in the Racial Struggle," *Southern Baptist Educator*, January 1957, 1.

145. "Hardin-Simmons University May Admit Negro Students," *Southern Baptist Educator*, December 1961, 6.

146. Ralph Phelps to T. B. Maston, 4 November 1958, Folder 905, T. B. Maston Papers.

147. "Statement Made by Dr. Ralph Phelps at Opening of Baptist High School at Little Rock, Arkansas, October 27, 1958," Folder 905, T. B. Maston Papers.

148. "Statement Made by Dr. Ralph Phelps at Opening of Baptist High School At Little Rock, Arkansas, October 27, 1958."

149. "Statement Made by Dr. Ralph Phelps at Opening of Baptist High School At

others who knew Phelps at Southwestern Seminary questioned whether their friend had abandoned both theological convictions and consistency when pressures increased.[150]

Integration and controversy continued in the 1960s. Wake Forest College removed all race barriers for undergraduate admission in 1962. The previous year it opened graduate schools, night school, and summer sessions to African Americans.[151] Baylor and Mercer Universities integrated in 1963 along with Howard Payne in 1964 and Mary Hardin-Baylor in 1965.[152] Furman enrolled its first black student in January 1965 after trustees announced in 1963 that they would consider all qualified applicants regardless of race and reaffirmed that policy in 1964.[153]

Baylor was a particularly noteworthy case of integration. President Abner McCall used politics, Christian theology, and social pressure to ease America's largest Southern Baptist university toward racial inclusiveness. Historian Vince Clark demonstrated that McCall "often told people that racism was not part of the true Christian philosophy and that all of society should have integrated long before the 1960s."[154] At the same time, McCall used a pragmatic leadership style that negotiated from the political center in disputes and said things to each party in the integration debate that the other side likely would have thought duplicitous.[155] On one side of the dispute, students and faculty wanted integration. Baylor students voted in 1954 and 1962 in support of integration, and the faculty did likewise in 1962.[156] Social pressures forced the debate forward in 1962 when Baylor's student newspaper, The Lariat, sent a reporter to the University

---

Little Rock, Arkansas, October 27, 1958."

150. T. B. Maston to Ralph Phelps, 22 October 1958, Folder 905, T. B. Maston Papers.

151. Baptist Press, "Wake Forest Drops Barriers," *Southern Baptist Educator*, May–June 1962, 2.

152. Baptist Press, "Mercer Accepts 3 Negro Students," *Southern Baptist Educator*, September–October 1963, 15; Baptist Press, "Baylor University Votes To Integrate," *Southern Baptist Educator*, December 1963, 11; "Howard Payne Admits All Races," *Southern Baptist Educator*, February 1964, 14; Baptist Press, "Mary Hardin-Baylor to Integrate," *Southern Baptist Educator*, January 1965, 9.

153. "Furman Enrolls First Negro Undergraduate," *Baptist Courier*, 11 February 1965, 18.

154. Clark, "Abner McCall and Civil Rights," 53.

155. Clark, "Abner McCall and Civil Rights," 54, 58.

156. Clark, "Abner McCall and Civil Rights," 54–55.

of Mississippi to cover that school's integration.¹⁵⁷ After a lengthy process of political maneuvering—including McCall's circulation of a letter from a Southern Baptist missionary in Nigeria claiming Baylor's failure to integrate hindered the spread of the gospel abroad—trustees voted November 1, 1963, by a sizeable margin to integrate.¹⁵⁸ The first black students enrolled in 1964, and McCall appealed to Christian theology in support of the action. In an address as president of the Baptist General Convention of Texas in 1964, McCall appealed to the social gospel as motivation for treating racial minorities with Christian love:

> Some of those to whom we now preach have heard our protestations that we worship and seek to do the will of a God of infinite love for all men regardless of race or color and that we strive to love all men as God does, but they have watched us carefully limit our religion in many instances to formal church activities and confine the application of our Christian principles to certain limited areas of life and to certain selected social problems. They often find that what we do thunders so loud that they cannot hear what we say.¹⁵⁹

The "social gospel," he continued, "calls for personal commitment, personal action, and personal sacrifice to help eliminate unnecessary . . . prejudice."¹⁶⁰ In a letter to a critic from the same time period, McCall cited the parable of the good Samaritan to argue that whites must take action to solve racial problems.¹⁶¹ At Baylor, appeal to theology played a role in racial integration.

Some Southern Baptists objected to integration of colleges during the 1960s. The general board of the South Carolina Baptist Convention asked Furman to defer action until a study could be made when the school's trustees voted to integrate.¹⁶² Subsequently at the 1964 state convention, South Carolina Baptists voted 908 to 575 to adopt a statement saying they did not want denominational colleges to admit black

---

157. Clark, "Abner McCall and Civil Rights," 54.

158. Clark, "Abner McCall and Civil Rights," 60–61.

159. Abner McCall, "President's Address to BGCT: Texas Baptists in 1964," *Baptist Standard*, 18 November 1964, 7.

160. McCall, "President's Address to BGCT," 7.

161. Clark, "Abner McCall and Civil Rights," 64.

162. "Carolina Board Asks Integration Delay," *Southern Baptist Educator*, November 1963, 13.

students.[163] In Mississippi, the 1966 meeting of the state convention rejected on a voice vote a resolution commending denominational colleges for admitting all qualified students regardless of race or national origin.[164] Three Mississippi Baptist Convention schools—Mississippi College, Blue Mountain College, and Clarke Memorial College—refused to sign "assurances of compliance" with the 1964 Civil Rights Act passed by Congress.[165] By 1969 all three schools admitted blacks.

In spite of the protests in some quarters, integration and other racial progress rolled on at Southern Baptist colleges through the 1960s, 1970s, and 1980s. Baylor hired its first full-time black professor in 1966. As of 1965, twenty-two senior colleges had integrated with eight additional colleges agreeing to integrate. Thirteen junior colleges affiliated with Southern Baptists either integrated or agreed to do so. Only seven senior colleges and six junior colleges had either made no decision or voted not to integrate as of 1965.[166] In the late 1960s, California Baptist College became the first Southern Baptist college to offer a course in black history.[167] By the 1980s, international students of all races were a common site on Baptist college campuses.[168] And whereas many Baptist colleges made intentional efforts to exclude black students two decades earlier, Wake Forest initiated a program in 1987 specifically to recruit black students. A faculty committee determined to strive for at least 10 percent black enrollment by 1992.[169] The university fell short of the goal, with 8 percent black undergraduate enrollment in the fall of 1992.[170]

Some of the factors at play in Southern Baptist seminaries also occurred in colleges on a smaller scale. Wayland and Baylor, for example, did not

---

163. "South Carolina Votes Against Integration," *Southern Baptist Educator*, December 1964, 5.

164. "Conventions Hold Important Sessions," *Baptist Courier*, 1 December 1966, 13–14.

165. "Colleges Differ on Compliance," *Southern Baptist Educator*, April 1965, 12.

166. Baptist Press, "Employs Negro Teacher," *Southern Baptist Educator*, July–August 1966, 12; McBeth, "A History of Southern Baptist Higher Education," 5-6.

167. Baptist Press, "Black History, Federal Aid Studies Set in California," *Southern Baptist Educator*, September–October 1969, 14.

168. Joyce A. DeRidder and Marion R. Webb, "The World Comes to the Baptist Campus," *Southern Baptist Educator*, May–June 1984, 3–5.

169. "Wake Forest University: Committed to Minority Enrollment," *Southern Baptist Educator*, December 1988, 3.

170. Office of Institutional Research, *Wake Forest University Fact Book 1992-93*, 20.

integrate apart from the force of theology. Baylor drew from social gospel theology to motivate its integration efforts. As with seminaries, racist Southern Baptists opposed integration in South Carolina and Mississippi.

Conclusion

Conservative theology alone did not lead to integration and racial progress in seminaries and colleges. But theology had something to do with it. Even when the leading advocates of racial progress were not conservative evangelicals in their overall theology, they drew from conservative theology to push forward their denomination and their institutions. The stories of Southwestern and Southern Seminaries, along with other Southern Baptist institutions of higher education show that appeals to theology advanced integration in the Southern Baptist Convention.

Chapter 5

African Americans and Southern Baptists

BETWEEN THE LATE 1950S and the early 1990s, there was no African American more involved in Southern Baptist life than Emmanuel McCall, the first black person brought on staff at any Southern Baptist agency. McCall worked at the Home Mission Board from 1968 until 1991 in the department charged with responding to racism, helping Southern Baptists relate cooperatively with National Baptists, and assisting Southern Baptist churches that wished to be inclusive in membership. McCall's impression of Southern Baptist progress between 1954 and 1995 illustrated the opinion of African-American Baptists in general. Though tension always existed between black and white Baptists, McCall said, black Baptists appreciated that the Southern Baptist Convention shifted to become gradually more affirming of African Americans.[1]

Black Baptists were ambivalent toward the Southern Baptist Convention. Some tension always existed between black Baptists and white Southern Baptists. Black Baptists thought the Southern Baptist Convention should have taken the Bible more seriously and in turn progressed more quickly. But black Baptists also depended on the financial help that they received from Southern Baptists and recognized the Southern Baptist Convention was changing gradually. The story of African Americans and Southern Baptists highlighted the Southern Baptist Convention's slowness to change and illustrated that black Baptists expected racial progress from those who claimed to believe the Bible.

---

1. Emmanuel McCall, telephone interview by author, digital recording, 24 April 2008.

African Americans and Missions

In mission work, blacks experienced tension with white Southern Baptists. African-American Baptists worked cooperatively with Southern Baptists on some fronts and at the same time expressed disappointment that Southern Baptists failed to advocate integration and social equality.

Southern Baptists considered relations between National Baptists and the Southern Baptist Convention to be a missions activity and assigned the work to a department within the Home Mission Board.[2] Originally known as the Department of Negro Work, that department changed its name to the Department of Work with National Baptists, then the Department of Cooperative Ministries with National Baptists, and finally the Black Church Relations Department.[3] This department saw relations between Southern Baptists and the three National Baptist conventions (the National Baptist Convention, U.S.A., Inc., the National Baptist Convention of America, and the Progressive National Baptist Convention) go through several stages.

Between the mid-1950s and the mid-1960s, National Baptists received Southern Baptist help with ministry endeavors and made positive public statements about the Southern Baptist Convention. Perhaps the most important Southern Baptist ministry endeavor with blacks during this period was the founding of Baptist Centers in urban areas. These centers were funded jointly by Southern and National Baptists but received the bulk of their operating budgets from the Southern Baptist Convention.[4] Approximately thirty centers across the nation offered black Baptists educational opportunities and a host of other services designed to aid black religious advancement. In 1954 the Home Mission Board reported that directors of centers and Southern Baptist "Teacher-Missionaries" enrolled 38,723 students in their classes at the centers and conducted 734 extension classes in black areas away from the centers.[5] The more successful centers, such as those in Louisville, Nashville, and Oklahoma City, helped local

---

2. Victor Glass, "Working With National Baptists," Box 15, Folder 50, W. C. Fields Papers.

3. "Filmstrip Script: Black Church Relations Department," "Emmanuel McCall, Black Baptists" Box, Unprocessed Home Mission Board Records.

4. McCall, interview by author, 24 April 2008.

5. "Home Mission Board, Southern Baptist Convention, Department of Work with Negroes, Guy Bellamy, Secretary," "Bellamy, Black Church Extension Department" Box, "Reports, Surveys, Black Church Relations Dept., Missions Ministries div." Folder, Unprocessed Home Mission Board Records.

African Americans adopt favorable attitudes toward Southern Baptists, according to McCall. He classified the centers as places "where Southern Baptists and black people had a great relationship developing" and said they catalyzed "positive feelings even though there was the anger related to what the social climate was."[6]

Meetings involving Southern and National Baptist leaders provided another forum for the development of relationships between the two groups. In a 1960 conference, for example, National Baptist leader Milton K. Curry said he was "impressed with the great amount of work being done for the Negro."[7] The *National Baptist Voice*, the official news organ of the National Baptist Convention, U.S.A., Inc., reported in dozens of articles between 1960 and 1965 on the activities of Southern Baptists, including the convention's public policy, missions, and administrative dealings.[8]

National Baptist impressions of Southern Baptists during this period were not all positive, though. During the previously mentioned 1960 conference, several black participants expressed frustration at the manner in which Southern Baptists carried out their mission work among African Americans. R. W. Puryear complained that Southern Baptists claimed to cooperate with National Baptists yet hardly ever consulted with National Baptist Convention leadership. National Baptist Convention, U.S.A., Inc., President Joseph H. Jackson said Southern Baptists would be more helpful if they stopped focusing their work on underprivileged black people and poured more money into providing college education for black Baptist leaders.[9] Black frustrations stemmed at least in part from notable failures of Southern Baptists to stand up for African-American rights during the civil rights movement. McCall recalled one episode in which the pastor of a county-seat First Baptist Church allegedly led an angry mob to disrupt a rally to integrate the public schools. The incident ended with a drunk in the mob relieving himself on civil rights leader Stokley Carmichael with the blessing of the local Southern Baptist pastor, McCall said. Such episodes had

---

6. McCall, interview by author, 24 April 2008.

7. "Memorandum – Joint Conference on Relations of Southern and National Baptists, Chicago, Illinois, December 28, 1960," Box 24, Folder 35, Executive Committee Administrative Records.

8. See the *National Baptist Voice*, Southern Baptist Historical Library and Archives, Nashville, Tennessee.

9. "Memorandum – Joint Conference on Relations of Southern and National Baptists, Chicago, Illinois, December 28, 1960," Box 24, Folder 35, Executive Committee Administrative Records.

a dramatic impact. McCall noted the contradiction: "Black Baptists could see whites who were doing the positive things," he said, "but the negative things kept looming so much larger than the positive things."[10]

Between the mid-1960s and the early 1980s, Southern Baptists continued to launch efforts to relate to National Baptists, but the relationship between the two groups grew increasingly strained. During this period the *National Baptist Voice* reduced its coverage of the Southern Baptist Convention dramatically, so that by 1985 there was hardly any notice of Southern Baptist activity at all. Southern Baptist W. R. Grigg reported that "National Baptists suspect that Southern Baptists are not really Christians at all, but racists hiding behind the church."[11] At a 1982 conference involving National and Southern Baptists, African-American leader J. Deotis Roberts warned Southern Baptists that "it's wrong to preach inerrancy and simultaneously approve of evil cultural structures." He also chided that "whites often find it difficult to repent because they do not understand fully the awesomeness of racism as a collective evil, or realize what it has done to its victims."[12] One Southern Baptist publication observed in 1984 that even though black churches and individuals joined the Southern Baptist Convention between 1960 and the 1980s, National Baptists and Southern Baptists "remained estranged" on the national level "despite overtures by the [Home Mission Board] Department of Black Church Relations."[13]

One likely cause of the increased tension between National and Southern Baptists was a personal conflict involving Joseph H. Jackson and the Southern Baptist Convention. At the 1965 meeting of the Baptist World Alliance, Jackson hoped to be elected the organization's president. Southern Baptists, however, largely threw their weight behind Liberian candidate William Tolbert, and Tolbert was elected. McCall said that after the election, Jackson "took a defensive attitude and began saying that everything Southern Baptists had done was intended to slam black Baptists in America." From that point on, Jackson "did everything that he could to generate that negative response against Southern Baptists."[14] The tension remained three years later

10. McCall, interview by author, 24 April 2008.

11. W. R. Grigg, "Keeping on the Road toward Freedom," "Emmanuel McCall, Black Baptists" Box, Unprocessed Home Mission Board Records.

12. J. Deotis Roberts, "A Theology of Reconciliation," in *Partners in Ministry*, "Emmanuel McCall, Black Baptists" Box, Unprocessed Home Mission Board Records.

13. Everett Hullum, "On a Path toward Reconciliation: National and Southern Baptists Begin Moves to Increase Cooperative Endeavors," *Ethnicity*, Spring 1984, 2–3.

14. McCall, interview by author, 24 April 2008.

when McCall was hired at the Home Mission Board as associate secretary of the Department of Work with National Baptists. At McCall's first meeting with Jackson, Jackson objected strongly both to McCall being hired by Southern Baptists and to Jackson not being consulted before the hire.[15] During the National Baptist Convention, U.S.A., Inc., annual meeting that year, Jackson publicly blasted McCall and called him Southern Baptists' "pawn boy."[16] Jackson persisted in his criticism of Southern Baptists throughout his tenure as convention president, which lasted until 1982. Other National Baptists followed Jackson's example and adopted an antagonistic posture toward Southern Baptists, McCall said.[17]

Tensions began to cool with the election of T. J. Jemison as president of the National Baptist Convention, U.S.A., Inc.[18] In 1984, Jemison gave an interview to the Southern Baptist publication *Ethnicity*, in which he expressed his willingness to work with Southern Baptists and his optimism regarding future cooperation between National Baptists and Southern Baptists:

> At first I thought, Southern Baptists have money and they've used it to pull some Blacks in. But they were not always sincere with their systems. Yet, as my contact with the SBC increases, I've found my earlier point of view was not correct. I can see a greater tie that binds the two conventions. I think our leadership should be dedicated enough to work together for the welfare of all peoples, White or Black or whatever race.[19]

During Jemison's tenure as president, Southern Baptists began to invite National Baptists to speak at Southern Baptist conferences and events. S. M. Lockeridge, E. V. Hill, Thomas Kilgore, J. Alfred Smith, Henry Mitchell, and Manuel Scott were among the National Baptists most often invited to preach.[20] According to T. Vaughn Walker, late professor of black church studies at the Southern Baptist Theological Seminary, Scott

---

15. McCall, interview by author, 24 April 2008.
16. McCall, interview by author, 24 April 2008.
17. McCall, interview by author, 24 April 2008.
18. "Black Baptists Elect Leader," *Nashville Tennessean*, 10 September 1982, Box 17, Folder 24, W. C. Fields Papers.
19. Hullum, "On a Path toward Reconciliation," 4.
20. See McCall, *When All God's Children Get Together*, 107; Sid Smith, telephone interview by author, digital recording, 24 April 2008.

preached at the denomination's annual meetings more than any other black person in history.[21]

Even during this period of decreased tension, however, strain between National and Southern Baptists was not altogether absent. During the same interview in which he praised Southern Baptists, Jemison also chided Southern Baptists for attempting to steal choice young leaders from his denomination and bring them to the Southern Baptist Convention.[22] Sid Smith, who worked in the 1980s as a consultant in the Ethnic Liaison Unit of the Southern Baptist Sunday School Board and beginning in 1988 as director of the Board's Black Church Development Section, said National Baptists particularly resented McCall's work at the Home Mission Board:

> They viewed him as an attempt of Southern Baptists to steal African-American leadership, especially trained leadership, so that we could get their churches away from them, which created a threat in their minds. And they did not understand the Southern Baptist position of not proselytizing churches. So they were skeptical.[23]

The use of National Baptist speakers by Southern Baptists also produced negative feelings on both sides. National Baptists feared that the Southern Baptist Convention invited the speakers in order to lure them into the denomination, and black Southern Baptists felt betrayed that their denomination would invite National Baptists over its own African-American members.[24]

In addition to cooperative missions endeavors with National Baptists, black Southern Baptists participated in home missions through their own denomination. As early as 1954, the Home Mission Board reported that Southern Baptists conducted home missions among African Americans in every state where there was a state convention affiliated with the Southern Baptist Convention.[25] Black churches had left the Southern Baptist Convention entirely, with the last black church exiting by the

21. T. Vaughn Walker, interview by author, digital recording, Louisville, Kentucky, 17 April 2008.

22. Hullum, "On a Path toward Reconcilation," 4.

23. Smith, interview by author, 24 April 2008.

24. Smith, interview by author, 24 April 2008; McCall, interview by author, 24 April 2008; Walker, interview by author, 17 April 2008.

25. "Home Mission Board, Southern Baptist Convention, Department of Work with Negroes, Guy Bellamy, Secretary," "Bellamy, Black Church Extension Division" Box, "Reports, Surveys, Black Church Relations Dept., Missions Ministries div." Folder, Unprocessed Home Mission Board Records.

early twentieth century, but they reappeared slowly beginning in 1951. Between 1960 and the early 1980s black Southern Baptist churches increased dramatically.[26] Black Southern Baptist churches participated in their own home mission endeavors with the result that some of those congregations grew to megachurch proportions. Houston's Brentwood Baptist Church, for example, grew to 4,200 members by 1985 on a steady diet of social action preaching by Pastor Joe Ratliff and ministries designed to liberate African Americans from problems they faced in everyday life.[27] Black Southern Baptist churches, Smith wrote, saw Scripture's missions mandate as including a call to fight racism and oppression in their communities, and they embraced that task with vigor.[28] T. Vaughn Walker, who had decades of experience as a black Southern Baptist pastor, said black Southern Baptists most often embraced home missions as opportunities for "meeting needs, sharing Christ." The great emphasis on home missions was due largely to the abundance of needs in the neighborhoods surrounding black Southern Baptist churches, he said.[29]

Foreign missions revealed a distinction between African-American Baptists and their white Southern Baptist counterparts. African Americans participated in Southern Baptist foreign missions to a small extent. In 1981, the Foreign Mission Board began a push to involve African Americans in world missions. Then in 1983, the board hired Willie Simmons as manager of the Black Church Relations Department with the assignment of increasing awareness of world missions among the seven hundred black Southern Baptist churches.[30] Still, by 1995, only five African Americans were serving as Southern Baptist foreign missionaries.[31] For blacks, home missions often came at the expense of foreign missions, both because of black Baptists' limited resources and the abundance of needs at home. Walker explained:

26. Sid Smith, "Black Church Growth as Denominational Alignment," *Ethnicity*, January/February 1985, 1; Hullum, "On a Path toward Reconciliation," 2; Emmanuel McCall, "From 1350 Spring St.," *Ethnicity*, March/April 1985, 2.

27. Steve Maynard, "Boom at Brentwood: Black SBC Congregation Thrives," *Ethnicity*, September/October 1985, 8–10.

28. Sid Smith, "Understanding the Black Southern Baptist Distinctives," *Ethnicity*, September/October 1985, 1–2.

29. Walker, interview by author, 17 April 2008.

30. "Foreign Mission Board Names Manager of Black Church Relations," *Ethnicity*, Winter 1984, 2.

31. Information from David Cornelius, former ethnic mobilization consultant, International Mission Board of the Southern Baptist Convention.

> African American Christians saw so many needs in their own neighborhood.... They did not come from a position that [said], "We don't care about helping others in other places." But with the limited resources that were available to the community, there was a greater emphasis on addressing Samaria [and] Jerusalem before you go to the uttermost parts of the world.... When you compare [African-American foreign missions] to international missions among Southern Baptists, it's miniscule.[32]

Another concern that limited black Baptist support of Southern Baptist Convention foreign missions was the apparent contradiction between Southern Baptists' concern with the blacks in Africa and their lack of concern for blacks in the United States. During the civil rights era, African Americans "could not understand Southern Baptists rushing to Africa . . . to help the Africans and yet objecting, as they did, to black freedom and concerns here in the states."[33] To make matters worse, white Southern Baptists at times granted Africans privileges they denied to American blacks. For example, Crescent Hill Baptist Church in Louisville received Nigerian Samuel T. O. Akande into its membership in the early 1960s before it received any African Americans. When Akande's wife needed hospital care, the Baptist hospital in Louisville received her even though it would not receive African Americans.[34] African Americans felt such hurt regarding Southern Baptist acceptance of Africans that African-American Baptist churches at times shunned or excluded Africans. For example, McCall once came into contact with an African church in Knoxville, Tennessee, started by a retired Southern Baptist missionary. When McCall urged the African church to develop a relationship with an African-American church nearby, the Mount Olive Baptist Church, he met with resistance. Mount Olive "wouldn't even talk to" the missionary, McCall said. "So we began probing as to what was behind the attitude. And they never would come right out and say they just did not like Africans. But that would give you an idea of how some contemporary African Americans think about Africans."[35]

32. Walker, interview by author, 17 April 2008.

33. McCall, interview by author, 24 April 2008.

34. McCall, interview by author, 24 April 2008; Andrew Rawls, telephone interview by author, 8 May 2008. Rawls, who serves as historian for Crescent Hill Baptist Church, confirmed that Akande was the first black member received at Crescent Hill.

35. McCall, interview by author, 24 April 2008. African Baptists appear, likewise, to have taken little interest in the civil rights concerns of African-American Baptists. Surveying *The Nigerian Baptist*, the newspaper of the Nigerian Baptist Convention, reveals

African Americans and Southern Baptists

In the area of missions, between 1954 and 1995, African Americans benefitted from some Southern Baptist efforts—yet never without feeling a degree of tension regarding Southern Baptists' social and racial positions. Constructive relationships between blacks and Southern Baptists increased, but Southern Baptists' racism prevented black Baptists from ever overcoming their reservations regarding the Southern Baptist Convention.

African Americans and the Seminaries

The relationship between black Baptists and the Southern Baptist Convention's six seminaries was another area in which blacks were ambivalent.[36] Beginning in 1947, the Inter-Convention Committee on Negro Ministerial Education worked to improve the general education level of black clergy—although within the segregated educational system of the day.[37] The first African American to attend a Southern Baptist seminary was Garland Offutt, who came to Southern Seminary in 1942. Though Kentucky's Day Law prevented him from legally attending classes with white students, Offutt earned two degrees from Southern by studying in professors' offices and listening in on lectures from a chair placed in the hall outside classrooms. In 1950, Southern admitted a group of black students, and racial restrictions were lifted from that time forward.[38] The other seminaries likewise opened their doors to African Americans students during the same era, and the opportunity for black Christians to study at Southern Baptist seminaries has been open ever since.

During the first decade of integrated education at Southern Baptist seminaries, African Americans voiced a number of positive reactions. McCall, who attended Southern Seminary between 1959 and 1963,

---

hardly any mention of civil rights causes in America between 1954 and 1995. Occasionally, the paper mentioned Africans attending Southern Baptist seminaries or colleges, but significant race-relations milestones hardly ever received notice by Nigerian Baptists. Southern Baptists approval of the Supreme Court's decision to desegregate public schools, for example, received no mention apart from one article about college students endorsing the decision (see Baptist Press, "Baptist Students Voice Approval of Court Ruling," *The Nigerian Baptist*, September 1954, 3).

36. See chapter 4.

37. "Report of Committee on Negro Ministerial Education," Box 74, "Negro Ministerial Education-1947–1950" Folder, Executive Committee Records.

38. Barnette, "The Southern Baptist Theological Seminary and the Civil Rights Movement: From 1859–1952," 537–41.

noted, "I don't recall ever hearing of a faculty member who exhibited an unchristian attitude toward race or who defended the status quo."[39] Marvin Griffin, the first black graduate of Southwestern Baptist Theological Seminary in 1955, recalled that the professors "were warm, particularly Dr. [T. B.] Maston and Dr. [J. M.] Price. They were concerned and helpful. I didn't have any incident where any student did anything to me. Nothing happened."[40] National Baptists endorsed the Southern Baptist seminaries. In the 1960s, the *National Baptist Voice* carried articles by Southern Baptist seminary professors, including a series on race by Southeastern Baptist Theological Seminary's Edward A. McDowell in 1968.[41] The main tensions during this period involved National Baptists, who, like J. H. Jackson, worried that the Southern Baptist Convention focused too little on college and seminary education and wasted valuable resources by ministering to the black underprivileged.[42]

Between 1970 and 1990 African Americans increased their enthusiasm for the seminaries. Working with McCall, the Woman's Missionary Union, an auxiliary of the Southern Baptist Convention, began in 1967 to fund seminary scholarships for National Baptist students as part of the Annie Armstrong Easter Offering emphasis.[43] In addition to the funds available at the national level for black students, state conventions began during the same era to provide scholarships of their own to African-American students.[44] The result of these scholarships was that, by the late 1970s, black enrollment at Southern Baptist seminaries increased. Black Baptists called Southern Seminary the "largest black seminary in the country," with an African-American enrollment exceeding that at most of America's

---

39. McCall, *When All God's Children Get Together*, 12.

40. Scott A. Collins, "Griffin Breaks Racial Barrier as Southwestern's First Black Graduate," *Black Church Development*, April–June 1991, 3–4.

41. See, for example, Edward A. McDowell, "The Historical Background of Race Prejudice," *National Baptist Voice*, May 1968, 2; Edward A. McDowell, "The Psychology of Race Prejudice," *National Baptist Voice*, May 1968, 2; Edward A. McDowell, "The Race Problem and the Gospel," *National Baptist Voice*, May 1968, 8. Two of the above articles appeared again in the June 1968 issue of the *National Baptist Voice*.

42. "Memorandum – Joint Conference on Relations of Southern and National Baptists, Chicago, Illinois, December 28, 1960," Box 24, Folder 35, Executive Committee Administrative Records.

43. McCall, *When All God's Children Get Together*, 119.

44. McCall, interview by author, 24 April 2008.

historically black seminaries.[45] In 1986, Southern Seminary hired Walker as the first full-time African-American Southern Baptist seminary professor.[46] Golden Gate Baptist Theological Seminary followed suit the following year by hiring African American Leroy Gainey to a full-time teaching position in Christian education.[47] The seminaries recruited black students. From the early 1980s through the early 1990s, the Sunday School Board's publication geared toward black audiences enthusiastically touted Southern Baptist seminaries, telling prospective black students that the schools understood how to contextualize orthodox Christian theology for the black community. Walker wrote in 1990 that Southern Baptist seminaries trained black ministers to preach "a message of deliverance through Jesus Christ of the whole person—not just simply one's soul."[48]

When the Southern Baptist Convention's conservative resurgence began to affect the seminaries in the late 1980s and early 1990s, some tension arose between African Americans and the white seminary leadership. The tensions included a theological component, but the main part of the tension was economic and political. Walker recounted that when he was a student at Southern Seminary in the mid-1980s, "there were a couple hundred or more African-American master's-level students on this campus." In 2008, however, "just visually, walking around, I can tell you that we have had a tremendous decrease in the number of African Americans." As for the cause of the decrease, Walker said, "I don't believe that's theological totally."[49] He attributed the decrease to several factors. First, when R. Albert Mohler Jr. took over as president at Southern Seminary in 1993, African Americans assumed that this new type of conservative would be "anti-black advancement."[50] Black Baptists were very much in favor of what the new conservatives believed about the Bible's inerrancy and had become "a little nervous" about the liberal theological leanings of moderate administrators and professors under the previous administration. However, they believed the conservatives were inappropriately tied to the Republican Party politically and adopted "a strong focus on personal sin but almost a lack

---

45. Walker, interview by author, 17 April 2008.

46. "Southern Seminary Names First Black Professor," *Ethnicity*, July/August 1986, 7.

47. Walker, interview by author, 17 April 2008.

48. T. Vaughn Walker, "Relevant Christian Ministry for the 21st Century," *Black Church Development*, November/December 1990, 3–4.

49. Walker, interview by author, 17 April 2008.

50. Walker, interview by author, 17 April 2008.

of acknowledgment of corporate sin [and] institutional sin."[51] The second reason for the decrease was economic, according to Walker. In 1995, the Southern Baptist Convention began to give seminary tuition breaks only to Southern Baptist students. Previously all Baptist students received reduced tuition rates.[52] Though the change was aimed at churches that supported the Cooperative Baptist Fellowship instead of the Southern Baptist Convention's Cooperative Program, it had the unintended effect of increasing costs for African-American students of other denominations and driving them away.[53] Also in the 1980s and 1990s, several new seminaries came into existence, both moderate and conservative. These schools also played a part in the decrease of black students at Southern Baptist seminaries by drawing away some of the already limited African-American pool of potential students.[54] The only directly theological cause of the decrease, according to Walker, was the conservatives' belief that women should not serve as pastors in local churches. Black women, both Baptist and non-Baptist, sought training at Southern under moderate administrations because they felt accepted and affirmed, Walker said. But as Southern Seminary shifted theologically, that perception changed:

> A lot of black women assumed this will not be a friendly place to come, although we kept preaching and speaking and saying, "All programs are open to all students." Now, over time, we've dropped women out of the school of theology as professors. We don't let women take preaching classes. And all of those things signal, then, less women coming.[55]

51. Walker, interview by author, 17 April 2008.

52. The Southern Baptist Theological Seminary, *For Such a Time as This: 1995–1996 Catalog*, 33.

53. Walker, interview by author, 17 April 2008.

54. Walker, interview by author, 17 April 2008.

55. Walker, interview by author, 17 April 2008. Walker was incorrect to claim that women could not take preaching classes under Mohler's administration. They had the option to substitute other courses for preaching courses but could take preaching if they chose. Black Southern Baptists often affirmed ordaining women to the pastorate. Feature articles in *Ethnicity* reported, for example, that Houston's Brentwood Baptist Church, one of the largest black Southern Baptist churches in the mid-1980s, had an ordained female minister (Steve Maynard, "Boom at Brentwood: Black SBC Congregation Thrives," *Ethnicity*, September/October 1985, 8–10). Willie Gaines, the first African American elected president of the California Southern Baptist Convention, said in *Ethnicity* that he supported women in ministry and had a female education minister that he would ordain if the church wished to do so. The publication reported, "Concerning the issue of women leaders in churches, Gaines said he believes it is a local church issue, probably more an

McCall agreed that the decrease was largely economic but thought it had more to do with a shift at the Home Mission Board than with any shift at the seminaries themselves. In the early 1990s, the board shifted its emphasis away from social ministries and increasingly toward church planting, McCall said. As part of the new emphasis, seminary scholarships for black students were cut. "When they cut out the scholarship," McCall said, "then the black students who would have gone to Southern or to an SBC seminary because the scholarship was available... didn't have the money. They began to decline."[56]

Despite the decline in numbers of black students, Southern Baptist seminaries continued to draw some African-American ministers throughout the conservative resurgence. Many black Baptists agreed with many of the theological stands Southern Baptists took and aligned themselves with the denomination's theological schools. Though the issue of women in ministry played a role in the tension that developed in the early 1990s, it was not the sole aspect of the tension. As with missions, tensions between African Americans and the Southern Baptist Convention centered on economic and social issues more than theological differences.

African Americans and the Conservative Resurgence

The reaction of African Americans to the Southern Baptist Convention's rightward theological shift varied. Those aligned solely with National Baptists reacted largely with indifference while African-American Southern Baptists tended to view the conflict as an exclusively white battle. In both cases, reaction to the resurgence revealed that black Baptists felt leery of supporting the Southern Baptist Convention.

Outside the Southern Baptist Convention, African Americans showed very little interest in the theological shift afoot in the denomination. The *National Baptist Voice* largely ignored the existence of the Southern Baptist Convention during the years of the resurgence, and increasingly so as time progressed. National Baptists without SBC ties, never "paid much attention to" the resurgence, McCall said. "It did not affect them, and there was no meaningful relationship going on. So it was

---

Anglo church issue than in Black churches. There have always been women leaders in the Black church, he added" (Herb Hollinger, "Gaines Says His Election California 'New Day,' *Ethnicity*, September/October 1985, 11–12).

56. McCall, interview by author, 24 April 2008.

not something I remember hearing black Baptists outside of the SBC talking about."[57] Walker, who was actively involved in National Baptist circles for the entire period between 1979 and 1995, likewise classified African Americans outside the Southern Baptist Convention as "ignorers" when it came to the conservative resurgence.[58]

Yet the ignoring did not reflect a theological aversion to the new Southern Baptist leadership. During the early years of the resurgence, National Baptists like Scott, Lockeridge, and Hill continued to receive invitations to speak at Southern Baptist events.[59] In fact, conservatives so admired Hill that one conservative leader planned to have Billy Graham nominate Hill for one of the convention's vice presidential slots in 1981. The plan fell through only when the conservative leader learned at the last minute that Hill was not a Southern Baptist.[60] Smith believed the Hill episode was illustrative of how popular a National Baptist could become among conservative Southern Baptists. "That's how influential Ed Hill was," Smith said. "I believe that he could have been the first African-American president of the Southern Baptist Convention."[61]

Within the Southern Baptist Convention, Houston pastor Joe Ratliff typified stance of African Americans when he said the conservative resurgence was "a white boys' fight, not ours."[62] Smith called the resurgence a "non-black issue" and compared African Americans' stance on the conservative-moderate fight to the attitude of the one black slave present at the battle of the Alamo. When given an opportunity to leave before the fighting heated up, the slave left, saying the battle was not his fight. The resurgence, Smith said, "was not the big issue for the African Americans though. Rather than being pro or against, they just said, 'You guys fight.'"[63]

---

57. McCall, interview by author, 24 April 2008.

58. Walker, interview by author, 17 April 2008.

59. Smith, interview by author, 24 April 2008. See also McCall, interview by author, 24 April 2008.

60. Smith, interview by author, 24 April 2008. Smith declined to provide the name of the leader who sought to nominate Hill because the leader was still alive at the time of the interview.

61. Smith, interview by author, 24 April 2008.

62. McCall, interview by author, 24 April 2008.

63. Smith, interview by author, 24 April 2008. Smith also cited the example of the lone black present at the Alamo in an interview cited by Barry Hankins in *Uneasy in Babylon*. See *Oral Memoirs of Sidney Smith Jr.*, interviewed by Barry Hankins, 13 June 2000, Religion and Culture Project, Baylor University Institute for Oral History, 2003, 4.

Walker agreed that black Southern Baptists were largely mere observers of the resurgence, but his perspective differed somewhat from that of Ratliff and Smith. As a seminary professor hired under the moderate leadership, Walker felt some nervousness regarding the security of his job as conservatives came to power.[64] McCall was perhaps the lone exception to the rule of black non-involvement in the conflict. Both in his role at the Home Mission Board and his duties as president of the Southern Seminary national alumni association, he grew disenchanted with the conservative leadership and left the Southern Baptist Convention. Yet, McCall admitted that his case was exceptional among African-American Southern Baptists.[65] Few others withdrew. Overall, black reaction within the convention involved observation rather than participation.

But black Southern Baptists did not refrain from participating in the controversy because they objected to the conservative theology of the white resurgence leadership. Most African American Southern Baptists, including McCall, classified themselves as theologically conservative.[66] Walker said, "The African-American Baptist is pretty much a conservative Baptist," while Smith classified black Southern Baptists as "more conservative" than moderate during the period of the resurgence.[67] As the resurgence gained momentum, Smith wrote in *Ethnicity* that black pastors were leading their churches to join the Southern Baptist Convention at least in part because of the convention's "sound doctrine."[68] Also under the leadership of conservatives, African Americans won election to convention offices at both the national and state-convention levels in record numbers. Gary Frost, Fred Luter, and E. W. McCall were all elected Southern Baptist Convention vice presidents, while more than twenty African Americans were elected state convention presidents in the final two decades of the twentieth century.[69] Both the increased involvement of African Americans in the denomination and the self-identification of black Baptists as conservative showed that any divide between the white participants in the resurgence and black Southern Baptists

---

64. Walker, interview by author, 17 April 2008.

65. McCall, interview by author, 24 April 2008. See also, McCall, *When All God's Children Get Together*, 139.

66. McCall, interview by author, 24 April 2008.

67. Walker, interview by author, 17 April 2008. Smith, interview by author, 24 April 2008.

68. Sid Smith, "Black Southern Baptist Church Growth as Denominational Alignment," *Ethnicity*, January/February 1985, 1.

69. Smith, interview by author, 24 April 2008.

was not primarily a matter of black objections to conservative theology. African Americans fit in so well among the conservatives that conservative churches during the resurgence era often had better records of integration than their moderate counterparts, according to Smith.[70]

Theology, however, did play some role in the division between black and white Southern Baptists. African Americans were willing to tolerate theological diversity to a greater extent than whites. Black Southern Baptists did not relate to the concerns of white conservative resurgence leaders partially because of the black concept of a free and open pulpit. The free pulpit referred to the reality that African-American preachers often had greater liberty than their white counterparts to espouse ideas with which the congregation disagreed. Walker explained:

> It's almost unheard of in an African-American church that a pastor would preach a sermon and the deacons call him in on Sunday night and fire him. To say that is almost ludicrous because what more likely would happen is the deacons would be sat down than the pastor. Now, the congregation might throw him out if he does something immoral, you know, something like that. But to preach something? As long as he could base it on Scripture—even misinterpretation of Scripture—the church is probably going to say, "I don't see it that way, but he has the right to preach it."[71]

Smith also acknowledged the reality of the free pulpit in an article from the late 1980s. "The Black pulpit is a brave pulpit," he wrote. "The preacher is free to preach whatever he feels God lays on his heart. He is not intimidated by the pew."[72] African-American preacher Otis Moss Jr. likewise described the black pulpit as "dynamic and free" as compared with the white pulpit, which was "circumscribed."[73] This heritage of a free pulpit allowed black Southern Baptists to embrace theologically moderate seminary professors and denominational employees more readily than did white conservatives. When white conservatives sought to clamp down on unscriptural preaching within the convention, black conservatives stood by, unable to understand why they should restrict the preaching of others. For example, though Walker regarded himself as the most theologically conservative professor on Southern Seminary's campus during the early days of the

---

70. Smith, interview by author, 24 April 2008.

71. Walker, interview by author, 17 April 2008.

72. Sid Smith, "Black Contributions to the Southern Baptist Convention," *Ethnicity*, July/August 1988, 3.

73. Otis Moss Jr., "Black Church Distinctives," in McCall, *Black Church Lifestyles*, 15.

campus's transition, he felt "pained" that the conservative resurgence cost the jobs of some professors who "really loved the Lord" but who held one or two unusual beliefs about the Bible or theology.[74]

Another source of the divide between white resurgence participants and black Southern Baptists was the perception among African Americans that white conservatives lacked concern for social justice. During the 1980s, black Southern Baptists repeatedly articulated their belief that the church should fight for social justice and that the white churches allowed civil rights to erode without showing adequate concern. In 1985, Smith warned that growing doubts about Southern Baptists' commitment to civil rights could jeopardize continued growth in the number of black Southern Baptist churches. "The black community," Smith said, "is largely convinced the United States is repeating an era of the erosion of civil rights of Blacks coincidental to the period of the ending of reconstruction during the last century."[75] Three years later, Smith suggested that black Southern Baptists exhibited a broader social justice consciousness and a better track record of fighting racism than whites in the denomination.[76] Again in 1989, he observed that African Americans "tend to bring a heightened sense of social justice to the Southern Baptist agenda."[77] Because of their understanding of social justice, black Southern Baptists had difficulty understanding why white conservatives within the denomination aligned themselves with the Republican Party and seemingly turned their backs on black concerns like affirmative action and economic equality. One weakness of the Southern Baptist Convention commonly cited by black pastors was the denomination's "close identity with conservative causes."[78] Walker identified the issues of "race," "affirmative action," and "social empowerment" as areas where theologically conservative, black Southern Baptists divided with theologically conservative, white Southern Baptists. Though black Southern Baptists agreed with white conservatives on issues like abortion and homosexuality, African Americans did not speak out on those issues along with whites because whites would not stand strongly

74. Walker, interview by author, 17 April 2008.

75. David Wilkinson, "White Baptists Urged to Appreciate Racial Distinctives," *Ethnicity*, March/April 1985, 6–7.

76. Smith, "Black Contributions to the Southern Baptist Convention," 3–4.

77. Sid Smith, "Black Southern Baptists: A New Generation of Baptists," *Ethnicity*, May/June 1989, 11.

78. "Bold New Work: Starting Southern Baptist Churches in Black Communities," "Emmanuel McCall, Black Baptists" Box, Unprocessed Home Mission Board Records.

with blacks on issues of economic justice, Walker said.[79] Some African Americans called the conservative resurgence nothing more than a shift from Democratic political alliances to Republican political alliances in convention. They saw Southern Baptists' shift of support from Jimmy Carter to Ronald Reagan as a shift toward a non-Christian president interested in keeping down the economic "have-nots."[80] According to some African-American observers, the only difference between Southern Seminary before the conservative resurgence and Southern Seminary after the resurgence was that the campus shifted from Democratic to Republican in its political affiliation.[81] Such perceptions that resurgence participants were unjustifiably Republican and unconcerned with issues of social justice contributed to black Southern Baptists' distancing themselves from the conservative turn in the Southern Baptist Convention.

When the Southern Baptist Convention passed its 1995 resolution on racial reconciliation, the divide between black Southern Baptists and the white conservatives evidenced itself again.[82] Theologically, parties from both races were on the same page. But skepticism regarding the white conservatives' commitment to social justice caused some black Southern Baptists to mix warnings with their praise of the resolution. Timothy James Johnson, a former Southern Seminary professor, voiced some of the harshest criticism of the resolution when he said, "It's like Hitler apologizing for what he had done to the Jews and Himmler accepting his apology."[83] McCall, who played a role in crafting the resolution, reported however that many African Americans "were rejoicing, especially within the SBC." Black Southern Baptists felt the resolution showed the convention's true feelings and "gave the guys who were in the SBC really a reason to feel proud."[84] But along with the positive responses, some black Southern Baptists "doubted the sincerity" of the resolution, saying that it was merely a ploy to draw additional black churches to the denomination.[85] Much of the negative sentiment among black Southern Baptists remained secret because of denominational political realities,

---

79. Walker, interview by author, 17 April 2008.

80. Walker, interview by author, 17 April 2008.

81. Walker, interview by author, 17 April 2008.

82. See chapter 7 below for a full discussion of how conservatives formulated the 1995 racial reconciliation resolution. The present discussion focuses only on African-American reactions to the resolution, in keeping with the theme of this chapter.

83. Hankins, *Uneasy in Babylon*, 252.

84. McCall, interview by author, 24 April 2008.

85. McCall, interview by author, 24 April 2008.

Walker said. But many African Americans, including Walker, believed the resolution had virtually no impact beyond the symbolic admission that Southern Baptists were wrong in the past.[86]

Both without and within the Southern Baptist Convention, African-American Baptists' reaction to the conservative resurgence demonstrated that there was very little conflict between the theology of rank-and-file white Southern Baptists and rank-and-file black Baptists. The conservative Southern Baptist movement and black Baptists shared a common theology, and there was never conflict between the two groups over central doctrinal issues. Social and political differences, however, revealed that even by the mid-1990s, relations between African Americans and the Southern Baptist Convention were not entirely repaired.

Conclusion

Between 1954 and 1995 African Americans were both optimistic and skeptical regarding the Southern Baptist Convention. Theologically, Southern Baptists held most of the same beliefs as black Baptists. Differences that existed generally related to the role of women in ministry and the freedom of the pulpit, but there was agreement on central doctrines of evangelical theology. Because of that theological agreement, black Baptists expected white Baptists to apply their theology to racial justice just as the black Christians did. When those expectations went unmet, black Baptists felt rather apart. Socially, no period between the *Brown* decision by the Supreme Court and the Southern Baptist Convention's resolution on racial reconciliation was free from tension between black and white Baptists. Smith typified the opinion of black Southern Baptists when he said that there was "significant change" among Southern Baptists by the 1980s, but "basically, African American Baptists perceived the SBC as a racist denomination" from the 1950s through the 1970s.[87] Even with the changes leading up to 1995, African Americans still felt they could not give Southern Baptists an entirely clean bill of health on the issue of race. Even Smith, who was among the African Americans that most ardently supported the convention, said in 2008, "I do not think that the Southern Baptist Convention has done enough in terms of racial progress."[88]

86. Walker, interview by author, 17 April 2008.
87. Smith, interview by author, 24 April 2008.
88. Smith, interview by author, 24 April 2008.

Chapter 6

Moderates and Race During the Southern Baptist Convention Controversy

BEGINNING IN 1979, A controversy that came to be known as the conservative resurgence blew apart the standing order of the Southern Baptist Convention. A conservative party pushed to control the denominational machinery and turn convention agencies back to what they saw as biblical orthodoxy. Moderates fought back to preserve what they saw as a traditional synthesis of diverse theological positions that served the cause of world missions and evangelism. The denominational rancor was severe. Baylor historian Barry Hankins called the controversy "one of the most contentious and significant denominational battles in American religious history."[1] Luther Copeland, a retired Southern Baptist missionary and missions professor, labeled it a period in which "rightists were successful in demanding sacrificial victims."[2] Moderate pastor Cecil Sherman summarized the controversy as a period when conservatives "were dividing the house."[3]

But when it came to the issue of race, there was little disagreement. Through three decades of progress prior to the controversy, Southern Baptists had applied conservative theology to matters of racial inequality and repudiated racial discrimination. During the controversy, both conservatives and moderates drew from this theological tradition to determine their thoughts

---

1. Hankins, *Uneasy in Babylon*, 2.
2. Copeland, *The Southern Baptist Convention and the Judgment of History*, 118.
3. Sherman, *By My Own Reckoning*, 134.

and actions regarding race. The present chapter discusses the moderate efforts relating to race while chapter 7 covers conservative efforts.

Moderates on Race

Moderates based their position on race explicitly on evangelical theology. Time and again moderates drew from scriptural principles to which even their most ardently conservative opponents did not object. Moderate seminary leader Larry L. McSwain was a case in point. Between the 1970s and the early 1990s, McSwain served at Southern Seminary in various capacities, including professor of church and community, dean of the School of Theology, and provost. In 1993 during the height of the controversy, he left Southern to assume the presidency of Shorter College in Rome, Georgia. McSwain had long advocated racial justice and improved race relations. He participated in demonstrations for open housing in Louisville in 1968, heard Martin Luther King speak the month before he was assassinated, and served for a semester as dean of Louisville's African-American Simmons University Bible College. While on a college Baptist Student Union trip in the early 1960s, he led a spontaneous and successful effort to force a segregated Amarillo, Texas, steakhouse to serve a black student.[4] Though he published only one article on race, McSwain highlighted racial justice in much of his teaching at Southern.[5] Like many moderate leaders, McSwain studied ethics in the T. B. Maston tradition at Southwestern Seminary. McSwain's views on racial equality and justice stemmed from a straightforward reading of the Bible. McSwain classified his views as consistent with "conservative theology" as articulated by the 1963 *Baptist Faith and Message*. Though not espousing the concept of biblical inerrancy, McSwain cited the Bible as "our ultimate authority" and "the ultimate source for theology and for daily living and for personal commitments."[6] Liberals would not have disagreed with McSwain on this point, but neither would conservatives.

---

4. Larry L. McSwain, telephone interview by author, digital recording, 5 September 2008.

5. See Larry McSwain, "Working with Secular Agencies and Institutions in Racial Concerns," in *Race: New Directions for a New Day, Addresses from the Christian Life Conference at Ridgecrest, June 1973*, 31–37, Box 35, Folder 21, Christian Life Commission Resource Files.

6. McSwain, interview by author, 5 September 2008.

When it came to race, McSwain said he derived his position from the "tenor of the times" growing up in Oklahoma of the 1950s and personal study of the Bible.[7] The doctrines of evangelism and the church played central roles in his thinking, with Galatians 3:28 serving as a key biblical text: "There is neither Jew nor Greek, there is neither slave nor free, there is no male and female, for you are all one in Christ Jesus." McSwain said of his Bible study early in life, "In a general sort of way I just saw Scripture as mandating universal proclamation of the gospel. The Great Commission and the Great Commandment were clear to me. They applied to all people."[8] The Bible appeared so clear to McSwain that he never considered nor was he ever aware of segregationist biblical arguments until he studied them in seminary. Martin Luther King Jr. became a favorite extrabiblical source for McSwain, but his admiration for King stemmed from the fact that King seemed "consistent with my understanding of Scripture," not from an affinity for any theological liberalism or neoorthodoxy espoused by the civil rights leader.[9]

Jimmy Allen, another moderate proponent of racial justice, like McSwain, described his views on race as deriving from a straightforward reading of Scripture that regarded the biblical text as totally authoritative. As executive director of the Baptist General Convention of Texas's Christian Life Commission from 1960 to 1968, Allen established a reputation as a racial activist and developed a large network of black Baptist friends. McSwain, who authored a biography of Allen, described Allen as one of five men who deserved the most credit for moving the Southern Baptist Convention toward a posture of greater racial inclusiveness.[10] As executive director of the Christian Life Commission, Allen held the first ever conference on race on the campus of Southwestern Seminary. When conservative pastor Fred Swank attempted to get Allen fired over the conference, Allen refused to apologize for advocating integration.[11] Through his relationships with Bill Moyers and Lyndon Johnson, Allen became an activist and advocate for the integration of Texas public schools between

---

7. McSwain, interview by author, 5 September 2008.
8. McSwain, interview by author, 5 September 2008.
9. McSwain, interview by author, 5 September 2008.
10. McSwain, interview by author, 5 September 2008. See McSwain, *Loving beyond Your Theology*.
11. McSwain, interview by author, 5 September 2008; Jimmy Allen, telephone interview by author, digital recording, 2 September 2008.

1960 and 1968. He also played an active role in the integration of public facilities in Texas. When he served as president of the Baptist General Convention of Texas, Allen cooperated with black and Hispanic Baptists in the state to organize an interracial gathering of 41,000 people in Houston's Astrodome. Allen's racial activism brought so many death threats that he and his wife established a secret pattern of rings for their home telephone in order to let their children know a parent was calling rather than a white supremacist with a death threat. Despite the threats, Allen continued courageously to press racial justice, appointing minorities to key committees when he served as president of the Southern Baptist Convention between 1977 and 1979.[12] He brought Coretta Scott King, widow of Martin Luther King Jr., to the 1978 Southern Baptist Convention meeting to speak on "America's need for spiritual awakening."[13]

Allen based his quest for racial justice on a straightforward reading of the Bible, which he viewed as completely authoritative for belief and practice. "My sense is that the Bible itself is our authority and our mandate and that the Bible is very clear about God creating all men in His image," he said. "And therefore there's a mandate in God's Word to oppose any kind of discrimination and racial prejudice."[14] In addition to the doctrine of creation, the doctrine of the church played a key role in Allen's thinking. He regarded Christians of all races as "one family" and believed they should treat each other "like brothers and sisters."[15] God's offer of salvation to people of all races was a major part of the argument Allen made to other Baptists when he urged them to racial inclusiveness. As a director of Royal Ambassador camps in Texas for two years, he exposed boys to people of other races and taught that segregation undermined the missionary impulse.[16] He insisted decades later as president of the Southern Baptist Convention that Southern Baptists should not neglect Native Americans in fulfilling the Great Commission.[17] The biblical command to protect the weak and helpless members of society also factored into Allen's dealings in racial justice.

12. McSwain, interview by author, 5 September 2008.
13. *1978 Southern Baptist Convention Annual*, 70, in "SBC Annuals."
14. Allen, interview by author, 2 September 2008.
15. Allen, interview by author, 2 September 2008.
16. Allen, interview by author, 2 September 2008.
17. Box 2, Folder 10, Jimmy Allen Papers.

During Allen's teenage years, liberal Southern Baptist preacher Clarence Jordan played a key role in convincing him to pursue racial reconciliation. After growing up with a father whom Allen described as a "mild segregationist," he attended a Young Men's Mission Conference at Ridgecrest Conference Center in North Carolina, where Jordan spoke. Jordan presented "uncomfortable truth" that caused Allen to rethink his position on race from that day forward. Jordan convinced Allen that through Scripture he "was mandated of God to deal with [race] as a major issue."[18] According to Allen, members of David Stricklin's "genealogy of dissent" never moved Southern Baptists on race with liberal ideas. Southern Baptists, including himself, responded to "Bible-believing, mission-minded, evangelistic-mandated people."[19] By his own testimony, Allen approached the race question with conservative theology.

James Dunn was another key moderate leader who derived his position on race from conservative theology. After serving as executive director of the Baptist General Convention of Texas's Christian Life Commission, Dunn became in 1980 executive director of the Baptist Joint Committee on Public Affairs, where he served until 1999. While not specifically dealing with issues of racial justice, Dunn partnered with many African-American Baptist leaders in his work on church-state issues. Through that work, Dunn established lifelong friendships with African Americans and began to see issues of racial justice "from their perspective." He remarked, "As I came to appreciate and work with them as friends, it was an entirely different way to relate to them."[20]

In a story similar to Allen's, Dunn changed his views on race after hearing a Baptist preacher address race from a biblical perspective. The change of perspective came in 1948 when Ralph Phelps, then an ethics professor at Southwestern Seminary, spoke to Dunn's youth group at Evans Avenue Baptist Church in Fort Worth. Phelps referenced the teaching of Acts 17:26 that God made all people "of one blood." He mentioned other New Testament passages about racial justice as well and drove the teenaged Dunn to a quiet, seething anger. Upon reflection, however, Dunn realized he was angry because Phelps hit "a weak spot" in his theology. "As I reflected on my response and why I had become so angry," Dunn said, "I realized how wrong I had

---

18. Allen, interview by author, 2 September 2008.
19. Allen, interview by author, 2 September 2008.
20. James Dunn, telephone interview by author, digital recording, 22 August 2008.

been" to hold any racist attitudes. The episode served as a turning point in Dunn's view of civil rights and racial justice.[21]

For the rest of his ministry, Dunn considered how historic evangelical doctrines applied to race relations. The doctrines of creation and sin factored into his racial views in particularly important ways. Because people of all races were created in the image of God, he reasoned from Psalm 8, "we should approach them with the same degree of willingness to relate to them as full-fledged humans beings."[22] As a function of their created status, people of all races are free to make moral decisions, he said. On the negative side, people of all races are equal because they are all sinners in need of the gospel, according to Dunn. "A theological anthropology that recognizes our great sinfulness and our great capacity as made in God's image is the way we should approach any persons of any race," he said.[23]

Cecil Sherman, a pastor and prominent leader of the resistance to the conservative resurgence, was another moderate leader who approached race from the standpoint of conservative theology. Sherman's most prominent stands for racial justice occurred while he was pastor of the First Baptist Church in Ashville, North Carolina. In September 1964, shortly after Sherman became pastor, an African-American woman presented herself as a candidate for church membership. Although Sherman favored admitting black members, many in the congregation felt differently, and a battle erupted. A majority of the congregation voted to admit the woman to membership, but she failed to receive the unanimous vote required by church bylaws and was thus denied. During the ordeal, Sherman courageously, though unsuccessfully, attempted to revise church bylaws so that only a seventy-five percent majority was required to admit new members. Again in 1965 the woman presented herself for membership only to be backed by Sherman but voted down by the congregation once again. Throughout the episode, Sherman and his family received accusations and insults. Finally in 1970, Sherman successfully led First Baptist to admit its first black member, Clarence Batts. Over the next ten years, the congregation's black membership rose to sixteen, and the issue of integration was closed.[24] Because of the church integration fight and other stands, Sherman gained a reputation for having a sense of social justice. He served two

---

21. Dunn, interview by author, 22 August 2008.
22. Dunn, interview by author, 22 August 2008.
23. Dunn, interview by author, 22 August 2008.
24. Sherman, *By My Own Reckoning*, 55–70.

terms on the Southern Baptist Convention's Christian Life Commission beginning in 1968, chairing the commission during his second term.[25] Sherman held to several theological positions at odds with the thinking of Southern Baptist conservatives, including his belief that the Bible contains scientific and historical errors.[26] Yet when it came to race, he drew his thinking from conservative theology.

From the integration episode in Ashville, Sherman said he learned "that the race issue is important. Racial inclusiveness is not petty morality. It is at the heart of Bible ideas. Violation of those Bible rules corrupts. Turning away people who have professed faith in Christ is out of step with the spirit of the New Testament."[27] In a 1968 sermon mourning the assassination of Martin Luther King Jr., Sherman argued that the hope for racial justice lay in Christianity rather than any message of liberalism or social reform. King experienced such dramatic success, Sherman said, because he gave a "Christian interpretation to the Negro struggle to be heard."[28] He said the inclusiveness of the New Testament's gospel appeal must be translated into racial openness in the church.[29]

William Tillman, an ethics professor at Southwestern Seminary presented another moderate treatment of race in his 1986 book, *Christian Ethics: A Primer*. He argued, "Possibly even more than other applied areas of Christian ethics, the area of human relations must be dealt with by way of biblical principles."[30] The first key principle in race relations, according to Tillman, was that God is equally the God of all people. He derived that principle from New and Old Testament passages, including Genesis 1:26–31, John 1:1–4, and Acts 17:27.[31] All humans are created in the image of God, he said, meaning that people of all races "have a sense of receptivity that may grow to faith in Christ."[32] In the Gospels, Jesus showed compassion to people of all races. In Acts and the epistles, the early church included people from all races. And the nature of the gospel itself is such that anyone

25. Sherman, *By My Own Reckoning*, 83.
26. Sherman, *By My Own Reckoning*, 139–40.
27. Sherman, *By My Own Reckoning*, 62.
28. Cecil Sherman, "The Way Things Are," 7 April 1968, p. 9, Box 19, Folder 74, Don B. Harbuck Papers.
29. Sherman, "The Way Things Are."
30. Tillman, *Christian Ethics*, 82.
31. Tillman, *Christian Ethics*, 82.
32. Tillman, *Christian Ethics*, 82–83.

of any race who believes will become a child of God.[33] Tillman concluded that, despite the exegetical gymnastics of some, neither the Old Testament nor the New Testament can be used to justify racism.[34]

For leading Southern Baptist moderates, the conservative evangelical reading of Scripture drove the agenda on the subject of race.

Agreement Despite Expulsion

By the late 1980s and early 1990s, conservatives won a sufficient number of Southern Baptist Convention presidential elections to change the makeup of denominational boards through the election of conservative trustees. When that occurred, the new denominational leadership gradually forced moderates out of power in all convention agencies, including the six Southern Baptist seminaries. They expelled moderate leaders because they believed that moderates departed from biblical norms and capitulated to norms of secular culture in their leadership of the denomination.[35] Yet conservatives never expelled moderates because of any disagreement on the race issue. In fact, conservative denominational leadership continued in the same stream of thinking on race as their moderate predecessors.[36]

The experience of Emmanuel McCall bore out this trend. Long an advocate for racial justice, McCall left the Southern Baptist Convention in the mid-1990s when he felt he was no longer welcome in the denomination's political circles. He recalled one episode in which conservative trustees at the Home Mission Board became angry when the board's Interfaith Witness department did not invite them to speak at an evangelistic conference in Israel. Despite attempted explanations from Home Mission Board officials, the trustees labeled the Interfaith Witness department as liberal from that time forward and stigmatized McCall for attempting to mediate the conflict, according to McCall.[37] He received additional evidence that he was no longer welcome in the denomination when he attempted to join a group of Southern Baptist representatives in a conversation at a Baptist World Alliance meeting. When McCall approached the group, it

33. Tillman, *Christian Ethics*, 83–84.
34. Tillman, *Christian Ethics*, 84–85.
35. Hankins, *Uneasy in Babylon*, 41–106.
36. Hankins, *Uneasy in Babylon*, 243.
37. Emmanuel McCall, telephone interview by author, digital recording, 24 April 2008.

disbanded almost instantly. When McCall asked for an explanation, he was told the issue was not race, but theology. The other Southern Baptist delegates perceived him to be a liberal and did not want him in their conversations, McCall said.[38] But the episode that finally convinced McCall there was no hope for him to be accepted in the convention occurred at a Baptist World Alliance meeting in Germany. Attending the meeting as a representative of the Southern Baptist Convention, McCall encountered several conservative resurgence leaders huddling and attempted to engage them in conversation. He recounted:

> There were about five of the SBC leaders together, and somebody did not know whether Judge [Paul] Pressler knew who I was. And I walked over to shake his hand and introduce myself to him. And in no uncertain terms I was told, "You aren't needed in the SBC anymore." And [from] the others that were in that presence, I expected some word of affirmation or some saying, "Well, you know, he's an OK guy." It didn't happen. And I decided, well, that's it for me. There's no point in trying anymore.[39]

So McCall exited Southern Baptist life and began to assume leadership roles in the moderate Cooperative Baptist Fellowship. Despite his emotional wounds over the controversy, McCall admitted that he and the conservatives were not at odds over race. "I didn't want to think that [conservative leaders' rejection] was racial," he said, "and it wasn't racial. But it was that the word had gone out that McCall is liberal."[40]

McCall's situation was not unique. Though they remained at odds on many other issues, moderates and conservatives agreed on race, both drawing their ideas from evangelical theology and striving for racial justice. Because of the theological agreement on race, a series of seemingly odd partnerships between the two sides sought to achieve racial equality. Until 1991 Richard Land, the staunchly conservative head of the Christian Life Commission, joined forces with moderates as an ex officio member of the Baptist Peace Fellowship of North America.[41] Timothy George, a conservative professor at Southern Seminary, also participated in the Baptist Peace Fellowship along with moderates like Dunn and ethicist Robert Parham.

38. McCall, interview by author, 24 April 2008.
39. McCall, interview by author, 24 April 2008.
40. McCall, interview by author, 24 April 2008.
41. Robert Parham, "The History of the Baptist Center for Ethics," in Shurden, *The Struggle for the Soul of the SBC*, 211–12.

THE SOUTHERN BAPTIST CONVENTION CONTROVERSY

During the 1980s the Baptist Peace Fellowship held an organizational gathering each year during the annual meeting of the Southern Baptist Convention, and both moderates and conservatives attended the gathering. The Baptist Peace Fellowship made racial justice a major priority, heard an address from Coretta Scott King in 1986, and addressed race relations at its annual conferences throughout the 1980s.[42]

When the Baptist Peace Fellowship revealed in 1993 that the Southern Baptist Convention Executive Committee wrongly handled a racially-charged situation in 1963, the conservative-led Christian Life Commission quickly joined the moderate Baptist Peace Fellowship in lamenting the Executive Committee's behavior. The Baptist Peace Fellowship reported that after the bombing of the African-American Sixteenth Street Baptist Church in Birmingham, Alabama, a member of the Executive Committee submitted a resolution in the administrative subcommittee expressing sympathy to the church and pledging efforts to heal the rift between blacks and whites. The subcommittee, under pressure by members from Alabama, rejected the resolution, substituted for it a more general resolution on race, and then requested that Baptist state paper editors not report the rejection of the initial resolution. Land credited the Baptist Peace Fellowship for uncovering the truth and stated his own feelings on the matter:

> As a 15-year old Southern Baptist, I was appalled at such barbarous savagery against little children in church. Had I known of the SBC Executive Committee's action then rejecting a strong and specific resolution condemning the bombings, I would have been both outraged and grieved. To learn of it now still fills me with an overwhelming sadness and grief at the sins of our past.[43]

Within the Christian Life Commission, another unlikely coalition existed during the conservative resurgence. Parham, who previously served as interim executive director, remained on staff through 1991 and partnered with Land to address racial issues. These opposite-minded ethicists on many issues coauthored an article urging Baptists to embrace the biblical vision of racial justice—in spite of the fact Parham thought people like Land addressed too few ethical issues, overlooked many social implications

---

42. See Box 1, Folders 10, 11, 39, and Box 2, Folders 5, 7, Baptist Peace Fellowship of North America Records.

43. Louis Moore, "Baptists Say Cover-Up Wrong, Urge Fight against Racism," Christian Life Commission news release, 1993, Box 2, Folder 22, Race Relations Collection.

of the gospel, and wrongly allied themselves with the Republican Party.[44] Eventually Parham helped found the Baptist Center for Ethics, a moderate counterpart to the Christian Life Commission. But on race, similar theologies allowed men from different ideological camps to partner.

Moderates and conservatives agreed on race. McSwain rejected any attempts to draw a distinction between the racial views of moderates and conservatives. "When you come to '79," McSwain said, "it does not seem to me that the new conservative leadership of the Southern Baptist Convention were less committed to racial justice than had been the . . . traditional synthesis leaders."[45] Allen agreed, noting that racism existed on both sides of the divide in an earlier era and progress existed on both sides by the time of the conservative resurgence. Segregation and racism had a "cultural base" rather than a "theological base," he said. When culture shifted in the era of the civil rights movement, both sides adopted a similar theological outlook and continued on the same trajectory through the 1970s and 1980s. Missions and evangelism were the key issues where the two camps congealed theologically and moved forward on race. Allen explained:

> If they believed in missions, they usually had enough drawing them to see what we were doing to our mission image and opportunity [by perpetuating racism], and they could rise to that. So a lot of people who were basically fundamentalist in their theology were mission-minded in their outreach, and they came to the table to help with some of the racial issues.[46]

Dunn critiqued conservatives harshly on their handling of race relations. He argued that it was "almost a joke" when conservative leadership passed resolutions advocating racial justice and that conservatives' affiliation with the Religious Right prevented them from realizing some contemporary applications of racial justice. Dunn also said moderates demonstrated a "comfort level" with the race issue that conservatives did not appear to have.[47] But even the highly critical Dunn concluded that by the conservative resurgence, both sides thought about race "pretty much the same,"

---

44. Richard Land and Robert Parham, "'God Pays No Attention to a Man's Skin' (Acts 10:34)," "Race Relations" Folder, Baptist History File; Parham, "The History of the Baptist Center for Ethics," 203, 218–19.

45. McSwain, interview by author, 5 September 2008.

46. Allen, interview by author, 2 September 2008.

47. Dunn, interview by author, 22 August 2008.

though he also said the consensus was pragmatic rather than due to philosophical and theological considerations.[48]

In the era of moderate exodus and expulsion from the leadership of the Southern Baptist Convention, moderates and conservatives held identical views concerning racial equality and sometimes partnered for racial justice. And both groups felt the strong influence of the doctrines of evangelism, the church, and creation when it came to race. That reality grew even clearer when moderates began to form their own organizations and continued to adopt a theologically conservative view of race—despite the fact that they no longer had to work with conservatives.

Race and Moderate Organizations

By 1990, conservative resurgence battles had gone the way of conservatives so many times that moderates began to form their own organizations rather than face defeat within the Southern Baptist Convention year after year. Organizations like the Cooperative Baptist Fellowship, the Baptist Center for Ethics, the Southern Baptist Alliance, and the Baptist Peace Fellowship of North America carried forward the moderate vision of Baptist identity. Within those organizations rhetoric against conservatives at times was harsh. But their public statements on race still rang with the same theology that drove Southern Baptist conservatives.

Few moderates characterized conservatives more harshly than did Cecil Sherman. He battled against the conservative resurgence beginning in 1980, when he invited a group of moderate pastors to a meeting in Gatlinburg, Tennessee, to formulate a strategy to oppose the resurgence.[49] He later became coordinator of the Cooperative Baptist Fellowship in 1992.[50] Sherman charged that conservative leader Adrian Rogers was so out of touch with biblical standards of racial justice that he spoke favorably of American slavery. During a meeting of the Southern Baptist Convention's Peace Committee, Sherman questioned Rogers' position that Baptists should read the Bible literally. "What do you do with those places in the New Testament that affirm slavery, like 1 Peter, Ephesians, and Colossians?" Sherman recalled asking. Rogers' response, according to Sherman, revealed a distressing logic in conservative reasoning:

48. Dunn, interview by author, 22 August 2008.
49. Sherman, *By My Own Reckoning*, 150–53.
50. Sherman, *By My Own Reckoning*, 225.

> He [Rogers] hesitated a moment then said, "Well, I believe slavery is a much maligned institution; if we had slavery today, we would not have this welfare mess." I had never heard anyone speak a good word for slavery; I went upstairs and wrote it down. Rogers was saying he believed slaves should be obedient to their masters just as he believed wives should be obedient to their husbands. Such was the biblical literalism of the people who controlled the Peace Committee.[51]

Parham likewise issued strong criticism of conservatives on the issue of race. Labeling the conservatives' approach to Christian ethics the "conqueror" mentality, Parham argued that "conquerors" overlooked the social implications of love for neighbor. Conquerors "crusade to preserve culture at its core," he said, including "white supremacy," "antiliberation efforts," and "anti-integration."[52] Parham said in an interview, "I will forever believe that the conservative takeover had its genesis among the Baptist segregationists, who claimed to read the Bible literally and hated the denominational bureaucracy for its progressive stance on race."[53] As evidence for his claim, Parham cited the case of Curtis Caine, a conservative Christian Life Commission trustee from Mississippi. In 1988 Caine said at a Christian Life Commission meeting that Martin Luther King Jr. was a fraud and that apartheid in South Africa was good. "Many commissioners nodded in agreement. None rebutted his statement," Parham said.[54] Rather than remove Caine from the commission, the conservative leadership recommended him for a second term, a move that "affirmed his position," according to Parham.[55]

However Sherman and Parham may have distanced themselves from conservatives, official moderate statements on race sounded similar to the 1995 resolution adopted by conservatives. The Southern Baptist Alliance adopted a resolution in 1990 repenting of the "sins of slavery and of condoning slavery," which are a "spiritual blight upon the relationships between African-Americans and whites in the south which has lasted unto this day."[56]

51. Sherman, *By My Own Reckoning*, 189.
52. Parham, "The History of the Baptist Center for Ethics," 203.
53. Robert Parham to author, email, 12 September 2008.
54. Robert Parham to author, email, 12 September 2008. See also Parham, "The History of the Baptist Center for Ethics," 210.
55. Robert Parham to author, email, 12 September 2008.
56. Dan Martin, "Alliance Resolution Repents of Slavery," *Baptist Press*, 13 March 1990, 8.

THE SOUTHERN BAPTIST CONVENTION CONTROVERSY

The Cooperative Baptist Fellowship followed suit in 1992, passing "A Statement of Confession and Repentance." In the statement, Fellowship Baptists repented "of the largely unconfessed sin of racism in our own heritage." The statement also acknowledged slavery as a factor in the formation of the Southern Baptist Convention and apologized to African Americans for Southern Baptist condoning of slavery. "We reject forthrightly," it said, "the racism which has persisted throughout our history as Southern Baptists, even to this present day."[57] The Baptist Peace Fellowship of North America in 1993 added its voice to the moderate groups speaking out on race. The group issued "The Birmingham Confession," which expressed sympathy to Sixteenth Street Baptist Church for the 1963 bombing that the Southern Baptist Convention's Executive Committee failed to acknowledge. The confession admitted a lack of faithful preaching on racial justice in Southern Baptist churches and that "racism impedes our own development as a people and discredits our own preaching." Referencing Martin Luther King Jr., the Birmingham Confession acknowledged "that the dream of the beloved community is painfully slow in coming."[58]

These moderate statements on race came before the conservatives issued their own resolution in 1995, but the similarities between the moderate statements and the 1995 Southern Baptist Convention resolution suggested that Allen and McSwain were correct—moderates and conservatives approached race in largely the same manner by the 1990s. The 1995 resolution acknowledged that "Our relationship to African-Americans has been hindered from the beginning by the role that slavery played in the formation of the Southern Baptist Convention." It also admitted that "in later years Southern Baptists failed, in many cases, to support, and in some cases opposed, legitimate initiatives to secure the civil rights of African-Americans." The resolution went on to "repudiate" historical acts of racism, "apologize" for perpetuating racism, and committed to fight racism.[59] In the resolution, echoes of moderate statements rang loudly and confirmed that consensus existed on race.

---

57. Cooperative Baptist Fellowship, "A Statement of Confession and Repentance," "Race: Southern Baptist Actions, 1990–1994" Folder, Christian Life Commission Records.

58. Baptist Peace Fellowship of North America, "The Birmingham Confession," "Race Relations" Folder, Baptist History File.

59. "On Racial Reconciliation on the 150th Anniversary of the Southern Baptist Convention," in *1995 Southern Baptist Convention Annual*, 80–81, in "SBC Annuals."

Moderate Southern Baptist organizations took on racial injustice in other ways as well. The Baptist Center for Ethics hosted a conference in the fall of 1993 entitled, "The Church's Challenge in a Multi-Racial and Multi-Ethnic Society." Conference speakers argued that racism was still present in society but that it took a more subtle form than in years past. Laws slanted against African Americans, economic pressures, and injustice in America's courts replaced overt segregation as the most common expressions of racism, speakers said. Just as with Baptists in past generations, conference speakers advocated the gospel as the remedy to racism. According to Cynthia Tucker, a conference speaker and columnist for the Atlanta Constitution, "Racism can only thrive where the gospel is ignored." Bill Leonard, another speaker and chairman of the religion department at Samford University, urged Americans to take Jesus as an example of confronting racial prejudice.[60]

Many moderates viewed involvement of minorities in leadership as the highest expression of racial justice and equality. Dunn said the most significant moderate action pertaining to race was the "no-fanfare, no-trumpets-blowing acceptance of African-American leadership." He noted that "almost all" of the newly formed moderate groups "have both employed and programmed African Americans without attention to race." Especially in the Cooperative Baptist Fellowship and the Baptist General Convention of Texas moderates are "willing not just to share leadership, but to follow the leadership of African Americans in things that we do together," Dunn said.[61] Allen, when asked about the greatest successes of the Cooperative Baptist Fellowship with regard to race, cited the "deliberate inclusion of leaders from all of the racial elements in the decision making of the organization."[62] McSwain answered almost identically when asked about the greatest successes of moderate groups pertaining to race. He cited Emmanuel McCall's service in Cooperative Baptist Fellowship leadership as "the most significant demonstration of the moderates' commitment to equality."[63]

For moderates, the inclusion of women in leadership related closely to the inclusion of minorities. In a significant departure from conservatives, moderates argued that it was inconsistent to argue racial equality from

---

60. Greg Warner, "Conferees Say '90s-Style' Racism Takes More Subtle, Insidious Forms," *Associated Baptist Press*, 28 October 1993.

61. Dunn, interview by author, 22 August 2008.

62. Allen, interview by author, 2 September 2008.

63. McSwain, interview by author, 5 September 2008.

Scripture if one was not also willing to argue that both men and women can fulfill all roles in the church equally. In their arguments about racial minorities and women, moderates continued to focus on the Bible; they interpreted the Bible differently than did conservatives, however. Moderates made biblical and theological arguments for the full equality of women in ministry and at times linked those arguments with arguments for the full equality of African Americans in ministry.[64] Allen drew a parallel between moderates' inclusion of racial minorities and their inclusion of women in leadership. Including both groups, he said, demonstrated the "non-discriminatory nature of the gospel."[65] McSwain explained that the issues of racial minorities and women were related for moderates because "you have to use the same biblical hermeneutic to make the case for race as you have to do to make the case for women. You can't read Paul and what Paul says about slavery without making some interpretive judgments that you also have to make when you read Paul on women."[66] Equality in Christ, as expressed in Galatians 3:28 and the book of Philippians, requires Christians to include both minorities and women at every level of leadership, McSwain said. To place restrictions on one group requires placing restrictions on both in order to be consistent, he said. To tout racial equality while limiting ordination to men is "just a totally inconsistent argument." McSwain called "the rejection of women in leadership of the church" the area "where this Baptist disagrees most profoundly with the new leadership of the SBC." McSwain summarized, "I could make a case for slavery if I read Paul in a certain way. And you have to read Paul that same way to make a case for a non-egalitarian relationship between men and women."[67]

Conservatives reached different conclusions than moderates on how the inclusion of racial minorities in leadership related to the inclusion of women. Conservative scholar Dorothy Patterson, for example, argued that Paul grounded female submission in God's created order but never grounded slavery in the created order. Instructions on slavery, Patterson said, were instructions on how to behave in the midst of a bad institution.[68] The differences between moderates and conservatives, while severe and significant, highlighted the fact that they both approached race similarly. Both sides

64. Hankins, *Uneasy in Babylon*, 204.
65. Allen, interview by author, 2 September 2008.
66. McSwain, interview by author, 5 September 2008.
67. McSwain, interview by author, 5 September 2008.
68. Hankins, *Uneasy in Babylon*, 211.

examined the Bible and based their conclusions on what they viewed to be the most logical and straightforward reading the scriptural texts. But moderates and conservatives found themselves closer to one another on racial issues than on other theological matters.

In their organizations, moderates consistently approached the race question from the perspective of evangelical theology. Their theology differed from conservatives on issues such as the inerrancy of Scripture and the ordination of women. But on race, moderates based their public statements on theological ideas held in common with conservatives.

Conclusion

William Tillman and Andrew Tillman argued that the ethical ideal of T. B. Maston and J. B. Weatherspoon passed to moderate Southern Baptist leaders like Foy Valentine then subsequently passed out of the Southern Baptist Convention into moderate groups like the Baptist General Convention of Texas and the Baptist Center for Ethics.[69] Whether their thesis is correct overall remains to be studied in another work. Within the narrow field of race relations though, their argument is partially accurate. The same theology utilized by Maston, Weatherspoon, and Valentine found its way into moderate Baptist life of the 1980s and 1990s, exerting an influence among the moderate side of the Southern Baptist Convention controversy and subsequently guiding the Cooperative Baptist Fellowship, Baptist Center for Ethics, and other moderate organizations. The Tillmans were incorrect, however, in attributing that ethical vision uniquely to moderates. The same theology fueled conservative treatments of race during the controversy as well, a fact which will become even more evident in the next chapter.

---

69. Tillman and Tillman, "The Rise, Decline, and Fall of Christian Life Commission Entities and Voices."

Chapter 7

Richard Land and Modern Conservatives on Race

CONSERVATIVES BASED THEIR VIEWS on race on their evangelical theology. Some historians have contested this. Barry Hankins, for example, argued that Southern Baptist conservatives initiated the conservative resurgence because the culture war had extended to the South and they needed to control the denominational machinery in order to combat the advance of secularism. On issues like abortion and women's ordination, Hankins said, conservatives acted consistently with their culture warrior mentality and opposed the mainstream view. But on race, they acted inconsistently and followed the cultural mainstream, he argued. The conservatives found their desire to pursue racial justice to be "colliding head on with their overall conservatism."[1] The fact that conservatives acted inconsistently with their ideological commitments made it difficult for them to pursue racial justice successfully, Hankins concluded.

But there is a more coherent explanation for conservatives' pursuit of racial justice. Rather than acting inconsistently with a culture warrior mentality, they acted consistently with their evangelical theology. The same theology that drove Southern Baptists on race for the previous half century drove the conservatives of the 1980s and early 1990s to strive for equality and justice for racial minorities. They differed with moderates at times on the best policies for achieving justice, but the theological premises for racial justice were the same for conservatives as for their moderate counterparts.

---

1. Hankins, *Uneasy in Babylon*, 250.

The biblical concepts of man's creation in the image of God and human equality before Christ motivated conservatives, under the leadership of Richard Land and the Christian Life Commission, to continue the convention's opposition to racism.

The Christian Life Commission under Land

The Christian Life Commission entered a new era in September 1988 when it elected Richard Land as its executive director by a vote of twenty-three to two.[2] Previously a vice president at Criswell College, Land identified openly with the conservative side of the Southern Baptist Convention controversy and represented a decisive shift away from the moderate Valentine and Baker administrations. But Land made clear to the commission before it hired him that he would not depart from Valentine's emphasis on racial justice. "I think one of the areas where the Christian Life Commission has historically taken an extremely courageous and strong stand has been on the issue of racial equality and the fact that racial prejudice is the antithesis of the gospel of Jesus Christ," Land said in his interview with the full commission.[3] Like Valentine, Land argued that race prejudice was inconsistent with the Bible.

In his interview, Land emphasized repeatedly that race relations would be a key issue in his administration and that faithfulness to the Bible demanded a proactive stance on race. Land recounted how segregation in his home state of Texas so bothered him as a teenager that he attended Princeton University in 1965 partly to get away from the South. "I told my parents when I left," he said, "that one of the reasons I was leaving was that I certainly didn't judge others who stayed, but that I could not live with that situation if it did not change."[4] His convictions about racial justice continued to develop during college as Land met African-Americans his own age for the first time in his life and studied under ethicist Paul Ramsey.[5] By the

    2. "Minutes of the Annual Meeting of the Christian Life Commission of the Southern Baptist Convention, September 13–14, 1988," p. 35, Box 5, Folder 1, Christian Life Commission Minutes.
    3. "Minutes of the Annual Meeting of the Christian Life Commission of the Southern Baptist Convention, September 13–14, 1988," 8.
    4. "Minutes of the Annual Meeting of the Christian Life Commission of the Southern Baptist Convention, September 13–14, 1988," 8.
    5. Richard Land, interview by author, digital recording, Indianapolis, Indiana, 11 June 2008; "Minutes of the Annual Meeting of the Christian Life Commission of the

time Land began his teaching career in Dallas, race was an important emphasis in his ministry. He told commission trustees that on the Dallas call-in radio show he hosted, race was among the top two topics callers wanted to discuss.[6] Land stressed that race relations in America had declined since the late 1970s and that he wanted no part of a Christian Life Commission that failed to emphasize racial justice. He said:

> I have been very deeply committed to racial equality and racial justice as a part of my Christian adventure since I was a teenager and I personally think that the Christian Life Commission has a greater need for visibility and impact upon Southern Baptists than ever before ... our witness has been compromised by our willingness to live with the blasphemy of racial prejudice being propagated in the name of the gospel of Jesus Christ. If the Christian Life Commission doesn't bear witness to that, it doesn't deserve existence.[7]

Such views, Land said, were not the maverick leanings of a Princeton elitist, but represented "a consensus in our Convention, a very strong one on racial equality and racial justice."[8] After the vote to hire him, Land told the press, just as he told the commission, that racial justice and equality would be strong emphases during his time at the commission's helm.[9]

Little did Land know that a controversy over race would arise even before he began his duties as executive director. During the same commission meeting in which Land was hired, conservative trustee Curtis Caine made his controversial comments about Martin Luther King Jr. said South African apartheid.[10] Regarding the Christian Life Commission's commitment to better race relations, Caine said:

> We must be careful not to end in the trap that's closing in around us about apartheid, which doesn't exist and wasn't bad when it did

---

Southern Baptist Convention, September 13–14, 1988," 4.

6. "Minutes of the Annual Meeting of the Christian Life Commission of the Southern Baptist Convention, September 13–14, 1988," 7.

7. "Minutes of the Annual Meeting of the Christian Life Commission of the Southern Baptist Convention, September 13–14, 1988," 28.

8. "Minutes of the Annual Meeting of the Christian Life Commission of the Southern Baptist Convention, September 13–14, 1988," 16.

9. Dan Martin, "Land Cites Pro-Life, Racial Equality as Key Concerns," *Baptist Press*, Box 5, Folder 2, Christian Life Commission Minutes.

10. Associated Press, "Baptists Condemn Official's Remarks on Apartheid, King," *Chattanooga Times*, 1 October 1988, B2; Marv Knox, "Racial Statements Distort SBC Stand, Ethicist Says," *Baptist Press*, 29 September 1988, 2–3.

exist because it meant separate development. We have to be very careful that we don't be caught up in the endorsement of—quote, the reverend, unquote—Martin Luther King.[11]

Interim executive director Robert Parham, a moderate, responded to Caine with sharp statements that echoed the themes Land brought up in his interview. Caine's statements, Parham said, "stand in sharp contrast with the accomplishments attained during the previous four decades, have offended many inside and outside the convention, have planted seeds of doubt about the authenticity of the Christian life of Southern Baptists and may prove injurious to the denomination's Christian witness at home and abroad."[12] Several commission members said they were embarrassed by Caine's remarks, and Chairman Fred Lackey said Caine "certainly did not speak for me. God is color-blind."[13] In the months that followed, several Baptist state conventions denounced Caine's statements and controversy became heated.[14]

In that context, Land entered the Christian Life Commission in October 1988. With controversy brewing and race relations as a top priority, Land began planning a conference on race his first day on the job. Announcing the conference a month later, he said, "Racism remains an entrenched moral problem in our society as well as within the Southern Baptist Convention. It discloses itself sometimes with directness and sometimes with great subtlety."[15] The conference occurred in January 1989 and showcased how conservative theology and progressive views on race worked hand in hand at Land's Christian Life Commission. The conference lasted two days, including the Martin Luther King holiday, and featured white and black Christian speakers. During a conference panel discussion, two participants

---

11. Associated Press, "Baptists Condemn Official's Remarks on Apartheid, King."

12. Robert Parham, "A Statement: Southern Baptists and Race Relations," Christian Life Commission news release, 28 September 1988.

13. Associated Press, "Baptists Condemn Official's Remarks on Apartheid, King."

14. Ray Waddle, "Rift Brews over Baptist Trustee's Apartheid Remark," *Tennessean*, 13 November 1988, 6; Ray Waddle, "State Baptists Pick Moderate, Denounce Racial Remarks," *Tennessean*, 17 November 1988, 1A; Ken Camp, "Texas CLC Opposes Comments Made by Southern Baptist CLC Members," *Baptist Press*, 26 September 1988, 5; All of these articles are located in Box 5, Folder 2, Christian Life Commission Minutes.

15. "Race Relations Conference Planned," Christian Life Commission news release, 28 November 1988.

condemned Caine's remarks and Land said Caine's view was not representative of the Christian Life Commission trustees.[16]

But addresses by conference speakers went beyond the Caine controversy to discuss the larger issue of how race relations fit into a fully developed Christian worldview. The fact that the conference included speakers from both camps in the denominational controversy provided evidence that both sides shared a common perspective on race. Perhaps the most surprising name to appear on the conference program was Foy Valentine. Though Land viewed Valentine as a theological liberal on nearly all other subjects, he praised Valentine at the conference as a vital player in the Southern Baptist struggle to achieve a biblical view of race.[17] Land said in an interview that Valentine's liberalism on other issues often prevented Southern Baptists from seeing him as holding a credible conservative stance on race, but he received a conference invitation because he was "the irreplaceable person" when it came to advocating a thoroughly biblical vision of equality and justice.[18] In his conference address, Valentine told how the gospel message shaped his opinions on racial justice. Valentine also argued that the gospel required the eradication of both personal racism and systemic racism.[19] Lynn Clayton, a moderate, former trustee at the commission and editor of Louisiana's *Baptist Message*, said in his conference address that conservative theology should not be wrongly confused with a desire to conserve the racial status quo. "We must not give in to falling prey to the misconception that conservative theology necessitates being conservative in bringing about racial equality and being compassionate to people in need socially, politically, or any other way," Clayton said.[20]

Conservatives on the program echoed the same sentiments. Jerry Sutton, a Nashville pastor who later served as a Southern Baptist Convention

16. Marv Knox, "CLC Panelist Advocates Inclusion, Not Restitution," Christian Life Commission news release, 17 January 1989.

17. Land, interview by author, 11 June 2008.

18. Land, interview by author, 11 June 2008.

19. Foy Valentine, "Reflections on a Journey Through the Racial Crisis," 9–13 in *Proceedings of Southern Baptists and Race: A Conference Sponsored by the Christian Life Commission of the Southern Baptist Convention, First Baptist Church, Nashville, Tennessee, January 16–17, 1989.*

20. Lynn P. Clayton, "Race Relations: A Historical Perspective From the Editor of a State Baptist Paper," 16–21 in *Proceedings of Southern Baptists and Race: A Conference Sponsored by the Christian Life Commission of the Southern Baptist Convention, First Baptist Church, Nashville, Tennessee, January 16–17, 1989.*

vice president, urged conference attendees to fight cultural racism. While overt, personal racism is largely gone, cultural racism is still an ingrained worldview for Southern Baptists, he said. Believers eradicate cultural racism by adopting a biblical worldview, including proper views of man, love for neighbor, and Christ's ministry of reconciliation, according to Sutton.[21] When Land addressed the conference, he equated the advances of the civil rights movement with the standards of racial justice required by the gospel. Prejudice is a "sin problem" and "a consequence of the fallen, sinful heart," Land said.[22] Martin Luther King Jr. combated racism effectively because he understood it as a spiritual problem that could not be solved apart from spiritual solutions, Land said.[23] The famous 1963 "I Have a Dream" speech was, Land said, an appeal to the same conservative evangelical doctrines Southern Baptists taught their children: "For what was Dr. King doing, but appealing to the truth I had imbibed in Sunday School? 'Red and yellow, black and white, They are precious in His sight. Jesus loves the little children of the world.'"[24] The secular media often misunderstood King, according to Land, because it failed to grasp his theological motivation.[25] Southern Baptists, motivated by the message of equality before Christ, must eradicate racism using both evangelism and crusades for social justice, he said.[26]

Land closed his address by proposing a series of resolutions on racial reconciliation. Among the resolutions were to establish "fraternal rather than paternal relationships" across racial boundaries, to repent of past bigotry and pray for those still within racism's "deadly clutches," and to witness to the devastating effects of racism on both "the persecutor and the persecuted."[27] Land also called on Southern Baptists "to urge their agencies and institutions to seek diligently to bring about greater

---

21. Jerry Sutton, "Theme Interpretation: The Bible Speaks on Race," 21–22 in *Proceedings of Southern Baptists and Race: A Conference Sponsored by the Christian Life Commission of the Southern Baptist Convention, First Baptist Church, Nashville, Tennessee, January 16–17, 1989.*

22. Richard D. Land, "The Racial Challenge and the Response of a Christian Ethicist," 39, in *Proceedings of Southern Baptists and Race: A Conference Sponsored by the Christian Life Commission of the Southern Baptist Convention, First Baptist Church, Nashville, Tennessee, January 16–17, 1989.*

23. Land, "The Racial Challenge and the Response of a Christian Ethicist," 39–40.

24. Land, "The Racial Challenge and the Response of a Christian Ethicist," 41.

25. Land, "The Racial Challenge and the Response of a Christian Ethicist," 40.

26. Land, "The Racial Challenge and the Response of a Christian Ethicist," 43.

27. Land, "The Racial Challenge and the Response of a Christian Ethicist," 43.

African-American representation at every level of Southern Baptist institutional life."[28] Two weeks following the conference, Christian Life Commission trustees adopted Land's resolutions for themselves.[29] At least some of the trustees apparently viewed the resolutions as connected to the Caine controversy. Following the vote, New Mexico trustee Richard Elkins asked Caine, "Considering your strong opinions on this subject, how can you serve on this commission?" Chairman Joe Atchison ruled Elkins out of order before Caine could respond, saying, "Our reply has been taken care of by this resolution." After the meeting, Caine did not speak to the media except to say that the vote for the resolutions was not unanimous, but "without a dissenting vote."[30] The obvious suggestion was the Caine did not vote for the resolutions.

In spite of Caine's disagreement, the rest of the conservative-controlled board continued to press for increased racial equality and justice. At a meeting later that same year, the commission approved a recommendation to produce an eight-page race relations action guide and mail it to every pastor in the Southern Baptist Convention to promote Race Relations Sunday. The commission also recommended that another race conference be held in late 1990.[31] The conference ended up on the schedule for mid-1991 and eventually was changed to a private consultation involving eighteen commission guests and staff members.[32] Despite its reduced scope and size, the consultation made some bold requests of the convention and its president, Morris Chapman of Wichita Falls, Texas. The consultation asked Chapman "prayerfully to consider appointing a multi-ethnic advisory committee to assist him and/or the Committee on Nominations to

28. Land, "The Racial Challenge and the Response of a Christian Ethicist," 43.

29. "Minutes of the Called Meeting of the Christian Life Commission of the Southern Baptist Convention, January 30–31, 1989," p. 7, Box 5, Folder 3, Christian Life Commission Minutes.

30. Ray Waddle, "Baptists Vow Racial Justice to Quiet Critics," *Tennessean*, 31 January 1989, 1A, 4A.

31. "Minutes of the Annual Meeting of the Christian Life Commission of the Southern Baptist Convention, September 12–13, 1989," pp. 7–8, Box 5, Folder 4, Christian Life Commission Minutes.

32. Memo from Richard Land to Christian Life Commission staff, 21 June 1990, "ERLC/CLC: Conferences & Consultations, Race Relations Consultation, 25th anniversary, Nashville, TN, 1991" Folder, Christian Life Commission Records. See also list of consultation participants in same folder. Louis Moore, "Minority Advisory Committee Suggested by Consultation," Christian Life Commission news release, 25 April 1991, Box 5, Folder 5, Christian Life Commission Minutes.

help achieve ... significant (more than token) multi-ethnic representation" on convention boards and professional staffs.[33] Consultation participants pointed out what they believed was a lack of racial minorities in key denominational leadership positions but did not establish precise numerical goals for minority representation. In addition, the consultation asked each convention agency to establish a mentorship program to "develop ethnic and/or African American persons for leadership positions," urged Southern Baptists to develop a greater appreciation for the racial diversity in their denomination, and suggested that the Christian Life Commission continue to hold periodic race consultations. Like their moderate counterparts had done for decades, the conservative-led consultation also reaffirmed Southern Baptists' commitment "to take the gospel to every person in the world regardless of racial/ethnic identity."[34]

The year 1992 brought racial tension to America when a group of Los Angeles police officers was acquitted of criminal charges after beating African-American Rodney King. Frustrated minorities rioted in response to the verdict and committed violence of their own against whites. Land responded to the riots with a statement criticizing people on both sides of the conflict. He "was sickened" by the Rodney King beating and believed the officers should have been convicted of criminal wrongdoing. On the other hand, he said he was "just as sickened" by the racial violence in the streets of Los Angeles after the verdict. Once again, Land argued that racism stemmed ultimately from man's fallen nature and that spiritual solutions were the only hope of eliminating racism: "We Christians have a special responsibility to remind our society that racism, as well as other problems, will not be solved without spiritual solutions."[35] Encouraging legislative and judicial remedies to alter *de jure* racism, Land argued that *de facto* racism was a matter of the heart that could not be solved apart from spiritual regeneration. "The ultimate answer to the plague of racism," he said, "is not Black Power, or White Power, but Gospel Power."[36]

The next two years brought more of the same—Land and the commission advocating racial justice based on their conservative convictions. Land reported to the commission's trustees in 1993 an unprecedented response to

---

33. Moore, "Minority Advisory Committee Suggested by Consultation."

34. Moore, "Minority Advisory Committee Suggested by Consultation."

35. Richard D. Land, "Racism," Christian Life Commission news release, 26 May 1992, "RACE: Southern Baptist Actions, 1990–94," Christian Life Commission Records.

36. Land, "Racism."

recently published literature, including materials promoting Race Relations Sunday. Literature sales were up 33 percent from the same period during the previous year.[37] In 1994 the commission adopted the advice of its own consultation and set a goal of increased minority representation on the staff and trustee board. Land told the commission that by 2001 he hoped to have "a more ethnically and sexually (gender) diverse program staff, support staff, and trustee board."[38] Land had already taken one step toward that goal by hiring Clarice Dixon to work for the commission. Though Land did not realize it at the time of her hiring, Dixon was the first African-American to work in the Southern Baptist Convention building in a non-custodial role.[39] Also at the commission's 1994 annual meeting, staff member Ben Mitchell expressed his hope that in the coming year the commission could produce "an analysis of the different types of racial reconciliation programs available to Southern Baptists" and how churches could use them to "deal with deep-seated racism and subconscious racism." Mitchell additionally hoped to produce a video showing Southern Baptists how to celebrate cultural and ethnic diversity without degenerating into cultural relativism.[40]

Throughout the late 1980s and early 1990s, the Christian Life Commission fought to show that its racial advocacy was consistent with a conservative theological viewpoint. "We had too many Southern Baptists," Land said, "who thought this [race] was a liberal issue, thought it was something we shouldn't be talking about."[41] Such a perception stemmed from the fact that for several decades prior to Land's arrival, the Christian Life Commission blended racial advocacy with other activities many conservative Southern Baptists perceived as displays of liberalism. For Land as well as for rank-and-file conservatives, past speakers at the commission's conferences and meetings advanced theological liberalism. Joseph Fletcher, the father of situational ethics; Sarah Weddington, a pro-choice lawyer who argued *Roe v. Wade* before the Supreme Court; former Democratic presidential

37. "Minutes of the Semi-Annual Meeting, Christian Life Commission, Southern Baptist Convention," March 4–5, 1993, pp. 1, 4, Box 6, Folder 1, Christian Life Commission Minutes.

38. "Minutes of the Annual Meeting of the Christian Life Commission, Southern Baptist Convention," September 13–14, 1994, p. 3, Box 6, Folder 2, Christian Life Commission Minutes.

39. Land, interview by author, 11 June 2008.

40. "Minutes of the Annual Meeting of the Christian Life Commission, Southern Baptist Convention," September 13–14, 1994, 6.

41. Land, interview by author, 11 June 2008.

candidates George McGovern and Ted Kennedy; and abortion rights activist Marian Wright Eddleman were among speakers who suggested to Land that Valentine's Christian Life Commission was out of step with the conservatism of most Southern Baptists.[42] To overcome the perception that racial justice was a cause advocated only by liberals, Land insisted it was "an issue of right and wrong" rather than "an issue of right and left."[43]

To a significant degree, Land succeeded in his quest to show that racial justice mixed well with conservative theology. Moderates and conservatives alike admitted that he drew his ideas from a conservative theological framework and that he genuinely seemed to care about the race issue. David P. Gushee, a participant in one of Land's race consultations who later identified with moderate Baptists, admitted, "Land really does care about the race issue. I mean, I'm convinced that he does, and I've almost never heard him speak publicly in which he does not mention it."[44] Hankins, who identified himself as a moderate Southern Baptist, admitted after historical scrutiny that Land did in fact make freedom to move forward on the race issue a condition of his appointment as executive director.[45] Larry McSwain commended Land for his work leading up to the 1995 racial reconciliation resolution.[46] But still, moderates were not without complaint on Land's handling of the race issue. While some moderates favored affirmative action, Land argued that it was a form of race prejudice and fundamentally wrong.[47] Parham argued that conservatives' willingness to nominate Caine for a second term on the commission after his racist statements showed a glaring deficiency in their ability to bring about racial justice.[48] James Dunn argued that Land's affiliation with the Republican Party harmed his ability to speak about racial justice effectively.[49]

---

42. Land, interview by author, 11 June 2008. On Land's perception of the Christian Life Commission's former liberalism, see also Sutton, *A Matter of Conviction*, 279.

43. Land, interview by author, 11 June 2008.

44. *Oral Memoirs of David P. Gushee*, interview by Barry Hankins, 16 June 1999, Religion and Culture Project, Baylor University Institute for Oral History, Waco, Texas, 2003.

45. Hankins, *Uneasy in Babylon*, 243.

46. Larry L. McSwain, telephone interview by author, digital recording, 5 September 2008.

47. See Hankins, *Uneasy in Babylon*, 263; Land, interview by author, 6 June 2008.

48. Robert Parham, "The History of the Baptist Center for Ethics," in Shurden, *The Struggle for the Soul of the SBC*, 211.

49. James Dunn, telephone interview by author, digital recording, 22 August 2008.

Other Conservatives on Race

Land and the Christian Life Commission were not the only conservatives taking action for racial justice during the denominational controversy. Others acted similarly and did so based on their conservative theology. One prominent opportunity for conservatives to display their convictions on race came when in 1992 convention president Ed Young appointed a Multi-Ethnic Advisory Study Group to help increase the ethnic diversity on denominational boards and develop a strategy for evangelism and church planting among minority groups.[50] The group, which consisted of Anglos, African Americans, Hispanics, Asians, and other ethnic minorities, met twice during late 1992 and early 1993 then presented a report.[51] The report expressed concern over the low number of black and other ethnic members of Southern Baptist Convention boards and committees and argued that belief in the gospel demanded that the denomination do better. The report concluded:

> While the Southern Baptist Convention is the most ethnically diverse evangelical group in America and is to be lauded for tremendous ethnic growth, if we are to effectively penetrate the multitude of ethnic and Black cultures in America with the Gospel, the Boards and Agencies of the Southern Baptist Convention must plan a unified strategy.[52]

The report began by lauding the Southern Baptist Convention's growth among racial and ethnic minorities since the beginning of the conservative resurgence. Between 1980 and 1991, congregations speaking a language other than English increased by 162 percent, baptisms among those churches increased by more than 12,000, and total membership increased by more than 200,000.[53] Citing church researcher Lyle Schaller, the report argued that the convention achieved such growth by evangelizing minorities rather than utilizing the less successful technique of bringing them

---

50. James Semple and George Harris to all Multi-Ethnic Advisory Study Group members, 9 November 1992, Box 18, Folder 5, H. Edwin Young Papers.

51. James Semple and George Harris to all Multi-Ethnic Advisory Study Group members, 9 November 1992, Box 18, Folder 5, H. Edwin Young Papers.

52. "Report of the Multi-Ethnic Advisory Study Group," 29 January 1993, p. 8, Box 18, Folder 5, H. Edwin Young Papers.

53. "Report of the Multi-Ethnic Advisory Study Group," 4.

into denominational leadership through affirmative action.[54] Despite the laudable efforts in minority evangelism, the report said, Southern Baptists would fail to reach millions of ethnic minorities in America if they did not increase the number of minorities in denominational leadership.[55] In 1992–1993, only thirty-two (3.26 percent) of the denomination's 982 total committee, commission, and board members were ethnic minorities.[56] The greatest number of ethnic members on any board was five at both the Home Mission Board and the American Seminary Commission. Ten boards had no ethnic members, including all six of the denomination's seminaries. "The Sunday School Board which supplies most of the programming for our churches has only one ethnic person on its 93-member Board," the report said. "The Stewardship Commission has one ethnic member on its Board and the Radio-Television Commission has two. The 68-member Committee on Nominations for Southern Baptist Convention entities has no ethnic or Black member."[57] Apart from remedying these deficiencies, Southern Baptists could not minister effectively, the report said: "There are several agencies that have almost no ethnic and Black representation where the ethnic and Black contextualization is vitally needed if we are to provide for the needs of ethnic and Black churches."[58]

To remedy these deficiencies, the report recommended that ethnic minorities be added to the Southern Baptist Convention annual meeting program and to every board, committee, and commission. Convention agencies should produce contextualized materials for ethnic and black churches, the report said, and the denomination should form an "Ethnic and Black Task Force" to help formulate a united strategy to involve Southern Baptists of all races in carrying out the Great Commission.[59] Appended to the report was a paper by study group member Daniel Sanchez, a professor at Southwestern Seminary. Sanchez underscored an essential component to reaching America for Christ, tapping qualified ethnic persons for leadership at the associational, state convention, and national levels.[60]

54. "Report of the Multi-Ethnic Advisory Study Group," 4.
55. "Report of the Multi-Ethnic Advisory Study Group," 4.
56. "Report of the Multi-Ethnic Advisory Study Group," 7.
57. "Report of the Multi-Ethnic Advisory Study Group," 7–8.
58. "Report of the Multi-Ethnic Advisory Study Group," 8.
59. "Report of the Multi-Ethnic Advisory Study Group," 8–9.
60. Daniel R. Sanchez, "The Challenge of American Diversity," appendix to the Report of the Multi-Ethnic Advisory Study Group," Box 18, Folder 5, H. Edwin Young

Richard Land and Modern Conservatives on Race

In addition to Young, at least two other conservative Southern Baptist Convention presidents pressed for racial advance. Jerry Vines, pastor of First Baptist Church in Jacksonville, Florida, published a sermon on racial inclusiveness as part of the Christian Life Commission's Race Relations Sunday materials for 1993. Taking Acts 10 as his text, Vines based his argument for racial equality on the equal need of all persons for the message of salvation by faith in Jesus Christ. He argued that the doctrine of redemption required those who believe it to treat equally people of all races. "The gospel is meant for all the world," Vines wrote. "No narrow, exclusive message is worthy of our Lord." The openness of the gospel invitation eliminated the possibility that God could view one race as superior to another, he argued: "There is no inferior race. God's grace is open to all. The blood of Christ extends its cleansing power to all people everywhere." The doctrine of the church, Vines said, also eliminated the possibility of prejudice because all believers enjoy equal standing in the congregation: "The walls which divide people today are brought down by the gospel." If God loved all people and offered the gospel to them all, His followers must do likewise, Vines concluded. "We must ask God to rid our hearts of any prejudice or wrong spirit," he said. "We must not allow narrow-minded views to keep us from carrying the gospel to people everywhere."[61] According to Land, Vines lived out the message he preached. First Baptist Jacksonville "is a significantly multi-racial church," Land said, because it practiced colorblind evangelism since at least the 1970s.[62] Jimmy Draper, the third conservative president elected during the controversy, also promoted racial inclusiveness. During Draper's presidency, Southern Baptists targeted ethnic minorities in a campaign to evangelize major American cities, planned to develop "Ethnic Leadership Development Centers" to train ethnic minorities for leadership, and experienced significant growth among minorities, according to the American Baptist News Service.[63] Draper's concern for multiracial ministry continued a decade later when Young announced the formation of the Multi-Ethnic Advisory Group. In

---

Papers.

61. Jerry Vines, "Suggested Sermon for Race Relations Sunday: Stop the Sermon!" 1993, "RACE: Southern Baptist Actions, 1990–94" Folder, Christian Life Commission Records.

62. Land, interview by author, 11 June 2008.

63. Ray Jennings, "As Tensions and Turmoil Plague Southern Baptists ABC Oldtimers Ask: Is This a Replay of the Forties?," *American Baptist News Service*, 1983, Folder 9, James T. Draper Jr. Papers.

a letter, Draper, then president of the Baptist Sunday School Board, commended Young and requested to be involved in the group. "Please know that I feel very strongly that we ought to be involved in such an advisory committee," Draper wrote. "Gene Mims, on my staff, is working in the area of ethnics and could be a great resource person for such a group. I hope you can include Gene, or someone, in that advisory committee."[64]

Despite the strides conservatives took toward racial inclusiveness, they also made missteps. One of the most prominent missteps occurred during the presidency of Bailey Smith, pastor of First Southern Baptist Church in Del City, Oklahoma. Twice in 1980, Smith made comments about Jewish people at which many took offense. Preaching at the National Affairs Briefing in Dallas, a conference that sought to involve evangelicals in American politics, Smith argued that God does not hear the prayers of any Jew who has not trusted Jesus Christ for his salvation:

> I'm telling you all other Gods besides Jehovah and his son Jesus Christ are strange Gods. It's interesting to me at great political battles how you have a Protestant to pray, and a Catholic to pray, and then you have a Jew to pray. With all due respect to those dear people, my friend God Almighty does not hear the prayer of a Jew. For how in the world can God hear the prayer of a man who says that Jesus Christ is not the true Messiah? It is blasphemous.[65]

The second statement occurred weeks later in a sermon at Smith's church, in which Smith commented that Jews have "funny looking noses."[66] Smith explained in a statement that a Jewish friend teased him before the worship service about a bald spot on Smith's head, saying, "Preacher, you've got a bald spot, and we Jews have funny noses." In turn, Smith said, he teased the friend during the sermon, which dealt with Jews being the "true people of God," by repeating the friend's comment about Jewish people's noses. The media "tried to create a story when there is none," Smith said.[67]

---

64. James T. Draper Jr. to H. Edwin Young, 28 July 1992, Box 18, Folder 5, H. Edwin Young Papers.

65. Transcript of statement by Bailey Smith 22 August 1980 at the National Affairs Briefing sponsored by the Religious Roundtable, Reunion Arena, Dallas, Texas, Box 1, Folder 32, Bailey Smith Papers.

66. Jim Newton, "Smith Expresses Regret, Condemns Anti-Semitism," *Baptist Press*, 19 December 1980, pp. 1–2, Box 1, Folder 5, Bailey Smith Papers.

67. Statement by Smith about the funny noses comment, Box 1, Folder 32, Bailey Smith Papers.

Unfortunately for Smith, others disagreed with his claim that the comments about Jews were insignificant. Moderate opponents claimed that the remarks were examples of racism. J. William Angell, professor of religion at Wake Forest University, repudiated the comments and argued that Smith "has joined himself to the nefarious company of Haman, Hitler, Arafat and Khomeini." Reasonable people should not try to reason with Smith, Angell said, because "logic and evidence do not influence such self-righteous bigots."[68] The faculty of Southeastern Baptist Theological Seminary joined the outcry by adopting a statement of "reaffirmation of our love and support for Jews." Without referencing Smith by name, the statement obviously came in response to his comments.[69] The outcry reached such a crescendo that Smith decided to meet with Jewish leaders in New York. After the meeting, Smith released a statement expressing regret for any hurt he caused the Jewish community and condemning anti-Semitism. Though Smith did not back down from this theological claims about faith in Jesus being the only avenue of access to God, he agreed to a working relationship with Jewish leaders in order to improve communication between Baptists and Jews.[70]

Smith and his conservative allies explained that the statement about God not hearing the prayers of a Jew was theological rather than racial in nature. Adrian Rogers, the first conservative to win the Southern Baptist Convention presidency during the controversy, attended the National Affairs Briefing where Smith made the statement and defended his friend. "[Smith] then said, while expressing his deep love and respect for the Jewish people, that God does not hear the prayers of Jews who reject Jesus, the Messiah. In saying that he was emphasizing the uniqueness of our faith," Rogers explained, adding, "Dr. Smith was not talking racially."[71] Smith echoed Rogers' explanation in one letter to a critic. "I was not speaking of the Jews as a race," he wrote, "but as a faith."[72] Though many remained upset at both of

---

68. J. William Angell to Rabbi Solomon S. Bernards, 12 September 1980, Box 1, Folder 19, Bailey Smith Papers.

69. "Seminary Faculty Reaffirms "Love, Support for Jews,'" *Baptist Press*, 6 November 1980, p. 4, Box 1, Folder 5, Bailey Smith Papers.

70. Newton, "Smith Expresses Regret, Condemns, Anti-Semitism." "News Release," 9 February 1981, Box 1, Folder 32, Bailey Smith Papers.

71. Adrian Rogers, "Pastor's Paragraphs," *Bellevue Messenger*, 31 October 1980, pp. 1, 3, Box 1, Folder 32, Bailey Smith Papers.

72. Bailey Smith to Shepard Jerome, 28 October 1980, Box 1, Folder 33, Bailey Smith Papers.

Smith's statements, for conservatives Smith's statements highlighted the centrality of the gospel in uniting all ethnic groups. They based racial equality in the exclusive claims of the Christian gospel to be the only and equal remedy for all persons and all races. The statements had racist overtones, but they reflected a rejection of non-Christian beliefs in favor of a gospel intended for every tongue, tribe, people, and race.

A second misstep on race aroused criticism from within the conservative ranks. When Young named the Multi-Ethnic Advisory Study Group in 1992, the group's co-chairs were both Anglo males, James Semple and George Harris. Three staff members at the Christian Life Commission thought it odd that a group tasked with bringing minority leadership into the Southern Baptist Convention did not itself include minority leadership. The staff members wrote their concerns in a memo to Land:

> We are certain that President Young has the best of intentions and that Drs. Harris and Semple are fine men. However, to establish a multi-ethnic advisory committee without an ethnic co-chair seems unwise at best. Also, since Black Southern Baptists have organized (African-American Baptist Fellowship), it would seem prudent to have representation from their group as well as from the Hispanic fellowship.[73]

The staff members added that "we are very concerned about the potential for bad press and for a strained relationship among the members of the group."[74] Land agreed with the concerns and passed them along to Young in a gentle but clearly worded letter. He asked regarding Harris and Semple, "Does making them co-chairs of the *multi*-ethnic advisory group run the risk of negatively impacting the work of the group?" Land suggested it would be well "for one of the chairmen to quietly drop out for the good of the cause." "How the remainder of the group is constituted will be extremely critical," Land said. "The committee must represent ethnic leadership from across the convention."[75] To Land's disappointment, Young decided not to replace either of the white co-chairs.

---

73. C. Ben Mitchell to Richard Land, 12 October 1992, Box 18, Folder 5, H. Edwin Young Papers.

74. C. Ben Mitchell to Richard Land, 12 October 1992, Box 18, Folder 5, H. Edwin Young Papers.

75. Richard Land to H. Edwin Young, 3 November 1992, Box 18, Folder 5, H. Edwin Young Papers.

Richard Land and Modern Conservatives on Race

Conservatives made an effort to find qualified minorities to fill leadership positions. This was true especially in the seminaries, where three presidents asked African-American leader Gary Frost to provide them with lists of qualified professors who were black.[76] In several cases, conservatives not only investigated potential black seminary professors, but hired them. Whether a black professor remained employed under the conservative regime, however, depended on his theological views. R. Logan Carson, a black theology professor at Southeastern Seminary, was a theological and political conservative with the strong support of conservative president Paige Patterson.[77] Similarly, T. Vaughn Walker, an African-American professor at Southern Seminary, was hired under a moderate administration but remained at the seminary under R. Albert Mohler Jr.'s administration. As the seminary transitioned to conservative control, Walker felt nervous about his future employment status before realizing that he shared most of the theological beliefs of the new leadership.[78] Professor Timothy James Johnson did not fare as well at Southern, and the difficulty was theological rather than racial. The seminary's moderate leaders recruited Johnson in 1991 with the promise of recommendation for tenure as soon as he completed his dissertation. When Mohler assumed the presidency though, he gave Johnson an eighteen-month contract and made no commitment to recommend him for tenure. Johnson acknowledged that the point at issue was largely theological. He was not conservative in his handling of the Bible. He also argued that an individual's sexual preference did not matter as long as he trusted Christ for salvation. Johnson's theological differences with the conservative administration resulted in his leaving Southern for Roberts Wesleyan College.[79] Emmanuel McCall was another African American turned away by conservative leaders, but not for racial reasons. When power shifted in the denomination, McCall's personal affiliation with some in the moderate camp caused conservatives to label him a theological liberal. Though McCall said he held conservative views on the Bible, he recognized that conservatives perceived him to be a liberal. That perception resulted in McCall being shunned by convention leaders and identifying himself

---

76. Hankins, *Uneasy in Babylon*, 254.

77. Hankins, *Uneasy in Babylon*, 267–68.

78. T. Vaughn Walker, interview by author, digital recording, Louisville, Kentucky, 17 April 2008.

79. Hankins, *Uneasy in Babylon*, 265–66.

with the Cooperative Baptist Fellowship.[80] Conservatives were more concerned with theology than race.

The Racial Reconciliation Resolution

As Southern Baptists approached their convention's sesquicentennial anniversary in 1995, they knew they needed to say something about the denomination's racist past of defending slavery and supporting legal segregation. That something ended up being a resolution "On Racial Reconciliation on the One Hundred and Fiftieth Anniversary of the Southern Baptist Convention" adopted at the convention's 1995 annual meeting in Atlanta. The resolution advocated racial justice based on a conservative reading of the Bible.

The idea for the 1995 resolution began to take shape as early as 1989, and a chief architect of the idea at that early date was Land. In preparation for the 1989 race conference, Land held a private consultation, in which he discussed race relations with a racially mixed group of Southern Baptists. At that consultation, Land recalled, a representative of the black participants said, "You need to understand how badly you have hurt us. We don't mean you personally. We mean white Christians. It's one thing to be discriminated against and ill treated by whites. It's another thing to be discriminated against and ill treated by fellow Christians."[81] Land thought about the man's statement and realized that Southern Baptists had never apologized or acknowledged the convention's complicity in perpetuating racism. Although the convention could not repent on behalf of its forebears, it could and should express regret, apologize, and ask for forgiveness, Land thought. "And so I began to look for an appropriate moment and venue to do that," Land said, adding, "I didn't tell anybody else. I just started plotting a strategy of when and where we could do it."[82] From that time forward, Land's public addresses and statements contained ideas that eventually found their way into the 1995 resolution. The resolutions Land

---

80. Emmanuel McCall, telephone interview by author, digital recording, 24 April 2008.

81. Land, interview by author, 11 June 2008. Precise quotation of Christian Life Commission race consultations is not provided because such consultations are "off the record" and have no official minutes. Commission rules stipulate that recounting of consultations must not include attribution of quotations to specific individuals.

82. Land, interview by author, 11 June 2008. Similarly, Land recounted his earliest plans for a resolution in Sutton, *A Matter of Conviction*, 280.

proposed at the end of his address during the 1989 race conference echoed themes that also emerged in 1995. Both statements called on Southern Baptists to "repent" of past bigotry. Both recognized that Southern Baptists did not always stand for racial justice. Both recognized that racism harmed the persecutor and the persecuted. And as the 1995 resolution denounced racism "in all its forms," Land's earlier statement denounced racism "whenever and wherever it occurs."[83] Land continued to contemplate when Southern Baptists should issue a major statement, and by 1992 he had the idea to adopt a statement during the convention's sesquicentennial meeting.[84] Through the early 1990s, he sounded a steady stream of themes that found their way into the 1995 resolution. The 1991 Christian Life Commission consultation on race, for example, reaffirmed the denomination's commitment "to take the gospel to every person in the world regardless of racial/ethnic identity"—a statement similar to the 1995 language, "we pledge our commitment to the Great Commission task of making disciples of all people." When early 1995 arrived, Gary Frost brought Land a copy of a failed resolution submitted to the 1994 annual meeting of the convention. Upon receiving the resolution, Land assembled a panel of eight whites and eight blacks to draft a resolution for the 1995 annual meeting.[85] The Southern Baptist Convention's resolution ended up nearly identical to the resolution produced by that consultation.[86]

Land, however, was not the only Southern Baptist promoting racial reconciliation leading up to the sesquicentennial anniversary. Jim Henry, pastor of First Baptist Church in Orlando, Florida, was elected Southern Baptist Convention president in 1994 and spoke six months prior to the 1995 annual meeting about the need to repent of racial prejudice. At an interdenominational prayer and fasting conference, Henry said he had come to a point in his Christian walk where he had to face his own prejudice. Though he admitted to shrugging off complaints of racism in the past, he announced his conviction that Christians, beginning with Southern

---

83. Land, "The Racial Challenge and the Response of a Christian Ethicist," 43; "On Racial Reconciliation on the 150th Anniversary of the Southern Baptist Convention," *1995 Southern Baptist Convention Annual*, 80–81, in "SBC Annuals."

84. Land, interview by author, 11 June 2008.

85. Hankins, *Uneasy in Babylon*, 244.

86. "Resolution on Racial Reconciliation on the 150th Anniversary of the Southern Baptist Convention, final draft, May 22, 1995, "ERLC/CLC: Conferences & Consultations, Race Relations Consultation, Nashville, Tennessee, 1995" Folder, Christian Life Commission Records.

Baptists, needed to repent of racism and prejudice. "I believe there is something to that," he said of complaints from ethnic minorities. "I think the sooner the Christian community deals with that and confesses it, the more bridges will be built and the more walls torn down—in healing, reaching across all colors, brothers and sisters, in fellowship and reaching the lost in our churches."[87] Henry, like Land and the moderate leaders before him, seized on the theme of evangelism to combat prejudice. Frost, a convention vice president and pastor of Rising Star Baptist Church in Youngstown, Ohio, spoke of a similar conviction during the Christian Life Commission's annual seminar in 1995. Racism, he said, made the fight to evangelize the inner city nearly impossible. Frost argued:

> The paralyzing sin of pride manifested in racism has in many cases rendered the witness of the corporate church almost totally ineffective. Until this racism is biblically and publicly dealt with amongst believers, there is no hope of a sweeping revival of the magnitude that is necessary to save our cities.[88]

With conservatives of all races supporting the reconciliation effort, momentum built as June approached. Leading up to the 1995 annual meeting, Henry felt concerned that the race issue would be a dark spot amid what looked to be an otherwise upbeat convention. So he agreed with Land that the resolutions committee should bring the racial reconciliation resolution to the convention floor before any celebration of the one hundred and fiftieth anniversary.[89]

When the 1995 resolution came to the floor, it was evident that conservatives were not the only people with a hand in shaping it. Some of the resolution's language echoed that used in moderate Baptist statements on race during the previous five years. The echoes were not the result of moderate theology on the part of the resolutions committee. On the contrary, moderates drew their thinking on race from similar theological commitments and thus issued statements with which conservatives generally agreed. In several instances the Southern Baptist Convention resolution used precisely the same language as statements from more moderate groups. For example, the 1993 "Birmingham Confession" by the

87. Ken Walker, "Henry Urges Repentance for Sins of 'Exculsivism,'" *Baptist Press* 15 December 1994, Box 10, Folder 4, Jim Henry Papers.

88. Dwayne Hastings, "Racism Stifles Church's Witness in Inner Cities, Frost Says," *Light*, May/June 1994, 14.

89. Land, interview by author, 11 June 2008. Hankins, *Uneasy in Babylon*, 245.

Baptist Peace Fellowship of North America, speaking of past evils, used the phrase, "We continue to reap a bitter harvest."[90] The exact same phrase appeared in the Southern Baptist Convention resolution. The "Birmingham Confession" also said to African Americans, "We ask for your forgiveness. In doing so, we acknowledge that our own healing is at stake."[91] Almost identically, the 1995 resolution said, "we ask for forgiveness from our African-American brothers and sisters, acknowledging that our own healing is at stake."[92] The "Declaration of Racial Repentance," drafted by a committee of Southern Baptist directors of mission in 1994, also exhibited striking similarities to the 1995 resolution. The declaration used a phrase very similar to the Baptist Peace Fellowship's language when it said, "We continue to reap the bitter harvest" of the inequality that resulted from slavery.[93] The directors of missions apologized for "perpetuating individual and systematic racism," which the 1995 resolution echoed closely with its apology for "perpetuating individual and systemic racism."[94] The "Declaration of Racial Repentance" additionally said racism "discredits the Gospel we proclaim."[95] The 1995 resolution struck a similar note when it said racism wrongly leads some Southern Baptists to believe "that racial prejudice and discrimination are compatible with the Gospel."[96] A "Declaration of Repentance and Rededication" by the Historical Commission of the Southern Baptist Convention was a third example of a statement by a more moderate group that ended up being quoted precisely in the 1995 resolution. The Historical Commission said, "The racism ... which plagues our culture today is tied to the past."[97] The Southern Baptist Convention

90. Baptist Peace Fellowship of North America, "The Birmingham Confession," 1993, "Race Relations – SBC 1995 Resolution" Folder, Baptist History File.

91. Baptist Peace Fellowship of North America, "The Birmingham Confession," 1993, "Race Relations – SBC 1995 Resolution" Folder, Baptist History File.

92. "On Racial Reconciliation on the 150th Anniversary of the Southern Baptist Convention."

93. Delroy A. Red-Salmon et al., "Declaration of Racial Repentance," "Race Relations – SBC 1995 Resolution" Folder, Baptist History File.

94. Delroy A. Red-Salmon et al., "Declaration of Racial Repentance"; "On Racial Reconciliation on the 150th Anniversary of the Southern Baptist Convention."

95. Delroy A. Red-Salmon et al., "Declaration of Racial Repentance."

96. "On Racial Reconciliation on the 150th Anniversary of the Southern Baptist Convention."

97. Historical Commission of the Southern Baptist Convention, "Declaration of Repentance and Rededication," 9 May 1995, "Race Relations – SBC 1995 Resolution" Folder, Baptist History File.

resolution proclaimed almost identically, "the racism which yet plagues our culture today is inextricably tied to the past."[98] On the issue of race the two sides operated out of similar theological convictions.

In addition to the obvious reliance on source documents, many of the phrases in the 1995 resolution appeared to be original. Those original phrases relied on evangelical theology derived from a literal reading of the Bible. Drawing on the doctrines of creation and salvation, the resolution said, "The Scriptures teach that Eve is the mother of all living (Genesis 3:20), and that God shows no partiality, but in every nation whoever fears him and works righteousness is accepted by him (Acts 10:34–35), and that God has made from one blood every nation of men to dwell on the face of the earth (Acts 17:26)."[99] Again applying the same two doctrines, the resolution affirmed "that every human life is sacred" and "of equal and immeasurable worth" and that "with respect to salvation through Christ, there is neither Jew nor Greek, there is neither slave nor free, there is neither male nor female, for (we) are all one in Christ Jesus."[100] One goal of racial reconciliation, according to the resolution, was for "people from every tribe and nation" to "stand together in restored family union as joint-heirs with Christ."[101] Such sentiments expressed the same doctrines that launched Southern Baptists in their journey toward racial equality more than forty years earlier, doctrines shared by nearly all who made significant contributions to the convention's view of race relations.

Conclusion

In the 1980s and early 1990s, conservatives gained control of the Southern Baptist Convention. When Richard Land was named executive director of the Christian Life Commission, moderates were rightly upset because they recognized that the agency would chart a new course.[102] In part their

---

98. "On Racial Reconciliation on the 150th Anniversary of the Southern Baptist Convention."

99. "On Racial Reconciliation on the 150th Anniversary of the Southern Baptist Convention."

100. "On Racial Reconciliation on the 150th Anniversary of the Southern Baptist Convention."

101. "On Racial Reconciliation on the 150th Anniversary of the Southern Baptist Convention."

102. Land, interview by author, 11 June 2008.

fears proved well founded. Land took the commission in a new direction on such issues as abortion, church-state separation, women's ordination, political concerns, and how to understand the Bible. But on the question of race, their fears never materialized. Land stayed the course that Foy Valentine and his moderate contemporaries had charted during the previous two decades. Drawing from a foundation of the doctrines of creation and salvation, Land and fellow conservatives across the denomination continued to advance the cause of race relations.

Chapter 8

Conclusion: The Way Forward

BETWEEN 1954 AND 1995, the Southern Baptist Convention shifted its position on race relations. The denomination that failed to challenge the Jim Crow status quo in late 1940s and early 1950s became by 1995 a denomination that apologized publicly for its racist past and gained the label of the most diverse religious denomination in America.[1] The change was gradual and multifaceted, but two catalysts brought it about. First, the social climate of the 1950s and 1960s caused Southern Baptists to rethink their views on race. Supreme Court rulings, the civil rights movement, and crises over school desegregation placed race relations on the front of every southerner's mind, including Southern Baptists. As Southern Baptists rethought the race issue, a second catalyst emerged. Leaders from a variety of ideological perspectives issued theological challenges that were consistent with Southern Baptists' conservative theology. The application of doctrines such as creation in the image of God and the universal offer of salvation in Christ gradually transformed segregationists into reluctant integrationists, and eventually into advocates for racial equality.

The decade prior to 1954 set the stage for this shift. Southern Baptists from across the theological spectrum advocated equality of the races, but most never considered the Bible's teachings on equality to be at odds with segregation. When the Supreme Court handed down its ruling in *Brown v. Board of Education*, the South's social climate changed and Southern

---

1. Wagner, *Your Spiritual Gifts Can Help Your Church Grow*, 202. More recently, Emmanuel McCall agreed with Wagner's assessment (McCall, *When All God's Children Get Together*, x).

Conclusion: The Way Forward

Baptists were forced to consider whether Scripture had anything to say about segregation and desegregation. Denominational leaders like Herschel Hobbs and W. A. Criswell began to see that the doctrines they long held required integration of churches. If all were welcome to receive salvation in Jesus, they reasoned, why should not all be welcome to join the church as well? The change in reasoning resulted in a change of practice. By the 1970s, many Southern Baptist churches welcomed African Americans into their memberships for the first time since Reconstruction.

The Christian Life Commission was one of the most important sources of theological prodding between the 1950s and the 1980s. Under the leadership of A. C. Miller and Foy Valentine, the commission gained a reputation for theological liberalism and on many occasions came under attack from the Southern Baptist rank and file. But on the issue of race, Valentine and his colleagues issued challenges consistent with the denomination's conservative theology. Living out the gospel taught in Scripture, they said, required granting equality to all races. The message sank in. Southern Baptists listened to the commission and civil rights gains began to materialize by the 1970s and 1980s.

The situation at Southern Baptist seminaries and colleges was similar. In the 1950s, social pressure mounted and trustees officially welcomed blacks into the seminaries. At each step in the integration of seminaries, administrators and trustees justified their actions with theology that resonated with conservative Southern Baptists. Such theological appeals continued to drive racial openness throughout the second half of the twentieth century as seminaries recruited black students and eventually launched courses in black church ministry. Seminaries met the greatest resistance when they moved away from evangelical theology and attempted to push their denomination with appeals based on theological liberalism. Similar patterns held at Southern Baptist colleges.

The reaction of black Baptists to the Southern Baptist Convention underscored the fact that conservative theology was consistent with racial progressiveness. Most black Baptists held conservative theology, like white Southern Baptists. But black Baptists frequently criticized Southern Baptists for not integrating more quickly. They reasoned that such theology led naturally to racial progress and did not understand why Southern Baptists failed to act consistently with the theology they professed to believe.

When denominational controversy erupted in the Southern Baptist Convention in the late 1980s and early 1990s, moderates and conservatives divided over myriad issues. Yet the two sides agreed on race relations, both displaying a willingness to press for equality and freedom for all. Such agreement existed because both sides accepted the theological basis of racial equality. Race relations remained far from perfect, but powerful theological arguments had built a consensus that controversy could not break. Any Southern Baptist who believed the Bible almost certainly also believed that churches, public facilities, and denominational agencies should be interracial.

Several implications arise from this study. First, it suggests that changing the Southern Baptist Convention requires appealing to the Bible. The denomination's shift on race relations, as well as the success of the conservative resurgence, showed that the most fruitful way to change Southern Baptists was to show them that the Bible required a change. Just as appeals to liberal theology or political expediency failed to move Southern Baptists in the civil rights era, appeals to pragmatism or modern philosophy are unlikely to move them today.

Second, this study suggests that the story which played out in the Southern Baptist Convention as a whole also played out in microcosm in thousands of Southern Baptist churches across the South. As David Chappell demonstrated, laypeople generally held on to segregation longer than did clergy across the South.[2] Cecil Sherman's experience at the First Baptist Church of Ashville, North Carolina, as well as K. Owen White's experience at the First Baptist Church of Houston exemplified that trend. Despite the slowness of some churches, however, such congregations as those of Herschel Hobbs and W. A. Criswell—and eventually the congregations of Sherman and White as well—showed that evangelical theology translated into racial progress at the local level. More research remains to be done, but it appears that challenging Baptists to live up to their biblical convictions had similar results in churches throughout the 1960s and 1970s.

Third, this study confirms the pervasiveness of sin in all people and organizations. It should humble Christians today to see how badly Southern Baptists missed the mark of racial justice even though they strove to apply God's Word to every area of their lives. Seeing the failures of well-intentioned Christians should open our own eyes to the prospect that our well-intentioned efforts at Christian service are touched by sin in ways we failed to imagine. The story of Southern Baptists and civil rights confirmed the prophet Jeremiah's statement, "The heart is deceitful above all things,

---

2. Chappell, *A Stone of Hope*, 131–35.

Conclusion: The Way Forward

and desperately sick; who can understand it?" (Jer 17:9). It is cause for thanksgiving though, that the story of Southern Baptists and civil rights also provided hope that looking to the Bible will eventually correct even the most deeply embedded patterns of sin.

The Southern Baptist Convention needs more progress in racial reconciliation. Though one in five Southern Baptist churches was non-Anglo by 2020, 85 percent of all Southern Baptist church members were Anglo.[3] In 2019, just 13 (0.3%) of the approximately 3,700 career missionaries serving with the International Mission Board were African American—a number Southern Baptist leaders hoped to increase.[4] Some black pastors within the convention have expressed frustration with the lack of African-American leaders at convention entities and in top elected positions (though they note Fred Luter, an African American, served as Southern Baptist Convention president from 2012 to 2014).[5] For all the progress, work remains to be done. If Southern Baptists are to complete the task of removing what two seminary professors have called "the stain of racism from the Southern Baptist Convention," the way forward must include a look back at methods that have worked.[6] Hopefully, this study represents a small step in that direction.

---

3. Roach, "Racial Reconciliation Is Not a 'Finished Project' 25 Years After Historic Resolution"; Fahmy, "7 Facts About Southern Baptists."

4. Roach, "Southern Baptists Have Only 13 African American Career Missionaries."

5. Roach, "Despite Racial Tensions, Black Southern Baptist Churches Still on the Rise."

6. Williams and Jones, *Removing the Stain of Racism from the Southern Baptist Convention*.

Bibliography

Allen, Catherine. *A Century to Celebrate: History of the Woman's Missionary Union*. Birmingham: Woman's Missionary Union, 1987.
Allen, Clifton J. Papers. Southern Baptist Historical Library and Archives, Nashville.
Allen, Jimmy. Papers. Southern Baptist Historical Library and Archives, Nashville.
Alvis, Joel L., Jr. *Religion and Race: Southern Presbyterians: 1946–1983*. Tuscaloosa: University of Alabama Press, 1994.
Ammerman, Nancy Tatom. *Baptist Battles: Social Change and Religious Conflict in the Southern Baptist Convention*. New Brunswick, NJ: Rutgers University Press, 1990.
———. "Southern Baptists and the New Christian Right." *Review of Religious Research* 32 (1991) 213–36.
———, ed. *Southern Baptists Observed: Multiple Perspectives on a Changing Denomination*. Knoxville: University of Tennessee Press, 1993.
Anderson, Margaret. *The Children of the South*. New York: Farrar, Strauss and Giroux, 1966.
Association of Theological Schools in the United States and Canada. *Fact Book on Theological Education 1980–1981*. Edited by Marvin J. Taylor. Vandalia, OH: Association of Theological Schools, 1981.
Bagwell, William. *School Desegregation in the Carolinas: Two Case Studies*. Columbia: University of South Carolina Press, 1972.
Bailey, Kenneth K. "The Post-Civil War Racial Separations in Southern Protestantism: Another Look." *Church History* 46 (1977) 453–73.
———. *Southern White Protestantism in the Twentieth Century*. New York: Harper & Row, 1964.
Baker, Robert A. *Tell the Generations Following: A History of Southwestern Baptist Theological Seminary, 1908–1983*. Nashville: Broadman, 1983.
Baptist History File. Southern Baptist Historical Library and Archives, Nashville.
Baptist Peace Fellowship of North America Records. Southern Baptist Historical Library and Archives, Nashville.
Barnette, Henlee. *Clarence Jordan: Turning Dreams into Deeds*. Greenville, SC: Smith & Helwys, 1992.
———. "Negro Students in Southern Baptist Seminaries." *Review and Expositor* 53 (1956) 207–10.
———. *A Pilgrimage of Faith: My Story*. Macon, GA: Mercer University Press, 2004.

Bibliography

———. "The Southern Baptist Theological Seminary and the Civil Rights Movement: From 1859–1952. Part One." *Review and Expositor* 90 (1993) 531–50.

———. "The Southern Baptist Theological Seminary and the Civil Rights Movement: The Visit of Martin Luther King, Jr. Part Two." *Review and Expositor* 93 (1996) 77–126.

Bartley, Numan V. *The New South, 1945–1980*. Baton Rouge: Louisiana State University Press, 1995.

———. *The Rise of Massive Resistance: Race and Politics in the South during the 1950s*. Baton Rouge: Louisiana State University Press, 1969.

Bass, Jack, and Walter DeVries. *The Transformation of Southern Politics: Social Change and Political Consequence Since 1945*. New York: Basic, 1976.

Beaver, R. Pierce, ed. *American Missions in Bicentennial Perspective*. Pasadena: William Carey Library, 1977.

Bebbington, David. *Evangelicalism in Modern Britain: A History from the 1730s to the 1980s*. London: Unwin Hyman, 1989.

Belew, Wendell. *A Missions People: The Southern Baptist Pilgrimage*. Nashville: Broadman, 1989.

Bennett, G. Willis. *Confronting A Crisis: A Depth Study of Southern Baptist Churches in Metropolitan Transitional Areas*. Atlanta: Home Mission Board, 1967.

Bennett, Lerone. *Before the Mayflower: A History of the Negro in America, 1619–1954*. New York: Penguin, 1966.

Black, Earl. *Southern Governors and Civil Rights: Racial Segregation as a Campaign Issue in the Second Reconstruction*. Cambridge: Harvard University Press, 1976.

Black, Earl, and Merle Black. *Politics and Society in the South*. Cambridge: Harvard University Press, 1987.

Bland, Thomas A., Jr., ed. *Servant Songs: Reflections on the History and Mission of Southeastern Baptist Theological Seminary, 1950–1988*. Macon, GA: Smyth & Helwys, 1994.

Bourne, Peter G. *Jimmy Carter: A Comprehensive Biography from Plains to Postpresidency*. New York: Scribner, 1997.

Bradley, J. C. "Profiles of Home Mission Board Executives." *Baptist History and Heritage* 30 (1995) 26–34.

Branch, Taylor. *At Canaan's Edge: America in the King Years: 1965–68*. New York: Simon and Schuster, 2006.

———. *Parting the Waters: America in the King Years, 1954–63*. New York: Simon and Schuster, 1988.

———. *Pillar of Fire: America in the King Years, 1963–65*. New York: Simon and Schuster, 1998.

Brown, Robert R. *Bigger Than Little Rock*. Greenwich, CT: Seabury, 1958.

Bryan, G. McLeod. *Dissenter in the Baptist Southland: Fifty Years in the Career of William Wallace Finlator*. Macon, GA: Mercer University Press, 1985.

Campbell, Ernest Q., and Thomas F. Pettigrew. *Christians in Racial Crisis: A Study of Little Rock's Ministry*. Washington, DC: Public Affairs, 1959.

———. "Racial and Moral Crisis: The Role of Little Rock Ministers." *American Journal of Sociology* 64 (1959) 509–16.

Campbell, Will D. *The Stem of Jesse: The Costs of Community at a 1960s Southern School*. Macon, GA: Mercer University Press, 1995.

Carey, John C. *Carlyle Marney: A Pilgrim's Progress*. Macon, GA: Mercer University Press, 1980.

Bibliography

Carter, Dan T. *The Politics of Rage: George Wallace, the Origins of the New Conservatism, and the Transformation of American Politics.* New York: Simon & Schuster, 1995.
Carter, Hodding, III. *The South Strikes Back.* Garden City, NY: Doubleday, 1959.
Carter, Jimmy. *Keeping the Faith: Memoirs of a President.* New York: Bantam, 1982.
———. *Why Not the Best?* Nashville: Broadman, 1975.
Carver, W. O. Papers. Southern Baptist Historical Library and Archives, Nashville.
Cauthen, Baker James, ed. *Advance: A History of Southern Baptist Foreign Missions.* Nashville: Broadman, 1970.
Cauthen, Kenneth. *The Impact of American Religious Liberalism.* New York: Harper & Row, 1962.
Chafe, William H. *Civilities and Civil Rights: Greensboro, North Carolina, and the Black Struggle for Freedom.* New York: Oxford University Press, 1981.
Chappell, David L. *Inside Agitators: White Southerners in the Civil Rights Movement.* Baltimore: Johns Hopkins Press, 1994.
———. *A Stone of Hope: Prophetic Religion and the Death of Jim Crow.* Chapel Hill: University of North Carolina Press, 2004.
Christian Life Commission Minutes. Southern Baptist Historical Library and Archives, Nashville.
Christian Life Commission Records. Ethics & Religious Liberty Commission of the Southern Baptist Convention, Nashville.
Christian Life Commission Resource Files. Southern Baptist Historical Library and Archives. Nashville.
Clark, Vince. "Abner McCall and Civil Rights: The Integration of Baylor University." *Texas Baptist History* 20 (2000) 53–69.
Cone, James H. *For My People: Black Theology and the Black Church.* Maryknoll, NY: Orbis, 1984.
Conkin, Paul. *American Originals: Varieties of Homemade Christianity.* Chapel Hill: University of North Carolina Press, 1997.
Cook, James Graham. *The Segregationists.* New York: Appleton-Century-Crofts, 1962.
Copeland, Luther. *The Southern Baptist Convention and the Judgment of History: The Taint of an Original Sin.* Lanham, MD: University Press of America, 1995.
Coppenger, Mark. "Herschel Hobbs." In *Baptist Theologians,* edited by Timothy George and David S. Dockery, 434–49. Nashville: Broadman, 1990.
Criswell, W. A. *Look Up, Brother!* Nashville: Broadman, 1970.
———. Press Conference at 1968 SBC Annual Meeting in Houston. Audio recording. Southern Baptist Historical Library and Archives, Nashville.
———. *Standing on the Promises: The Autobiography of W. A. Criswell.* Dallas: Word, 1990.
Day, Richard Ellsworth. *Rhapsody in Black: The Life Story of John Jasper.* Valley Forge, PA: Judson, 1953.
Dehoney, Wayne, ed. *Baptists See Black.* Waco: Word, 1969.
———. Papers. Southern Baptist Historical Library and Archives, Nashville.
Dittmer, John. *Local People: The Struggle for Civil Rights in Mississippi.* Urbana: University of Illinois Press, 1995.
Dorgan, Howard. "Response of the Main-Line Southern White Protestant Pulpit to *Brown v Board of Education,* 1954–1965." In *A New Diversity in Contemporary Southern Rhetoric,* edited by Calvin M. Logue and Howard Dorgan, 15–51. Baton Rouge: Louisiana State University Press, 1987.

Bibliography

Draper, James T., Jr. Papers. Southern Baptist Historical Library and Archives, Nashville.
Du Bois, W. E. B. *W. E. B. Du Bois: Writings*. Edited by Nathan Huggins. New York: Library of America, 1986.
Edgar, Walter B. *South Carolina in the Modern Age*. Columbia: University of South Carolina Press, 1992.
Egerton, John. *Promise of Progress: Memphis School Desegregation, 1972–1973*. Atlanta: Southern Regional Council, 1973.
Eighmy, John Lee. *Churches in Cultural Captivity: A History of the Social Attitudes of Southern Baptists*. Revised by Samuel S. Hill. Knoxville: University of Tennessee Press, 1987.
———. "Recent Changes in the Racial Attitudes of Southern Baptists." *Foundations* 5 (1962) 354–60.
Ely, James W., Jr. *The Crisis of Conservative Virginia: The Byrd Organization and the Politics of Massive Resistance*. Knoxville: University of Tennessee Press, 1976.
Estep, William R. *Whole Gospel Whole World: The Foreign Mission Board of the Southern Baptist Convention, 1845–1995*. Nashville: Broadman & Holman, 1994.
Executive Committee Records. Southern Baptist Historical Library and Archives, Nashville.
Ezell, Humphrey K. *The Christian Problem of Racial Segregation*. New York: Greenwich, 1959.
Fahmy, Dalia. "7 Facts About Southern Baptists." *Pew Research Center*, June 7, 2019. https://www.pewresearch.org/fact-tank/2019/06/07/7-facts-about-southern-baptists/.
Fairclough, Adam. *Race & Democracy: The Civil Rights Struggle in Louisiana, 1915–1972*. Athens: University of Georgia Press, 1995.
Fields, W. C. Papers. Southern Baptist Historical Library and Archives, Nashville.
Findlay, James F., Jr. *Church People in the Struggle: The National Council of Churches and the Black Freedom Movement, 1950–1970*. Oxford: Oxford University Press, 1993.
Fletcher, Jesse C. *Baker James Cauthen: A Man for All Nations*. Nashville: Broadman, 1977.
Flynt, Wayne. *Alabama Baptists: Southern Baptists in the Heart of Dixie*. Tuscaloosa: University of Alabama Press, 1998.
Freeman, Curtis W. "'Never Had I Been So Blind': W. A. Criswell's 'Change' on Racial Segregation." *Journal of Southern Religion* 10 (2007) 1–12.
Gaillard, Frye. *The Dream Long Deferred*. Chapel Hill: University of North Carolina Press, 1988.
Garrett, James Leo. Papers. Southwestern Baptist Theological Seminary.
Genovese, Eugene E. *Consuming Fire: The Fall of the Confederacy in the White Christian South*. Athens: University of Georgia Press, 1998.
Gilmore, J. Herbert, Jr. *They Chose to Live: The Racial Agony of an American Church*. Grand Rapids: Eerdmans, 1972.
Glaser, James M. "Back to the Black Belt: Racial Environment and White Racial Attitudes in the South." *Journal of Politics* 56 (1994) 21–41.
Goldfield, David R. *Black, White, and Southern: Race Relations and Southern Culture, 1940 to the Present*. Baton Rouge: Louisiana State University Press, 1991.
Gould, Stephen Jay. *The Mismeasure of Man*. Rev. and exp. ed. New York: Norton, 1996.
Graham, Hugh Davis. *Crisis in Print: Desegregation and the Press in Tennessee*. Nashville: Vanderbilt University Press, 1967.
Grant, Donald L. *The Way It Was in the South: The Black Experience in Georgia*. New York: Birch Lane, 1993.

Bibliography

Graves, Harold K. *Into the Wind: Personal Reflections on the Early Years of Golden Gate Baptist Theological Seminary.* Nashville: Broadman, 1983.

Greene, Glen Lee. *House upon a Rock: About Southern Baptists in Louisiana.* Alexandria: Executive Board of the Louisiana Baptist Convention, 1973.

Gregory, Joel. *Too Great a Temptation: The Seductive Power of America's Super Church.* Fort Worth: Summit Group, 1994.

Griffin, Marvin C., ed. *The President Speaks: Annual Addresses Delivered to the National Baptist Convention of America, 1898-1986.* Nashville: National Baptist Convention of America, 1989.

Gushee, David P. Oral Memoir. Texas Collection. Baylor University.

Hamby, Alonzo L. *Liberalism and Its Challengers: F.D.R. to Reagan.* New York: Oxford University Press, 1985.

Hankins, Barry. "Southern Baptists and Northern Evangelicals: Cultural Factors and the Nature of Religious Alliances." *Religion and American Culture* 7 (1997) 271-98.

———. *Uneasy in Babylon: Southern Baptist Conservatives and American Culture.* Tuscaloosa: University of Alabama Press, 2002.

Harbuck, Don B. Papers. Southern Baptist Historical Library and Archives, Nashville.

Harper, Keith. *The Quality of Mercy: Southern Baptists and Social Christianity, 1890-1920.* Tuscaloosa: University of Alabama Press, 1996.

Harper, Keith, and Steve McKinion. *Then and Now: A Compilation and Celebration of Fifty Years at Southeastern Baptist Theological Seminary.* Wake Forest: Southeastern Baptist Theological Seminary, 2000.

Harvey, Paul. *Freedom's Coming: Religious Culture and the Shaping of the South from the Civil War Through the Civil Rights Era.* Chapel Hill: University of North Carolina Press, 2005.

———. *Redeeming the South: Religious Cultures and Racial Identities among Southern Baptists, 1865-1925.* Chapel Hill: University of North Carolina Press, 1997.

———. "Religion in the American South Since the Civil War." In *A Companion to the American South*, edited by John B. Boles, 387-408. Malden, MA: Blackwell, 2002.

Hays, Brooks. *A Southern Moderate Speaks.* Chapel Hill: University of North Carolina Press, 1959.

———. *This World: A Christian's Workshop.* Nashville: Broadman, 1958.

Henry, Jim. Papers. Southern Baptist Historical Library and Archives, Nashville.

Hill, Samuel S. *Religion and the Solid South.* Nashville: Abingdon, 1972.

———. *Southern Churches in Crisis.* New York: Holt, Rinehart and Winston, 1967.

Hobbs, Herschel H. *My Faith and Message: An Autobiography.* Nashville: Broadman & Holman, 1993.

———. Papers. Southern Baptist Historical Library and Archives, Nashville.

Hobson, Fred. *But Now I See: The White Southern Racial Conversion Narrative.* Baton Rouge: Louisiana State University Press, 1999.

Holmes, Thomas J. *Ashes for Breakfast.* Valley Forge, PA: Judson, 1969.

Home Mission Board Records. Southern Baptist Historical Library and Archives, Nashville.

Horowitz, David Alan. "White Southerners' Alienation and Civil Rights: The Response to Corporate Liberalism, 1956-1965." *Journal of Southern History* 54 (1988) 173-200.

Howe, Claude L., Jr. *Seventy-Five Years of Providence and Prayer.* New Orleans: New Orleans Baptist Theological Seminary, 1993.

Hunt, Alma. *Reflections from Alma Hunt.* Birmingham: Woman's Missionary Union, 1987.

Bibliography

Hutchison, William R. *The Modernist Impulse in American Protestantism*. Cambridge: Harvard University Press, 1976.

Irvin, Michael T. "J. B. Weatherspoon: Christian Statesman." *Quarterly Review* 42 (1982) 45–53.

Jackson, Hermione Dannelly. *Women of Vision*. Montgomery: Alabama Woman's Missionary Union, 1964.

Jones, Estill, John J. Owens, Henry Turlington, and Wayne Ward. Oral History Interview. Interview by Becky England and Diana Frederick, April 1986, Southern Seminary Audio Visual Archives CA 8314 & 8316, Transcription by Michele B. Fowler, 2003.

Jordan, Clarence. "Christian Community in the South." *Journal of Religious Thought* 14 (1956–57) 27–36.

Jordan, Winthrop D. *The White Man's Burden: Historical Origins of Racism in the United States*. New York: Oxford University Press, 1974.

Keith, Billy. *W. A. Criswell: The Authorized Biography*. Old Tappan, NJ: Revell, 1973.

Kelley, Jonathan. "The Politics of School Busing." *Public Opinion Quarterly* 38 (1974) 23–39.

Kelsey, George D. "Christian Love and Race Relations." *Quarterly Review* (1947) 38–41.

———. *Social Ethics among Southern Baptists, 1917–1969*. Metuchen, NJ: Scarecrow, 1972.

K'Meyer, Tracy Elaine. *Interracialism and Christian Community in the Postwar South: The Story of Koinonia Farm*. Charlottesville: University Press of Virginia, 1997.

Lee, Dallas. *The Cotton Patch Evidence*. New York: Harper & Row, 1971.

Leonard, Bill J. *Baptists in America*. New York: Columbia University Press, 2005.

———. *God's Last and Only Hope: The Fragmentation of the Southern Baptist Convention*. Grand Rapids: Eerdmans, 1990.

Lincoln, C. Eric, and Lawrence Mamiya. *The Black Church in the African-American Experience*. Durham: Duke University Press, 1990.

Link, William A. *The Paradox of Southern Progressivism, 1880–1930*. Chapel Hill: University of North Carolina Press, 1992.

Manis, Andrew Michael. "Silence or Shockwaves: Southern Baptist Responses to the Assassination of Martin Luther King Jr." *Baptist History and Heritage* 15 (1980) 19–27, 35.

———. *Southern Civil Religions in Conflict: Black and White Baptists and Civil Rights, 1947–1957*. Athens: University Press of Georgia, 1987.

Manza, Jeff, and Clem Brooks. "The Religious Factor in U.S. Presidential Elections, 1960–1992." *American Journal of Sociology* 103 (1997) 38–81.

Marable, Manning. *Race, Rebellion and Reform: The Second Reconstruction in Black America, 1945–1990*. 2nd ed. Jackson: University Press of Mississippi, 1991.

Marius, Richard. "The War Between the Baptists." *Esquire* 96 (1981) 46, 48–50, 53, 55.

Marney, Carlyle. Papers. Duke University.

Marsh, Charles. *The Beloved Community: How Faith Shapes Social Justice, from the Civil Rights Movement to Today*. New York: Basic, 2005.

———. *God's Long Summer: Stories of Faith and Civil Rights*. Princeton: Princeton University Press, 1997.

———. *The Last Days: A Son's Story of Sin and Segregation at the Dawn of a New South*. New York: Basic, 2001.

Marty, Martin E. *Pilgrims in Their Own Land: 500 Years of Religion in America*. New York: Penguin, 1984.

Bibliography

Maston, T. B. *The Bible and Race*. Nashville: Broadman, 1959.
———. *"Of One": A Study of Christian Principles and Race Relations*. Atlanta: Home Mission Board, 1946.
———. Oral Memoirs. Texas Collection. Baylor University.
———. Papers. Southwestern Baptist Theological Seminary.
———. *Segregation and Desegregation: A Christian Approach*. New York: Macmillan, 1959.
Mathews, Shailer. *The Faith of Modernism*. New York: Macmillan, 1924.
McBeth, Leon. "Origin of the Christian Life Commission." *Baptist History and Heritage* 1 (1966) 29–36.
———. "Southern Baptists and Race Since 1947." *Baptist History and Heritage* 7 (1972) 155–69.
McCain, R. Ray. "Reactions to the United States Supreme Court Segregation Decision of 1954." *Georgia Historical Quarterly* 52 (1968) 371–87.
McCall, Duke K. *Duke McCall: An Oral History with A. Ronald Tonks*. Nashville: Baptist History and Heritage Society and Fields, 2001.
———. Papers. The Southern Baptist Theological Seminary.
McCall, Emmanuel L. *Black Church Lifestyles*. Nashville: Broadman, 1986.
———. "Home Mission Board Ministry in the Black Community." *Baptist History and Heritage* 16 (1981) 29–40.
———. *When All God's Children Get Together: A Memoir of Race and Baptists*. Macon, GA: Mercer University Press, 2007.
McClellan, Albert. *The Executive Committee of the Southern Baptist Convention, 1917–1984*. Nashville: Broadman, 1985.
McCullough, Charles Franklin. "An Evaluation of the Biblical Hermeneutic of T. B. Maston." PhD diss., Southwestern Baptist Theological Seminary, 1987.
McDonald, Erwin L. *Across the Editor's Desk: The Story of the State Baptist Papers*. Nashville: Broadman, 1966.
McMillen, Neil R. *The Citizens' Councils: Organized Resistance to the Second Reconstruction, 1954–1964*. Urbana: University of Illinois Press, 1971.
McSwain, Larry L. *Loving beyond Your Theology: The Life and Ministry of Jimmy Raymond Allen*. Macon, GA: Mercer University Press, 2010.
———, ed. *Twentieth-Century Shapers of Baptist Social Ethics*. Macon, GA: Mercer University Press, 2008.
Miller, Acker C. Oral Memoir. Texas Collection. Baylor University.
Moore, R. Laurence. *Selling God: American Religion in the Marketplace of Culture*. New York: Oxford University Press, 1994.
Moore, Russell D. "Crucifying Jim Crow: Conservative Christianity and the Quest for Racial Justice." *Southern Baptist Journal of Theology* 8.2 (2004) 4–23.
Moore, William T. *His Heart Is Black*. Atlanta: Home Mission Board, 1979.
Mueller, William A. *A History of Southern Baptist Theological Seminary*. Nashville: Broadman, 1959.
———. *The School of Providence and Prayer: A History of the New Orleans Baptist Theological Seminary*. New Orleans: New Orleans Baptist Theological Seminary, 1969.
Myrdal, Gunnar. *An American Dilemma: The Negro Problem and Modern Democracy*. 2 vols. New York: Harper & Brothers, 1944.
Naylor, Robert E. Papers. Southwestern Baptist Theological Seminary.

BIBLIOGRAPHY

Nevin, David, and Robert E. Bills. *The Schools That Fear Built: Segregationist Academies in the South.* Washington, DC: Acropolis, 1976.

Newman, Mark. "The Alabama Baptist State Convention and Desegregation, 1954–1980." *Alabama Baptist Historian* 35 (1999) 3–40.

———. "The Arkansas Baptist State Convention and Desegregation, 1954–1968." *Arkansas Historical Quarterly* 56 (1997) 294–313.

———. "The Baptist General Association of Virginia and Desegregation, 1931–1980." *Virginia Magazine of History and Biography* 105 (1997) 257–86.

———. "The Baptist State Convention of North Carolina and Desegregation, 1945–1980." *North Carolina Historical Review* 75 (1998) 1–28.

———. "The Baptist State Convention of South Carolina, 1954–1971." *Baptist History and Heritage* 34 (1999) 56–72.

———. *The Civil Rights Movement.* Edinburgh: Edinburgh University Press, 2004.

———. "The Florida Baptist Convention and Desegregation, 1945–1980." *Florida Historical Quarterly* 78 (1999) 1–22.

———. "The Georgia Baptist Convention and Desegregation, 1945–1980." *Georgia Historical Quarterly* 83 (1999) 683–711.

———. *Getting Right with God: Southern Baptists and Desegregation, 1945–1995.* Tuscaloosa: University of Alabama Press, 2001.

———. "The Mississippi Baptist Convention and Desegregation, 1945–1980." *Journal of Mississippi History* 59 (1997) 1–31.

———. "The Tennessee Baptist Convention and Desegregation, 1954–1980." *Tennessee Historical Quarterly* 57 (1998) 236–57.

Nettles, Tom. *The Baptists: Key People Involved in Forming a Baptist Identity.* Vol. 1, *Beginnings in Britain.* Fearn: Mentor, 2005.

Noll, Mark A. *The Scandal of the Evangelical Mind.* Grand Rapids: Eerdmans, 1994.

Office of Institutional Research. *Wake Forest University Fact Book 1992–93.* Wake Forest: Wake Forest University, 1993.

Omi, Michael, and Howard Winant. *Racial Formation in the United States: From the 1960s to the 1980s.* New York: Routledge & Paul, 1986.

Orser, W. Edward. "Racial Attitudes in Wartime: The Protestant Churches During the Second Wald War." *Church History* 41 (1972) 337–53.

Parham, Robert. "A. C. Miller: The Bible Speaks on Race." *Baptist History and Heritage* 27 (1992) 32–43.

Paschall, H. Franklin. Papers. Southern Baptist Historical Library and Archives, Nashville.

Peirce, Neal R. *The Deep South States of America: People, Politics, and Power in the Seven Deep South States.* New York: Norton, 1974.

Pinson, William P., Jr., comp. *An Approach to Christian Ethics: The Life, Contribution, and Thought of T. B. Maston.* Nashville: Broadman, 1979.

Porter, Lee. "Southern Baptists and Race Relations, 1948–1963." ThD diss., Southwestern Baptist Theological Seminary, 1965.

Proceedings of Southern Baptists and Race: A Conference Sponsored by the Christian Life Commission of the Southern Baptist Convention, First Baptist Church, Nashville, Tennessee, January 16–17, 1989. Box 11, Folder 5, Southern Baptist Convention Christian Life Commission/Ethics and Religious Liberty Commission Seminar Proceedings Collection. Southern Baptist Historical Library and Archives, Nashville.

Queen, Edward L., II. *In the South Baptists Are the Center of Gravity: Southern Baptists and Social Change, 1930–1980.* Brooklyn: Carlson, 1991.

Bibliography

Quint, Howard H. *Profile in Black and White: A Frank Portrait of South Carolina*. Washington, DC: Public Affairs, 1958.

Race Relations Collection. Southern Baptist Historical Library and Archives, Nashville.

Ragsdale, B. C. *The Story of Georgia Baptists*. Atlanta: Executive Committee of the Georgia Baptist Convention, 1938.

Rauschenbusch, Walter. *A Theology for the Social Gospel*. New York: Macmillan, 1917.

Record, Wilson, and Jane Cassels Record, eds. *Little Rock, U.S.A.: Materials for Analysis*. San Francisco: Chandler, 1960.

Records of the Executive Office of the Sunday School Board. Southern Baptist Historical Library and Archives, Nashville.

Reed, John Shelton. *The Enduring South: Subcultural Persistence in Mass Society*. Chapel Hill: University of North Carolina Press, 1993.

———. "How Southerners Gave Up Jim Crow." *New Perspectives* 17 (1985) 15–19.

———. *Surveying the South: Studies in Regional Sociology*. Columbia: University of Missouri Press, 1993.

Reid, A. Hamilton. *Baptists in Alabama: Their Organization and Witness*. Montgomery: Paragon, 1967.

Reimers, David M. *White Protestantism and the Negro*. New York: Oxford University Press, 1965.

Roach, David. "Despite Racial Tensions, Black Southern Baptist Churches Still on the Rise." *Christianity Today*, August 21, 2020. https://www.christianitytoday.com/news/2020/august/southern-baptist-black-church-growth-race-sbc.html.

———. "Racial Reconciliation Not a 'Finished Project' 25 Years After Historic Resolution." *Baptist Press*, June 19, 2020. https://www.baptistpress.com/resource-library/news/racial-reconciliation-not-a-finished-project-25-years-after-historic-resolution/.

———. "The Southern Baptist Convention and Civil Rights, 1954–1995." PhD diss., Southern Baptist Theological Seminary, 2009.

———. "Southern Baptists Have Only 13 African American Career Missionaries. What Will It Take to Mobilize More?" *Christianity Today*, February 28, 2020. https://www.christianitytoday.com/news/2020/february/southern-baptist-imb-african-american-missionaries.html.

Roberts, Anthony Dale. "Jesse Burton Weatherspoon: The Ethics of Advocacy in a Southern Baptist Context." ThD thesis, Southern Baptist Theological Seminary, 1983.

Sapp, Phyllis. *The Long Bridge*. Atlanta: Home Mission Board, 1957.

Sarratt, Reed. *The Ordeal of Desegregation: The First Decade*. New York: Harper & Row, 1966.

"SBC Annuals." Southern Baptist Historical Library and Archives, Nashville. https://sbhla.org/digital-resources/sbc-annuals/.

SBC Press Kits Collection. Southern Baptist Historical Library and Archives, Nashville.

Sernett, Milton. *Black Religion and American Evangelicalism*. Metuchen, NJ: Scarecrow, 1975.

Sherman, Cecil. *By My Own Reckoning*. Macon, GA: Smyth & Helwys, 2008.

Shurden, Walter B. *Not a Silent People*. Nashville: Broadman, 1972.

———, ed. *The Struggle for the Soul of the SBC: Moderate Responses to the Fundamentalist Movement*. Macon, GA: Mercer University Press, 1993.

Singal, Daniel Joseph. *The War from Within: From Victorian to Modernist Thought in the South, 1919–1945*. Chapel Hill: University of North Carolina Press, 1982.

Smith, Bailey. Papers. Southern Baptist Historical Library and Archives, Nashville.

Bibliography

Smith, H. Shelton. *In His Image, But...: Racism in Southern Religion, 1780-1910*. Durham: Duke University Press, 1972.

Smith, Sid. "Growth of Black Southern Baptist Churches in the Inner City." *Baptist History and Heritage* 16 (1981) 49-60.

———. Oral Memoir. Texas Collection. Baylor University.

Snider, Philip Joel. "The 'Cotton Patch' Gospel: The Proclamation of Clarence Jordan." Ph.D. diss., Southern Baptist Theological Seminary, 1984.

———. *The "Cotton Patch" Gospel: The Proclamation of Clarence Jordan*. Lanham, MD: University Press of America, 1985.

Southern Baptist Theological Seminary. *For Such a Time as This: 1995-1996 Catalog*. Louisville: Southern Baptist Theological Seminary, 1995.

Spain, Rufus B. *At Ease in Zion: A Social History of Southern Baptists, 1865-1900*. Nashville: Vanderbilt University Press, 1967.

Storey, John W. *Texas Baptist Leadership and Social Christianity, 1900-1980*. College Station: Texas A&M University Press, 1986.

———. "That's Our Name... Why Not Call it the Christian Life Commission?" *Texas Baptist History* 20 (2000) 1-52.

Storey, John W., and Ronald C. Ellison. *The Southern Baptists of Southeast Texas: A Centennial History, 1888-1988*. Beaumont, TX: Golden Triangle Baptist Association, 1988.

Stricklin, David. *A Genealogy of Dissent: Southern Baptist Protest in the Twentieth Century*. Lexington: University Press of Kentucky, 1999.

Sullivan, Clayton. *Called to Preach, Condemned to Survive: The Education of Clayton Sullivan*. Macon, GA: Mercer University Press, 1985.

Sullivan, James L. *God Is My Record*. Nashville: Broadman, 1974.

Sutton, Jerry. *A Matter of Conviction: A History of Southern Baptist Engagement with the Culture*. Nashville: B&H, 2008.

Thompson, Ernest Trice. *Presbyterians in the South*. Vol. 3. Richmond, VA: John Knox, 1973.

Thurman, Howard. *Jesus and the Disinherited*. New York: Abingdon, 1949.

Tillman, William M., Jr. "T. B. Maston: The Conscience of Texas Baptists." *Texas Baptist History* 20 (2000) 71-85.

Tillman, William M., Jr., with Timothy D. Gilbert. *Christian Ethics: A Primer*. Nashville: Broadman, 1986.

Tillman, William M., Jr., and W. Andrew Tillman. "The Rise, Decline, and Fall of Christian Life Commission Entities and Voices." *Baptist History and Heritage* 41 (2006) 21-34.

Turner, James. *Without God, without Creed: The Origins of Unbelief in America*. Baltimore: Johns Hopkins University Press, 1985.

Valentine, Foy D. "Baptist Polity and Social Pronouncements." *Baptist History and Heritage* 14 (1979) 52-61.

———, ed. *Christian Faith in Action: Fourteen Sermons on Current Moral Issues*. Nashville: Broadman, 1956.

———. *A Historical Study of Southern Baptists and Race Relations, 1917-1947*. New York: Arno, 1980.

———. Oral Memoirs. Texas Collection. Baylor University.

———. Papers. Texas Collection. Baylor University.

———. *T. B. Maston: Shaper of Ethics and Social Concern*. Nashville: Historical Commission of the Southern Baptist Convention, 1987.

Bibliography

Wagner, C. Peter. *Your Spiritual Gifts Can Help Your Church Grow*. Glendale, CA: G/L Publications, 1970.

Wagy, Tom R. *Governor LeRoy Collins of Florida: Spokesman of the New South*. Tuscaloosa: University of Alabama Press, 1985.

Weatherspoon, J. B. Papers. The Southern Baptist Theological Seminary.

Wheeler, Edward L. "An Overview of Black Southern Baptist Involvements." *Baptist History and Heritage* 16 (1981) 3–11, 40.

White, K. Owen. Papers. Southern Baptist Historical Library and Archives, Nashville.

Williams, J. Howard. Papers. Southwestern Baptist Theological Seminary.

Williams, Jarvis J., and Kevin M. Jones, eds. *Removing the Stain of Racism from the Southern Baptist Convention*. Nashville: B&H Academic, 2017.

Williamson, Joel. *The Crucible of Race: Black-White Relations in the American South Since Emancipation*. New York: Oxford University Press, 1984.

———. *A Rage for Order: Black-White Relations in the American South Since Emancipation*. New York: Oxford University Press, 1986.

Willis, Alan Scot. "A Baptist Dilemma: Christianity, Discrimination, and the Desegregation of Mercer University." *Georgia Historical Quarterly* 80 (1996) 595–615.

Wills, Gregory A. *Southern Baptist Theological Seminary, 1859–2009*. New York: Oxford University Press, 2009.

Wilson, Charles Reagan. *Baptized in the Blood: The Religion of the Lost Cause, 1865–1920*. Athens: University of Georgia Press, 1980.

Wood, James R. "Authority and Controversial Policy: The Churches and Civil Rights." *American Sociological Review* 35 (1970) 1057–69.

Woodward, C. Vann. *The Burden of Southern History*. 3rd ed. Baton Rouge: Louisiana State University Press, 1991.

———. *Origins of the New South, 1877–1913*. Baton Rouge: Louisiana State University Press, 1951.

———. *The Strange Career of Jim Crow*. New York: Oxford University Press, 1955.

Wuthnow, Robert. *The Restructuring of American Religion: Society and Faith Since World War Two*. Princeton: Princeton University Press, 1998.

Young, Andrew. *An Easy Burden: The Civil Rights Movement and the Transformation of America*. 2nd ed. Waco: Baylor University Press, 2008.

Young, H. Edwin. Papers. Southern Baptist Historical Library and Archives, Nashville.

www.ingramcontent.com/pod-product-compliance
Lightning Source LLC
Chambersburg PA
CBHW051745230426
43670CB00012B/2163